John Calvin's Exegesis
of the Old Testament

COLUMBIA SERIES IN REFORMED THEOLOGY

The Columbia Series in Reformed Theology represents a joint commitment of Columbia Theological Seminary and Westminster John Knox Press to provide theological resources for the church today.

The Reformed tradition has always sought to discern what the living God revealed in scripture is saying and doing in every new time and situation. Volumes in this series examine significant individuals, events, and issues in the development of this tradition and explore their implications for contemporary Christian faith and life.

This series is addressed to scholars, pastors, and laypersons. The Editorial Board hopes that these volumes will contribute to the continuing reformation of the church.

EDITORIAL BOARD

Shirley Guthrie, Columbia Theological Seminary

George Stroup, Columbia Theological Seminary

Donald K. McKim, Memphis Theological Seminary

B. A. Gerrish, University of Chicago

Amy Plantinga Pauw,
Louisville Presbyterian Theological Seminary

Columbia Theological Seminary wishes to express its appreciation to the following churches for supporting this joint publishing venture:

First Presbyterian Church, Tupelo, Mississippi

First Presbyterian Church, Nashville, Tennessee

Trinity Presbyterian Church, Atlanta, Georgia

Spring Hill Presbyterian Church, Mobile, Alabama

St. Stephen Presbyterian Church, Fort Worth, Texas

COLUMBIA SERIES IN REFORMED THEOLOGY

John Calvin's Exegesis of the Old Testament

DAVID L. PUCKETT

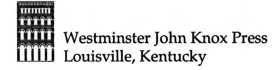 Westminster John Knox Press
Louisville, Kentucky

Book and cover design by Drew Stevens

First edition

Published by Westminster John Knox Press
Louisville, Kentucky

This book is printed on acid-free paper that meets the American National Standards Institute Z39.48 standard. ♾

PRINTED IN THE UNITED STATES OF AMERICA
95 96 97 98 99 00 01 02 03 04 — 10 9 8 7 6 5 4 3 2 1

Library of Congress Cataloging-in-Publication Data

Puckett, David Lee, date.
    John Calvin's exegesis of the Old Testament / David L. Puckett. — 1st ed.
        p.   cm. — (Columbia series in Reformed theology)
    Revision of thesis (Ph.D.)—University of Chicago, 1992.
    Includes bibliographical references.
    ISBN 0-664-22044-4 (alk. paper)
    1. Calvin, Jean, 1509–1564—Views on the Old Testament. 2. Bible. O.T.—Criticism, interpretation, etc.—History—16th century. I. Title. II. Series.
BX9418.P83   1995
221.6'092—dc20   94-31595

To Tandi, Amy, and Dori

CONTENTS

PREFACE

This book originated during the first year of my doctoral studies at the University of Chicago. One day while I was walking across the main Quadrangle reading a copy of T.H.L. Parker's *Calvin's New Testament Commentaries,* I felt my heart strangely warmed. I knew that I wanted to study the history of exegesis; more specifically, I knew that I wanted to study Calvin's exegesis. Now, over a decade later, I remain grateful to my teachers for providing encouragement and very competent guidance as I pursued this interest. The late Eric Cochrane kindly allowed me to extend Italy northward just a bit in order to write a paper on Calvin's exegesis for his Italian Renaissance seminar. Professor Donald Lach quite accurately observed on one occasion that in every course I took with him I always ended up writing about the history of the Bible; he graciously allowed me to persist in my single-mindedness. Professor Bernard McGinn first introduced me to the idea that the history of Christian thought may be understood as the history of biblical interpretation. This has remained my gateway into the history of theology. Finally, I must say that it was a rare privilege to study and to write my dissertation under the guidance of Professor Brian Gerrish. He has exemplified dedication and excellence in teaching and scholarship. More importantly for me, he has been a model of patience, encouragement, and grace.

1

INTRODUCTION

As the sixteenth century was drawing to a close, Aegidius Hunnius, a prominent Lutheran theologian, hurled a brickbat entitled "Calvin the Judaizer: Judaistic Glosses and Corruptions by Which John Calvin Did Not Fear to Corrupt the Clearest Passages of Sacred Scripture and Its Witness to the Glorious Trinity, the Deity of Christ and the Holy Spirit, including the Predictions of the Prophets concerning the Coming of the Messiah, His Birth, Passion, Resurrection, Ascension to Heaven, and Session at the Right Hand of God, in a Detestable Fashion."[1] Three decades earlier John Calvin had been buried in Geneva; Hunnius must have regretted that Calvin's writings were not buried with him. He was deeply troubled by Calvin's Judaistic approach to the Old Testament—an approach that threatened to undermine sound Christian doctrine.

Calvin would not have been surprised by such criticism. In his later years he was accustomed to being attacked by Lutheran polemicists, and the charge of "Judaizing" was a favorite insult of all parties in sixteenth-century Christian polemics. Friedman sums it up well:

> The Lutheran author Hunnius described John Calvin as a judaizer much as Calvin believed Lutheran liturgy was highly judaistic. On the other hand, Roman Catholic spokesmen thought Lutheran preoccupation with scriptural literalism was judaistic while both Reformed and Lutheran thinkers assumed Roman Catholic interest in ceremony and ritual reflected judaizing tendencies. Expressing a rare ecumenism, all agreed that Michael Servetus was a severe judaizer by any and all standards. For his part, Servetus lamented his being persecuted by judaizing Christians, Calvin in particular.[2]

Hunnius's charge that Calvin was a "Judaizer" was a sixteenth-century expression of a long-standing problem in the Christian church. The charge suggests that the ambiguity and tension that had existed throughout the Christian era concerning the role of the Old Testament in the life and

1

thought of the church was not yet resolved.[3] Indeed, the abundance of modern literature on the subject suggests that the problem is still far from being resolved.[4]

From its birth the Christian church claimed as its inheritance the Jewish holy writings. But with them came a problem: how to understand the writings in light of the reality that Jesus Christ had fulfilled what was promised or foreshadowed there. Oberman describes the tension produced when the church claimed the Old Testament as its own:

> Since early in the history of the Christian Church, the Old Testament has posed the chief exegetical problem to the biblical interpreters. The New Testament seemed clear and straightforward by comparison. The Gospels contain the history of Jesus Christ, while the other writings principally contain the interpretation of this history and its application to the life of the Church. But how can one apply the Old Testament to Christ, how can one make good the claim of the Church that the Books of Moses are her books?[5]

The church of the first century, according to Greer, had no difficulty determining how to use the Jewish scriptures. It used them to prove that Jesus Christ was the fulfillment of Israel's hope by interpreting the Old Testament as prophecy, typology, and allegory.[6]

> Three somewhat differing approaches were taken. The Hebrew Scriptures prophesy Christ and the events surrounding his life and fate. Or the Hebrew Scriptures foreshadow Christ. It is the type, the mark of the seal ring in the wax of the past, that points to the reality of Christ. Or, finally, the relationship of the old and new is transformed into the relationship of earthly to heavenly; and the Hebrew Scriptures become a mysterious allegory of Christian truths.[7]

The approach was not very different in the second century. Hanson explains that "the main exegetical preoccupation of the writers of this period was to show that the Law and the Prophets and the Writings are fulfilled in Jesus Christ, that they find their ultimate significance in him.[8]" However, the confidence with which Christian writers interpreted the Old Testament was being challenged on several fronts. Grant argues that the problem of how the church should understand and use the Old Testament was a major disputed issue in the development of second-century Christian theology.

> First came the question of the Old Testament, a question raised most forcefully by Marcion, who argued that the Old Testament had to be rejected since it contradicts the true gospel of Jesus and of Paul. When the Church sought refuge in its traditional allegorical method, it encoun-

that it really corresponded to their own theories of the aeons and of human nature. The Church then relied on its interpretation of the Old Testament as predictive rather than philosophical allegory, only to meet the third question, that of the Montanists. If the Old Testament was prophecy, so was the New. These predictions of a coming Paraclete were fulfilled in their leader Montanus. Out of these conflicts arose the Christian theology of the late second century.[9]

In the fourth century, problems of Old Testament interpretation were still plaguing Christian thinkers. This may be seen in the church's conflict over Arianism. Kannengiesser argues that the Arian crisis was at its heart a hermeneutical problem.

> The Arian crisis is, in my understanding, the specifically Alexandrian crisis of biblical interpretation. It bears directly on the principles of understanding Scripture, as formulated by Philo on the Jewish side and Origen on the Christian side. The crisis is essentially one of hermeneutics. This means that Arius' teaching led to conflicts within the ecclesiastical community about the interpretation of certain biblical passages.[10]

The biblical passages in dispute were as likely to be from the Old Testament as the New, with a major difference of opinion on precisely how the interpretation of the New Testament was to be brought to bear on the Old. Both sides understood Psalm 44:7–8 to refer to Christ; they did not agree on what it taught about him ("But thou hast saved us from our foes, and hast put to confusion those who hate us. In God we have boasted continually, and we will give thanks to thy name for ever"). Proverbs 8:22 ("The LORD created me at the beginning of his work, the first of his acts of old") was a key text in the Arian arsenal. It seemed to clearly teach that Christ was a part of creation. Athanasius objected to this interpretation, arguing that the Arians failed to understand the text in the framework provided by the New Testament—specifically John 1:14 and Philippians 2:5–11.[11]

After almost two millennia of Christian history it is clear that the interpretation of the Old Testament has posed a perennial problem for Christian exegetes and theologians. Two major concerns have been expressed: first, how to understand the Old Testament in light of the newer and more complete revelation recorded in the writings of the New Testament; second, how to handle the seeming imperfections of the Old Testament—chronological irregularities, apparent contradictions, stories of excessive brutality on the part of God's people, and misleading descriptions of God and his character. For many Christians, a historical understanding of the Old Testament has been difficult to harmonize with either of these concerns.[12] In the first millennium and a half of the church's history the scales of Christian Old Testament interpretation were often tipped away from a historical exegetical method. Such a method, it was believed, did not consistently produce results that were doctrinally orthodox and spiritually edifying. Preus suggests that "in a very important—perhaps fatal—sense, ... the Fathers agreed with Marcion: taken in its literal, historical meaning, the Old Testament has little to offer as a book for Christians."[13] Augustine, in his *De doctrina Christiana*, offered a defense for a spiritual approach to the interpretation of scripture. He warned that the reader must be careful not to take certain texts literally[14] and offered a simple method for determining if a passage is to be taken literally or figuratively: if the literal meaning does not edify in virtue or faith, the passage must be taken figuratively.[15] Medieval exegetes who tried to follow Augustine's rather imprecise counsel continued to struggle with the question of how to interpret the Old Testament and apply it in the life of the church.[16]

By the sixteenth century the chronic problem of the Old Testament had become acute. With the rise of humanism in the Renaissance, the need for careful literary and historical interpretation of ancient literature was widely recognized. But the writings contained in scripture were considered to be unique. Did they lend themselves to the same methods used in the study of Aristotle, Seneca, and the fathers of the church? The particular form the issue took in the Reformation period can be expressed as a question: Is the Old Testament to be interpreted according to normal principles for understanding human literature or does its special status as divine revelation forming a part of the Christian canon demand that a different approach be adopted? Friedman pointedly articulates the problem that faced Christian interpreters of that day:

> The unresolved, and unstated, problem was that the OT understood in its own historical context away from the NT, did not give strong support for the Christological positions and formulations Christians drew from the NT. In other words, if the OT was understood as possessing its own integrity and autonomy and was interpreted within its own conceptual context and not that of the NT, it is possible that large parts of the OT would oppose much of the NT.[17]

THE EXEGETICAL CONTINUUM

Sixteenth-century Christian solutions to the problem of the Old Testament formed a continuum. At one end were those who wished to interpret it on its own terms with a minimum of New Testament input; at the other end were those who seemed ready to read the New Testament into every nook and cranny of the Old Testament, with little consideration of how the Old Testament would have been understood in its day.

Hunnius's attack on Calvin illustrates the viewpoint from one end of the continuum. From his vantage point as a defender of Christian doctrine, it seemed that Calvin made numerous interpretative mistakes in his commentaries—mistakes that dangerously compromised Trinitarian orthodoxy. Calvin's Judaistic exegesis began with his interpretation of the very first verse of the Bible. It was obvious to Hunnius that the plural grammatical form *Elohim* in the creation account of Genesis 1:1 was pregnant with theological significance: here was a clear reference to the Trinity. Calvin, however, argued that the plural construction had nothing to do with the plurality of the godhead. It simply expressed the great power God had exercised in creating the cosmos. He cautioned his readers to beware of a violent gloss that would infer from this text the three persons of the godhead. Such an interpretation, he insisted, was overly subtle and actually proved too much, because it placed the believer in the uncomfortable position of using an argument against Arianism that could easily be used in support of Sabellianism. "If we suppose three persons to be here denoted, there will be no distinction among them."[18] Hunnius was unconvinced. In Calvin's denial of this obvious reference to the Trinity, was it not he who was guilty of the violent gloss? Moses in using the plural form clearly intended to teach that the world was created by all three persons of the Trinity—Father, Son, and Holy Spirit.[19]

Calvin's interpretations were no more satisfactory elsewhere. Hunnius found a clear example of Judaistic exegesis in the interpretation of Haggai 2:7 ("And I will shake all nations, and the desire of all nations shall come"). Calvin acknowledged the plausibility of either of two interpretations. The phrase "the desire of all nations" could be understood as a prophecy of Christ (the traditional Christian view). "We indeed know that Christ was the expectation of the whole world, according to what is said by Isaiah." But a second interpretation seemed simpler and was thus preferable: "that nations shall come and bring with them everything that is precious, in order to consecrate it to the service of God."[20] This interpretation, according to Hunnius, was clearly a Jewish gloss—an inexcusable one, because it was an error that Luther himself had earlier refuted.[21]

Hunnius found fault with Calvin's exegesis of a score of other Old Testament texts.[22] One such instance involves the interpretation of Micah 5:2 ("But you, O Bethlehem Ephrathah, who are little to be among the clans of Judah, from you shall come forth for me one who is to be ruler in Israel, whose origin is from of old, from ancient days"). Calvin questioned the traditional Christian view that this text was a solid proof of the eternal existence and thus the deity of the Messiah, Jesus Christ. He readily granted that the passage was rightly understood by Christians as evidence for the eternal existence of the Son, but he did not consider the evidence to be strong enough to be of any polemical value against the Jews. "I willingly own that the divinity of Christ is here proved to us, but as this will never be maintained by the Jews, I prefer taking the words simply as they are—that Christ will not come forth unexpectedly from Bethlehem, as though God had previously determined nothing respecting him."[23] Hunnius could not fathom how a Christian writer could willingly compromise the truth by conceding so much to the Jews.[24]

Hunnius also rejected Calvin's interpretation of the language of Genesis 19:24 ("Then the LORD rained on Sodom and Gomorrah brimstone and fire from the LORD out of heaven"). Hunnius believed that earlier interpreters were correct in understanding that the two occurrences of "LORD" in this verse referred to the first two persons of the Trinity.[25] Calvin argued that Christian writers were mistaken in believing that this verse provided a strong argument for the Trinity against the Jews. While it was certainly true that God always acted by his Son, in this passage Moses was simply trying to elevate the minds of his readers so they might contemplate the power of God. The repetition in the verse simply emphasized the extraordinary nature of what happened—that the rain of fire and brimstone came from God, not from natural causes.[26]

Even worse in Hunnius's judgment was Calvin's assault on the true interpretation of Isaiah 63:1 ("Who is this that comes from Edom, in crimson garments from Bozrah, he that is glorious in his apparel, marching in the greatness of his strength?"). Calvin believed that Christian interpreters were guilty of violently twisting (*violenter torserunt*) the text when they concluded that the reference to crimson garments was a picture of the blood of Christ. "They have imagined that here Christ is red, because he was wet with his own blood which he shed on the cross."[27] He maintained that the prophet was referring not to Christ but to God. According to Hunnius, Calvin was in this instance guilty of the most blatant kind of Judaizing. For in addition to scoffing at the traditional interpretation offered by pious Christian interpreters, he showed a total disregard for the authority of the apostle John, who clearly applied this text of scripture to Christ in Revelation 19.[28]

It is evident from these examples that Calvin and Hunnius were operating with very different approaches to understanding the Old Testament. Calvin appeared to be more critical of the Christian exegetical tradition;[29] he was also more likely to adopt interpretations that did not on the surface appear to provide the strongest support for Christian doctrine.[30] He believed Christian exegetes, in their eagerness to relate the Old Testament to Christian doctrine, were often guilty of twisting the text to an unnatural interpretation. Hunnius, however, argued that Calvin was a Judaizer because he, like the Jews, violated the genuine sense of scripture in his denial of the christological meaning of the Old Testament.

At the end of the continuum opposite Hunnius was Calvin's archenemy Michael Servetus—"the antitrinitarian Judaizer."[31] Servetus argued that Trinitarianism found no support in the Bible. He believed that the Achilles heel of Trinitarian Christianity was its failure to properly understand the Old Testament. This failure was caused in part by early Christian thinkers' ignorance of the Hebrew language. A belief as absurd as the doctrine of the Trinity might never have been invented if the "philosophers" who were defending early Christianity against heresies had possessed an adequate knowledge of Hebrew. "Paul of Samosata, . . . being entirely ignorant of the mysteries of Christ which are hidden in the Hebrew, . . . scandalized the Greek philosophers, who were also ignorant of Hebrew, and infected by the contagion of Aristotle, and forced them to ascend to heaven without wings."[32] According to Friedman, Servetus's concern in attacking the Christian exegetical tradition went much deeper than matters of the Hebrew language. His goal was nothing less than to free Old Testament interpretation from the domination of New Testament theology. His approach was "predicated upon a diminished sense of OT prophecy of Christ coupled with a heightened awareness of the historical context as the proper agency of scriptural interpretation."[33] Newman argues that Servetus normally accepted as the proper interpretation "the primary, immediate, and literal reference to the age in which it was composed, to the personages, events and circumstances amid which its authors lived."[34] While there is some truth to the view that one distinguishing mark of his method was the great emphasis he placed on historical interpretation, Servetus's use of the Old Testament in *On the Errors of the Trinity* and *Dialogues on the Trinity* does show him to be consciously in the Christian camp. Though he did fault Christian interpreters for reading erroneous interpretations of the New Testament back into the Old Testament and for failing to treat Old Testament prophecies in a soundly historical manner, he too found prophecies of Christ and types of Christ in the Old Testament.[35]

Calvin resides somewhere on the continuum that stretches from Hunnius to Servetus. In this study I will attempt to locate him through an extensive examination of his method of exegetical reasoning as it appears in his Old Testament commentaries. In the following section I will briefly survey some of the more significant scholarly literature on his method of exegesis. Then I will offer a justification for the method of this study.

MODERN EVALUATIONS
OF CALVIN'S EXEGESIS

It is the fact that Calvin rejected traditional Christian exegesis that accounts for the current popularity of his commentaries with some Christian biblical interpreters. He is applauded for his attempt to interpret scripture on its own terms. Childs suggests that the student of the Old Testament would do well to supplement von Rad's exposition of Genesis with Calvin's "magnificent Genesis commentary," a work characterized by "its sober attempt to render the literal sense of the book."[36] He recommends Calvin's Psalms commentary, even though modern readers ask different questions of the text. "The one with the theological maturity to discern Calvin's questions will soon be caught up in the sheer brilliance of this exposition."[37]

In his massive commentary on Paul's epistle to the Romans, Cranfield praises Calvin for his solid exposition of the book. "He takes care not to allow his commentary to come between the text and the reader, seeking to unfold the mind of Paul as expressed in the written words as faithfully, simply and succinctly as he can." Calvin's commentary is characterized by "an outstanding degree of that humility before the text which is shared to some degree by every commentator on a historical document who is of any worth, the humility which seeks, not to master and manipulate, but to understand and to elucidate."[38]

Kraeling offers a less flattering perspective of Calvin's merits as an exegete. While it is true that at times Calvin showed remarkable insight into the historical conditioning of the Bible, his approach as a whole must be rejected, for he mistakenly read the Old Testament through "the coloured glasses of the author of the Epistle to the Hebrews." His view that there was only one covenant and one people of God meant that he failed to see the discontinuity between Old and New Testaments. "The plain fact is that Calvin has Christianized the Old Testament and Judaized the New Testament."[39]

Kraus, in a frequently cited study of Calvin's exegesis, argues that eight exegetical principles can be derived from Calvin's work: (1) the principle of brevity and clarity; (2) the principle of determining the intention of the author; (3) the principle of investigating the historical, geographical, and institutional circumstances that are determinative for the author's situation; (4) the principle of setting forth the real meaning of a passage (also called the original, true, simple, or grammatical meaning); (5) the principle of investigating the context of a passage; (6) the principle of establishing standards concerning the extent to which exegesis can go beyond the literal biblical wording of a text; (7) the principle of recognizing metaphorical language; (8) the principle of reading the Old Testament with the purpose of finding Christ there. Principles two through five constitute what may be called historical exegesis and provide the basis for Kraus's conclusion that "Calvin's exegesis is grounded in humanistic studies and was much more strictly oriented to history than was Luther's."[40]

Ganoczy and Scheld attempt to understand Calvin's hermeneutics by viewing his work against the backdrop of the exegetical traditions of the

Middle Ages, the Renaissance, and the Reformation. Their work surveys a number of areas of his thought and practice, including his philological orientation, his use of typology, and his rejection of allegory. It includes a helpful section on his historical exegesis and investigates in some detail his hermeneutics in several theologically sensitive areas. The authors conclude that his exegesis reflects the fact that he was torn between biblical exegesis and systematic theology. Calvin's exegetical work cannot finally be reduced to a single principle but is a blend of historical and dogmatic exegesis.[41]

Parker, in a study devoted to Calvin's Old Testament exegesis, argues for the historical and contextual orientation of his work. He "binds himself to the conditions of the respective authors and their subjects. This is another way of saying that he faithfully observes the context." Parker is quick to point out, however, that one cannot say that Calvin adheres strictly to the immediate historical context. "The context of any single book is the rest of the Holy Scripture. No book can be interpreted as if it stood outside the Bible." Contextual interpretation expands to include the entire canon.[42] Parker suggests that Calvin's commentaries are characterized by abrupt moves from one end of the exegetical continuum to the other: "For page after page he can look like *Calvinus Judaeus* and then suddenly show that, in his voluntary exile among the men of the Old Covenant, living with them in shades and shadows, he has not forgotten the Sun of righteousness who, as he himself already knows, will in their future rise with healing in his wings."[43]

Torrance places Calvin's hermeneutics in the context of late medieval theories of knowledge, linking him directly to the thought of John Major (and indirectly to Duns Scotus). Torrance is primarily interested in Calvin's hermeneutical ideas as they are reflected in his biblical-theological work—the *Institutes*. He credits Calvin with laying the basis for the modern science of interpretation and exposition. "Every technical tool of language and thought is applied to the subject matter in order to make it as perspicuous as possible."[44] Calvin represents the very best in humanist scholarship. "Language and matter, form and content were to be distinguished but they were not to be handled in abstraction from one another: linguistic interpretation and epistemological clarification had to go hand in hand."[45]

Some of the most intriguing approaches to Calvin's exegesis come from writers who have highlighted the tension (or even inconsistency) resulting from what are thought to be irreconcilable differences between his historical exegesis and his doctrine of scripture. Dowey sees "two Calvins"—the theologian and the humanist scholar. Calvin the theologian strongly affirms the verbal inerrancy of the Bible; Calvin the critical scholar is able to recognize mistakes "with a disarming ingenuousness."

Dowey finds in Calvin "an instance of the incomplete assimilation of a traditional doctrine with the new manner of approaching the text."[46] In other words, Calvin was inconsistent—an understandable problem in view of the fact that he lived between two ages that approached scripture very differently. The implications of humanistic scholarship had not yet been carried over into the doctrine of scripture. Although Dowey is not primarily interested in Calvin's exegetical work, the tension he observes does raise questions about the harmony of Calvin's exegesis with his theology.

No one has made the case for a radical discontinuity between Calvin's doctrine of scripture and his method of exegesis more forcefully than Fullerton, who calls him "the first scientific interpreter in the history of the Christian church." He argues that Calvin, like Luther, enunciates the "exegetical principle of the grammatico-historical sense," but unlike Luther, actually follows through in his exegetical practice:

> Adopting the same principles of interpretation as Luther did, he consistently applied them in his commentaries as Luther did not. This is all the more astonishing as Calvin held many theological presuppositions which would have logically led to a complete abandonment of the historical meaning of the Old Testament in general and of prophecy in particular. The most astonishing difference between Luther and Calvin is that, whereas Luther's religious canon of interpretation, the Christocentric theory of Scripture, dominated his exegetical method at every turn, Calvin's dogmatic theories of Scripture controlled his exegesis only to a limited extent. In the case of no great commentator is it more necessary to distinguish between the theologian and the exegete than in the case of Calvin.[47]

Fullerton notes that Calvin's view of the Old Testament is as unhistorical as Luther's since, like Luther, he understands it to be a Christian book. Yet he finds Calvin disregarding his "theory" at every turn. It is significant, he suggests, that Calvin, who "in theory regarded the historical events of the Old Testament as typical," does not succumb to the temptation to whitewash the sins of the patriarchs by explaining them away as holy mysteries.[48] His exposition of the forms and ceremonies of the Mosaic law lacks the "mystical exegesis of details" one would expect to find with a commentator who believes in typology.[49] In his exposition of the Psalms, he "arrives at a Messianic reference only indirectly through typology"— further evidence of his exegetical freedom from dogma.[50] Finally, and most significantly, Calvin demonstrates his candor in his even-handed treatment of the citations in which the New Testament writers appear to have misunderstood (or misapplied) the Old Testament. "The admission of the appearance of evil was forced from Calvin by his exegetical conscience; the denial of its reality by his dogmatic presuppositions."

How did Calvin reconcile New Testament theology and Old Testament exegesis? According to Fullerton, "he refused to allow the New Testament method of citation to determine the historical sense of the Old Testament passage. . . . Calvin as an exegete, in his fearless application of the Reformation principle of exegesis, had succeeded in emasculating the New Testament ἵνα πληρωθῇ of any distinctive meaning."[51]

Interestingly, Forstman arrives at almost the opposite conclusion in his study of Calvin's doctrine of biblical authority. He argues that Calvin was far from consistent in his commitment to historical interpretation. His consistency was entirely in the other direction. He was so committed to the unity and perfection of scripture that he was not averse to taking recourse to "rather devious techniques and notions in order to maintain his theory."[52] Forstman's analysis of Calvin's exegetical commitment is in stark contrast to that of Fullerton.

> It is a foregone conclusion that all exegesis must uphold the divinity and, therefore, the unity and perfection of scripture. In this respect Calvin was remarkably consistent. If this consistency meant that at times he had to depart from what seems to the contemporary reader the natural meaning of the text, it can only be countered that to Calvin the natural meaning of a text is that which upholds the divine authorship of scripture. Because of this, Calvin as an exegete was free to read into a passage whatever might be necessary in order to arrive at the foregone conclusion.[53]

Forstman is able to cite numerous instances in which Calvin seemed to depart from the literal meaning of the Old Testament text. He notes Calvin's frequent appeal to the principle of accommodation (God's condescension in adapting his message to limited human understanding), and argues that this was his usual means of escape when scripture seemed to speak of God in an unworthy way. Whenever he comes to a verse that raises questions about the immutability or transcendence of God by attributing human activities or senses to God, "he takes pains to make unmistakably clear that the language is improper and that the author doesn't really mean what he says, but that the Holy Spirit is here accommodating his language to our low capacities."[54] Forstman argues that Calvin's frequent appeals to synecdoche (putting a part for the whole), hysteron proteron (putting the first last or the last first), and a number of other devices were attempts to avoid having to admit that there were errors in the text. The major problem with his approach, as Forstman sees it, is its subjectivity. It is devoid of any key for determining when a figure is used and of "clearly determining which meaning the figure is to have in any one place."[55] He finds it ironic that in his effort to maintain the divine authorship of scripture Calvin "was driven to a form of exegesis in which the literal meaning of the text was often denied and in which it became the task of the exegete to add, subtract, or create, depending on the nature of the case."[56] In Forstman's judgment, Calvin should not be viewed as a practitioner of historical exegesis because his exegetical method cannot properly be considered apart from his doctrine of scripture.

> The entire Bible is the work of the Holy Spirit and consequently an internally consistent unity. For one who holds such a conviction an explicit norm of interpretation external to the Bible itself is unthinkable, and it is noteworthy that Calvin does not articulate one.[57]

Thus Calvin should not be viewed as committed to any method that might operate independently of his doctrine of the divine inspiration, unity, and perfection of scripture. He frequently broke with canons of historical interpretation, adopting what Forstman calls "flexible hermeneutical guides."

In spite of the radically different conclusions reached by Fullerton and Forstman, they do have one thing in common: both see tension between Calvin's doctrine of scripture and a historical exegetical method. Fullerton applauds him for his commitment to historical exegesis in the face of pressure from his doctrine of scripture to compromise. Forstman gently chastises him for abandoning objective historical exegesis in his effort to maintain the unity and perfection of scripture. He suggests that Calvin's goal of arriving at the natural meaning of the text should not be confused with the goal of arriving at the historical meaning. The natural meaning is simply "that which upholds the divine authorship of Scripture."[58]

METHOD OF THIS STUDY

In the early 1960s Hall complained, with some justification, that the history of biblical interpretation "is one of the most neglected topics in the history of the church and its doctrines." The neglect of the exegetical work of the sixteenth-century Reformers was particularly glaring. It is remarkable, he observed, that "the passionate devotion to biblical studies in the sixteenth century, which involved the commitment of men and whole communities to ways of living based on their interpretation of the Scriptures, has aroused so little interest among historians."[59] In the early seventies Parker observed that "the literature on Calvin's New Testament commentaries is meagre and disappointing."[60] Almost two decades later, Steinmetz echoed the same sentiment:

> Historians have paid very little attention to the history of the interpretation of the Bible in the sixteenth century. The career of John Calvin (1509–1564) provides an excellent example of such neglect. Although

Calvin considered himself to be primarily an interpreter of the Bible, and although his sermons and commentaries outnumber in length and quantity his systematic and polemical writings, far more is known about Calvin as a systematical or polemical theologian than as an interpreter of the Bible.[61]

Perhaps one of the reasons his exegetical method suffered neglect is found in the fact that Calvin never bothered to explain it in any systematic way. Parker notes that one of the difficulties in studying him is "his un-humanistic reticence on intention and method. We have to piece it all together from incidental remarks."[62] One such remark was made by Calvin to his friend Simon Grynaeus in the preface of his Romans commentary:

> I remember that three years ago we had a friendly discussion about the best way of interpreting scripture. The plan which you particularly favoured was also the one which at that time I preferred to any others. Both of us felt that the chief virtue of an interpreter lies in lucid brevity [*in perspicua brevitate*]. Since it is almost his only task to unfold the mind of the writer whom he has undertaken to expound, he misses his mark, or at least strays outside his limits, by the extent to which he leads his readers away from the meaning of his author.[63]

Parker suggests that in the few sentences of this preface "are revealed Calvin's views on method."[64] The methodological issues addressed in the preface are rhetorical and interpretative, expositional and exegetical. This is a statement of both the goal of exegesis ("to unfold the mind of the writer") and of how to present the results of one's exegesis ("lucid brevity").[65] It does not explain, however, how Calvin hopes to reach his goal. In fact nowhere does Calvin spell out precisely how he makes exegetical judgments. If his exegetical decisions are to be understood, an alternative approach will be necessary—one that does not rely on what Parker calls his "incidental remarks" about method.

My approach in this study is based upon my belief that Calvin reveals his method most clearly in the reasoning he offers for rejecting the interpretations of others. Throughout the study I will make extensive use of Calvin's criticisms of the work of other interpreters.[66] However, before I can proceed, a possible objection to this approach must be addressed. Calvin, it is sometimes argued, does not usually like to refute the opinions of other commentators. Gamble suggests that this reticence is a significant aspect of his hermeneutic.

> We note that Calvin keeps his teaching style simple and that he generally abstains from refuting opponents, a particularly enjoyable sixteenth-century pastime! This information is by no means unimportant in analyzing Calvin's method; it should be noted that as a general

rule Calvin refuses to enter into debate with opponents in his commentaries and for that matter also deletes opinions that support him.[67]

It is true that Calvin frequently expresses a desire to avoid exegetical disputes. In his commentary on Daniel he writes, "I do not usually refer to conflicting opinions, because I take no pleasure in refuting them, and the simple method which I adopt pleases me best, namely to expound what I think was delivered by the Spirit of God."[68] In his Genesis commentary he confirms that he tries to avoid criticizing the interpretations of others. "It is not my intention to relate the ravings or the dreams of every writer, nor would I have the reader to expect this from me; here and there I allude to them, though sparingly."[69]

Among the reasons Calvin offers for wishing to avoid interpretative disputes is the inevitability of differences of opinion. Christian interpreters have always differed among themselves. "There is by no means universal agreement even among those who have not been found wanting in zeal for godliness, or piety and moderation in discussing the mysteries of God." Calvin is resigned to the fact that such differences will always exist. "Even though it were otherwise highly desirable, we are not to look in the present life for lasting agreement among us on the exposition of passages of scripture." Nor should we expect full agreement, because God's people do not possess "full and perfect knowledge" in this life.[70]

In the preface to his Psalms commentary Calvin offers several additional reasons for avoiding controversy with other interpreters: first, his goal of communicating clearly and simply; second, his desire not to appear ostentatious; third, his belief that polemics do not contribute greatly to the edification of the church.

> I have not only observed throughout a simple style of teaching, but in order to be removed the farther from all ostentation, I have also generally abstained from refuting the opinions of others, although this presented a favorable opportunity for plausible display, and of acquiring the applause of those who shall favor my book with a perusal. I have never touched upon opposite opinions, unless there was reason to fear that by being silent respecting them, I might leave my readers in doubt and perplexity. At the same time, I am sensible that it would have been much more agreeable to the taste of many, had I heaped together a great mass of materials which has great show, and acquires fame for the writer, but I have felt nothing to be of more importance than to have a regard to the edification of the church.[71]

Calvin appears to believe that if one's own view is correct and well stated, it should not normally be necessary to correct other interpreters. In his commentary on the Psalms he explains: "It would not be for edification to recount all the interpretations which have been given of this clause, for when I have established its true and genuine import, it would be quite superfluous to enter upon a refutation of others."[72] He reaffirms this approach in his commentary on Isaiah: "I do not relate all the expositions of this passage, for that would be too tedious, and I consider the true exposition to be so well supported that it will easily refute all others."[73] In his commentary on Jeremiah, he writes: "Interpreters differ as to the meaning of the words. I will not repeat their views, nor is it necessary: I will only state what seems to me to be the genuine sense."[74]

In light of such statements, which clearly discount the value of refuting other interpretations, it is easy to understand how Kraus could suggest that Calvin "saw himself as bound by and indebted to the exegetical tradition of the church, above all the early church, especially Augustine. He was unwilling to give up the consensus of interpretation."[75]

Sometimes though, Calvin indicates that it is necessary to correct the views of those who have gone before. Sometimes he feels he must depart from the Christian exegetical tradition. "If it be considered a sin to corrupt what has been dedicated to God, we assuredly cannot tolerate anyone who handles that most sacred of all things on earth with unclean or even ill-prepared hands."[76] In such cases the interpreter must carefully examine his motives.

> When, therefore, we depart from the views of our predecessors, we are not to be stimulated by any passion for innovation, impelled by any desire to slander others, aroused by any hatred, or prompted by any ambition. Necessity alone is to compel us, and we are to have no other object than that of doing good.[77]

Calvin may have truly believed that he hid the disagreements he had with other interpreters—most Calvin scholars have been willing to take his word for it. But despite his protestations, throughout his commentaries he expresses dissatisfaction with the conclusions reached by other interpreters. He frequently corrects the exegesis of interpreters who are not taking due care in the exposition of scripture. In this study I will examine many instances where he substantiates or defends the validity of his exegesis against the views of other interpreters.

Calvin does not like to name commentators when he refutes their exegesis.[78] In a letter in which he defends himself against the charge that he has been overly critical of Luther's exegesis, he explains that he prefers to protect the anonymity of those interpreters with whom he differs.

> I mention sparingly and soberly things that anyone who was given to display would make a great fuss about. If others have gone wrong on something, I reprove it without mentioning names and without violence, and indeed I bury errors in silence unless necessity forces.[79]

He expresses a similar desire in his commentary on Daniel 9:25. "I am willing to spare the names of surviving commentators, and of those who have lived during our own times, yet I must say what will prove useful to my readers."[80] Calvin is fairly consistent in following this approach. He usually raises opposing views and refutes them without naming the individuals who hold the erroneous views. Bouwsma argues that, even if Calvin's sources could be successfully identified, the exercise would be "unlikely to yield major returns" since, like other cultivated men of the age, he was open to many influences. "The important question is less what he read than why he preferred and made a part of himself some works and authors rather than others."[81] Although a study of Calvin's exegetical sources might be more fruitful than Bouwsma's statement would suggest, the task of the present study will not be to examine whose work Calvin read and used but why he preferred certain interpreters and interpretations.

It has been argued that the two parties Calvin consciously opposed in the theological arena—Roman Catholics and Anabaptists—were also his principal rivals as he exegeted the Old Testament.[82] It appears to me, however, that Calvin's confrontation with these parties is not especially prominent in his Old Testament commentaries. While he does explicitly criticize the interpretations of supporters of the papacy and the Anabaptists, such critiques are relatively infrequent. Much more common are his criticisms of interpretations that he believes represent Jewish and Christian exegetical traditions. Indeed, these appear to be the polar opposites against which he often chooses to articulate his own interpretations. This study will highlight the prominence of the the Jewish/Christian polarity in Calvin's exegesis.

Calvin recognizes that often he is not simply evaluating the interpretations of individuals but is critiquing whole traditions of exegesis—Christian and Jewish. In his commentary on Daniel 7:27 ("And the kingdom and the dominion and the greatness of the kingdoms under the whole heaven shall be given to the people of the saints of the Most High; their kingdom shall be an everlasting kingdom, and all dominions shall serve and obey them"), he notes that almost everyone except the Jews mistakenly relate the prophecy to Christ's final advent. "All Christian interpreters agree in this; but as I have shown before, they pervert the prophet's genuine sense [*pervertunt genuinum prophetae sensum*]." If Christian writers pervert the prophet's meaning, what of the Jewish interpreters? "As to the Jews, theirs is no explanation at all, for they are not only foolish and stupid, but even mad."[83]

Calvin is often uncomfortable with both Jewish and Christian explanations, especially of those Old Testament texts usually taken by Jews as prophecies of earthly deliverance from captivity and by Christians as

promises of spiritual deliverance through Christ. In his interpretation of
Isaiah 43:19 ("Behold I am doing a new thing; now it springs forth, do you
not perceive it? I will make a way in the wilderness and rivers in the
desert") he notes that almost all Christian commentators understand the
passage to refer to the coming of Christ. In this they are "undoubtedly
mistaken." The Jews are just as mistaken "when they limit it to the
redemption from Babylon."[84] He finds the same problem with Jewish and
Christian interpretations of Isaiah 52:10 ("The LORD has bared his holy
arm before the eyes of all the nations; and all the ends of the earth shall see
the salvation of our God"). "This prophecy is maliciously restricted by the
Jews to the deliverance from Babylon, and is wrongly restricted by
Christians to the spiritual redemption which we obtain through Christ."[85]
In a similar vein is his critique of Jewish and Christian interpretations of
Psalm 87:4 ("Among those who know me I mention Rahab and Babylon;
behold, Philistia and Tyre, with Ethiopia—'This one was born there,' they
say"). The Jewish view, "that there shall spring from other nations very
few who shall excel either in mental endowment or in virtuous attain-
ment, but that in Israel such persons will be very numerous," is so forced
that it needs no refutation; the almost unanimous interpretation of the
Christian doctors that these words refer to Christ is ingenious and at first
sight plausible, but is not solid.[86]

The difference between Jewish exegesis and Christian exegesis is not
simply the fact that Jewish interpreters follow a more historical approach
while Christians are prone to spiritualizing. Both traditions, Calvin insists,
have been guilty of adopting weak interpretations of scripture. In his
exposition of Hosea 6:2, after charging that Jewish interpretations are
frivolous and Christian interpretations overly subtle, he offers one of his
rare statements of exegetical principle:

> Subtle speculations [*argutae speculationes*] please at first sight, but after-
> wards vanish. Let every one, then, who desires to be proficient in the
> Scriptures always keep to this rule—to gather from the Prophets and
> Apostles what is solid [*solidum*].[87]

The remainder of this study will consist of an examination of Calvin's
exegetical reasoning as he tries to determine what is solid and what is not.
But first, the presuppositions that lie behind his exegesis need to be
discussed. Chapter 2 examines his view of the Bible: first, his understanding of its divine and human authorship; second, his understanding of its
unity and diversity. Chapter 3 examines the elements of his exegesis that
might have given his work a "Jewish" appearance to critics such as
Hunnius: first, his rejection of traditional Christian exegesis; second, his
commitment to historical reasoning in interpretation. Chapter 4 examines
two elements in his exegetical practice that most clearly show the

Christian character of his work: first, his criticism of Jewish exegesis; second, his use of the New Testament as an exegetical guide. Chapter 5 examines his exegetical reasoning in three areas that often divided Jewish and Christian interpreters: the use of allegorical interpretation, the use of typological interpretation, and the interpretation of Old Testament promises or prophecies. The character of Calvin's exegesis as a *via media* will become clear through this investigation of his dialogue with Jewish and Christian exegetical traditions. He attempts to chart a middle course—one which betrays neither his historical sensitivities nor his theological commitments.[88] A proposal concerning how Calvin's method of exegetical reasoning may relate to the question of the role of the Holy Spirit in interpretation is offered in the concluding chapter.

NOTES

1. Aegidius Hunnius, *Calvinus Iudaizans, Hoc est: Iudaicae Glossae et Corruptilae, Quibus Iohannes Calvinus illustrissima Scripturae sacrae loca & Testimonia, de gloriosa Trinitate, Deitate Christi, & Spiritus sancti, eum primis autem vaticinia Prophetarum de Adventu Messiae, nativitate eius, passione, resurrectione, ascensione in coelos & sessione ad dextram Dei, detestandum in modum corrumpere non exhorruit. Addita est corruptelarum confutatio* (Wittenberg, 1595).

2. Jerome Friedman, *The Most Ancient Testimony: Sixteenth-Century Christian-Hebraica in the Age of Renaissance Nostalgia* (Athens, Ohio: Ohio University Press, 1983), 182.

3. The problem of how to interpret and apply the Hebrew Bible existed even before the rise of Christianity. Fishbane describes how biblical interpretation was already taking place in the biblical writings themselves as those who composed scripture sought to demonstrate "the capacity of Scripture to regulate all areas of life and thought" (Michael Fishbane, *Biblical Interpretation in Ancient Israel* [Oxford: Clarendon Press, 1985], 3). The older standard work on the history of Old Testament interpretation in the church is Ludwig Diestel, *Geschichte des Alten Testaments in der christlichen Kirche* (Jena, 1869). For the use of the Hebrew Bible in early Judaism and Christianity, see Martin Jan Mulder and Harry Sysling, eds., *Mikra: Text, Translation, Reading, and Interpretation of the Hebrew Bible in Ancient Judaism and Early Christianity*, Compendia Rerum Iudaicarum ad Novum Testamentum (Philadelphia: Fortress Press, 1988), vol. 1, section 2. See also James L. Kugel and Rowan A. Greer, *Early Biblical Interpretation*, Library of Early Christianity (Philadelphia: Westminster Press, 1986). For a general treatment of the interpretation of the Old Testament by New Testament writers, see Richard Longenecker, *Biblical Exegesis in the Apostolic Period* (Grand Rapids: Wm. B. Eerdmans Publishing Co., 1975). Rogerson surveys the history of Old Testament study from New Testament times to the present in John Rogerson, Christopher Rowland, and Barnabas Lindars, *The Study and Use of the Bible*, ed. Paul Avis, vol. 2 of History of Christian Theology series (Grand Rapids, Mich.: Wm. B. Eerdmans Publishing Co., 1988), 3–150. For the history of the problem of the Old Testament

in the Middle Ages, see James Samuel Preus, *From Shadow to Promise: Old Testament Interpretation from Augustine to the Young Luther* (Cambridge, Mass.: Harvard University Press, Belknap Press, 1969). For the impact of Renaissance philological scholarship on Old Testament interpretation, see Friedman, *The Most Ancient Testimony*.

4. The modern problem of the Old Testament is not limited to any particular tradition. For tensions among modern Old Testament scholars, see James Barr, *Old and New in Interpretation: A Study of the Two Testaments* (London: SCM Press, 1982); "The Literal, the Allegorical, and Modern Biblical Scholarship," *Journal for the Study of the Old Testament* 44 (1989): 3–17. See also Brevard Childs, "The Sensus Literalis of Scripture: An Ancient and Modern Problem," in *Beiträge zur alttestamentlichen Theologie*, ed. Herbert Donner, Robert Hanhart, and Rudolf Smend (Göttingen: Vandenhoeck & Ruprecht, 1977). Among Catholic scholars much of the discussion has revolved around the question of the *sensus plenior*. See Raymond E. Brown, "The History and Development of the Theory of a Sensus Plenior," *Catholic Biblical Quarterly* 15 (1953): 141–62; *The Sensus Plenior of Sacred Scripture* (Baltimore: St. Mary's University, 1955); "The Sensus Plenior in the Last Ten Years," *Catholic Biblical Quarterly* 25 (1963): 262–85; "The Problems of the Sensus Plenior," in *Exégèse et théologie: Les saintes Ecritures et leur interprétation théologique*, ed G. Thils and R. E. Brown (Gembloux: J. Duculot, 1968), 72–81. See also Denis Farkasfalvy, "The Case for Spiritual Exegesis," *Communio* 10 (winter 1983): 332–50. For the state of the issue in American evangelicalism, see John S. Feinberg, ed., *Continuity and Discontinuity: Perspectives on the Relationship between the Old and New Testaments* (Westchester, Ill.: Crossway Books, 1988); Douglas J. Moo, "The Problem of Sensus Plenior," in *Hermeneutics, Authority, and Canon*, ed. D. A. Carson and J. Woodbridge (Grand Rapids: Zondervan Publishing House, 1986), 178–211; Darrell L. Bock, "Evangelicals and the Use of the Old Testament in the New," parts 1 and 2, *Bibliotheca Sacra* 142 (1985): 209–23, 306–19; Vern Sheridan Poythress, "Divine Meaning of Scripture," *Westminster Theological Journal* 48 (1986): 241–79. Also of interest on the subject are G.W.H. Lampe, "The Reasonableness of Typology," in *Essays on Typology*, ed. G.W.H. Lampe and K. J. Woollcombe (Naperville, Ill.: Alec R. Allenson, 1957); Rolf Rendtorff, "Towards a New Christian Reading of the Hebrew Bible," *Immanuel* 15 (winter 1982–83): 13–21; Charles J. Scalise, "The 'Sensus Literalis': A Hermeneutical Key to Biblical Exegesis," *Scottish Journal of Theology* 42 (1989): 45–65; David C. Steinmetz, "The Superiority of Precritical Exegesis," *Theology Today* (1980): 27–38. For a very full bibliographical essay, see Henning Graf Reventlow, *Problems of Biblical Theology in the Twentieth Century*, trans. John Bowden (Philadelphia: Fortress Press, 1986).

5. Heiko Augustinus Oberman, *Forerunners of the Reformation: The Shape of Late Medieval Thought Illustrated by Key Documents* (Philadelphia: Fortress Press, 1981), 281.

6. Chapter 5 will examine Calvin's treatment of prophecy, typology, and allegory.

7. Kugel and Greer, *Early Biblical Interpretation*, 3:127. See also D. A. Carson and H.G.M. Williamson, *It Is Written: Scripture Citing Scripture* (Cambridge: Cambridge University Press, 1988).

8. R.P.C. Hanson, "Biblical Exegesis in the Early Church," in *The Cambridge History of the Bible*, vol. 1: *From the Beginnings to Jerome*, ed. P. R. Ackroyd and C. F. Evans (Cambridge: Cambridge University Press, 1970), 414. See also Willis A.

Shotwell, *The Biblical Exegesis of Justin Martyr* (London: SPCK, 1965). For Origen's exegesis, see R.P.C. Hanson, *Allegory and Event: A Study of the Sources and Significance of Origen's Interpretation of Scripture* (Richmond: John Knox Press, 1959); Henri de Lubac, *Histoire et esprit: L'intelligence de l'Ecriture d'après Origène* (Paris: Editions Montaigne, 1950); plus various articles in Charles Kannengiesser and William L. Petersen, eds., *Origen of Alexandria: His World and His Legacy* (Notre Dame, Ind.: University of Notre Dame Press, 1988).

9. R. M. Grant, *The Letter and the Spirit* (London: SPCK, 1957), 62.

10. Charles Kannengiesser, *Holy Scripture and Hellenistic Hermeneutics in Alexandrian Christology: The Arian Crisis* (Berkeley, Calif.: Center for Hermeneutical Studies, 1982), 1.

11. Craig Alan Blaising, "Athanasius of Alexandria: Studies in the Theological Contents and Structure of the *Contra Arianos* with Special Reference to Method" (Ph.D. diss., University of Aberdeen, 1987), 277–90, 317–60.

12. In this study I normally use the term *historical interpretation* to designate an approach to the Old Testament that attempts to determine what the text meant in the context in which it was originally produced. An Old Testament exegete who makes such an attempt may be said to practice "historical interpretation." Such an approach does not necessarily preclude an attempt to interpret a text in its broader canonical context or in the context of the teaching of the Christian church, nor does it preclude the recognition of *sensus plenior*. Chapter 3 of the present work is devoted to Calvin's efforts to interpret the Old Testament historically.

13. Preus, *From Shadow to Promise*, 10.

14. Augustine, *De doctrina Christiana* III.v.9.

15. Ibid. III.x.14.

16. The development of Old Testament hermeneutics in the Middle Ages is described in Preus, *From Shadow to Promise*. See also Henri de Lubac, *Exégèse médiévale: Les quatre sens de l'Ecriture*, 4 vols. (Paris: Aubier, 1959–64); Beryl Smalley, *The Study of the Bible in the Middle Ages* (Oxford: Basil Blackwell Publisher, 1952); G. R. Evans, *The Language and Logic of the Bible*, 2 vols. (Cambridge: Cambridge University Press, 1984–85). For the twelfth century, see M. D. Chenu, *Nature, Man, and Society in the Twelfth Century: Essays on New Theological Perspectives in the Latin West*, trans. and ed. Jerome Taylor and Lester K. Little (Chicago: University of Chicago Press, 1968), 146–61. For the study of the Old Testament in the monasteries, see Jean LeClercq, *The Love of Learning and the Desire for God: A Study of Monastic Culture*, trans. Catharine Misrahi (New York: Fordham University Press, 1982), 79–83.

17. Jerome Friedman, "Servetus and the Psalms: The Exegesis of Heresy" in *Histoire de l'exégèse au XVIe siècle*, ed. Olivier Fatio and Pierre Fraenkel, Etudes de Philologie et d'Histoire, no. 34 (Geneva: Librairie Droz, 1978), 166.

18. Comm. Gen. 1:1 (C.O. 23.15). Citations from Calvin's commentaries will include the biblical reference followed by the volume and column (or page) number in *Ioannis Calvini opera quae supersunt omnia*, ed. W. Baum, E. Cunitz, and E. Reuss, 59 vols. (Braunschweig, 1863–1900), hereafter C.O. Where the verse numbers in the C.O. differ from the standard English numbering, the latter will be followed. References to the *Institutes* will include the book, chapter, and section followed by the page number of the 1559 edition in *Joannis Calvini Opera Selecta*, ed. by Peter Barth and Wilhelm Niesel, 5 vols. (Munich: Chr. Kaiser Verlag, 1926–62), hereafter O.S. Normally I have chosen to follow the English translations

of the Calvin Translation Society edition of Calvin's Old Testament commentaries, the more recent translation of *Calvin's New Testament Commentaries*, edited by David W. Torrance and Thomas F. Torrance, and the edition of Calvin's *Institutes* edited by John T. McNeill and translated by Ford Lewis Battles. While the Calvin Translation Society is usually reliable, I sometimes depart from its punctuation and diction for the sake of accuracy and clarity.

19. Hunnius, *Calvinus Iudaizans*, 9–10.

20. Comm. Hag. 2:7 (C.O. 72.106).

21. Hunnius, *Calvinus Iudaizans*, 74–79.

22. Hunnius explicitly rejects Calvin's exegesis of the following Old Testament texts: Ps. 8:5; 16:10; 22:16; 45:6; 68:18; 110:1; Isa. 6:3; 40:3; 43:25; 61:1; Jer. 31:22; Hos. 6:12; 13:14; Micah 2:12–13; Hag. 2:7; Zech. 9:9; 9:11; 11:12–14; 13:7; 14:4.

23. Comm. Micah 5:2 (C.O. 43.368).

24. Hunnius, *Calvinus Iudaizans*, 33–36.

25. Ibid., 15–16.

26. Comm. Gen. 19:24 (C.O. 23.277–78).

27. Comm. Isa. 63:1 (C.O. 37.392).

28. Hunnius, *Calvinus Iudaizans*, 132–34.

29. That Calvin gave some weight to the work of Christian exegetes is clear from his interpretation of Ps. 7:11, where he offers as one of his reasons for holding his interpretation that it is the view of "most learned divines" (C.O. 31.84).

30. Calvin was not in every case opposed to considering the doctrinal implications of exegesis. In his interpretation of Gen. 4:26, he suggests that one of his reasons for adopting his view is the fact that it contains a useful teaching (C.O. 23.103).

31. This label is found in Louis Israel Newman, *Jewish Influence on Christian Reform Movements*, Columbia University Oriental Studies, no. 23 (New York: Columbia University Press, 1925), 511.

32. Michael Servetus, *The Two Treatises of Servetus on the Trinity*, trans. Earl Morse Wilbur, Harvard Theological Studies, no. 24 (Cambridge, Mass.: Harvard University Press, 1932), 173. This is a translation of *Trinitatis erroribus libri septum* and *Dialogorum de Trinitate libri duo*.

33. Friedman, *The Most Ancient Testimony*, 138. Friedman describes the conflict between Lutheran Hebraists of the Wittenberg school and Reformed Hebraists of the Strassburg-Basel-Zurich school. This conflict appears to be evidence of tension between Lutheran and Reformed methods that later led Hunnius to attack Calvin. The method of Servetus is radical compared to that of either school.

34. Newman, *Jewish Influence*, 531.

35. Servetus exhibits considerable independence in his Old Testament interpretation. His attacks on Trinitarianism make it clear that his use of the Old Testament was different from that of most Christian writers. He was embarrassed by traditional Christian exegesis of the Old Testament. He was indebted to Jewish interpreters and clearly believed their arguments against the doctrine of the Trinity to be compelling, yet he differs from them in his high regard for Christ and his willingness to allow the New Testament to inform his Old Testament exegesis. See Servetus, *The Two Treatises of Servetus on the Trinity*, 199ff.

36. Brevard S. Childs, *Old Testament Books for Pastor and Teacher* (Philadelphia: Westminster Press, 1977), 36.

37. Ibid., 63.

38. C.E.B. Cranfield, *A Critical and Exegetical Commentary on the Epistle to the Romans*, International Critical Commentary (Edinburgh: T. & T. Clark, 1975), 1:40.

39. Emil G. Kraeling, *The Old Testament since the Reformation* (London: Lutterworth Press, 1955), 32. Interestingly, Kraeling's concern about Calvin's Old Testament exegesis is the opposite of Hunnius's concern.

40. Hans-Joachim Kraus, "Calvin's Exegetical Principles," *Interpretation* 31 (January 1977): 8–18. This article is a translation of "Calvins exegetische Prinzipien," *Zeitschrift für Kirchengeschichte* 79 (1968): 329–41.

41. Alexandre Ganoczy and Stefan Scheld, *Die Hermeneutik Calvins: Geistesgeschichtliche Voraussetzungen und Grundzüge*, Veröffentlichungen des Instituts für Europäische Geschichte Mainz, ed. Peter Manns, no. 114 (Wiesbaden: Franz Steiner, 1983).

42. T.H.L. Parker, *Calvin's Old Testament Commentaries* (Edinburgh: T. & T. Clark, 1986), 80.

43. Ibid., 7.

44. Thomas F. Torrance, *The Hermeneutics of John Calvin* (Edinburgh: Scottish Academic Press, 1988), 155.

45. Ibid., 161.

46. Edward A. Dowey, Jr., *The Knowledge of God in Calvin's Theology* (New York: Columbia University Press, 1952), 104.

47. Kemper Fullerton, *Prophecy and Authority: A Study in the History of the Doctrine and Interpretation of Scripture* (New York: Macmillan, 1919), 133.

48. Ibid., 139.

49. Ibid., 141–42.

50. Ibid., 148.

51. Ibid., 160–61.

52. H. Jackson Forstman, *Word and Spirit: Calvin's Doctrine of Biblical Authority* (Stanford, Calif.: Stanford University Press, 1962), 123.

53. Ibid., 109.

54. Ibid., 115.

55. Ibid., 107–8.

56. Ibid., 112.

57. Ibid., 106.

58. Ibid., 109.

59. Basil Hall, "Biblical Scholarship: Editions and Commentaries," in *The Cambridge History of the Bible*, vol. 3: *The West from the Reformation to the Present Day*, ed. S. L. Greenslade (Cambridge: Cambridge University Press, 1963), 76.

60. T.H.L. Parker, *Calvin's New Testament Commentaries* (Grand Rapids: Wm. B. Eerdmans Publishing Co., 1971), ix.

61. David C. Steinmetz, "Calvin and Abraham: The Interpretation of Romans 4 in the Sixteenth Century," *Church History* 57 (December 1988): 443–55.

62. Parker, *Calvin's New Testament Commentaries*, 49.

63. Calvin to Simon Grynaeus, Oct. 18, 1539 (C.O. 10.403).

64. Parker, *Calvin's New Testament Commentaries*, 50.

65. Calvin describes the qualities of a good commentary in this preface by contrasting his ideal with the work of Philip Melanchthon and Martin Bucer. He gently criticizes Melanchthon for neglecting many points that deserve attention and Bucer for being verbose. He faults neither for failing to arrive at the true meaning of the text. Calvin's rationale for adopting his method of commentary

writing is discussed in Richard C. Gamble, "Brevitas et Facilitas: Toward an understanding of Calvin's Hermeneutic," *Westminster Theological Journal* 47 (1985): 1–17. Gamble argues that there are significant areas of discontinuity between Calvin's early commentary on Seneca and his later commentaries on scripture. See also Parker, *Calvin's New Testament Commentaries*, 50–56.

66. The data upon which the argument of this study is based are drawn largely from Calvin's published lectures and commentaries. This is because he frequently justifies his exegetical decisions in these works. A brief history of the publication of Calvin's lectures and commentaries is provided in the appendix.

67. Gamble, "Brevitas et Facilitas," 3.

68. Comm. Dan. 9:24 (C.O. 41.167). Calvin makes this statement to introduce a long refutation of incorrect exegesis he is about to undertake. "But I cannot escape the necessity of confuting various views of the present passage." He indicates that he is mainly concerned to show how incorrect the Jews are in their understanding of the passage. He will bring their errors to light with what he identifies as firm and certain reasons.

69. Comm. Gen. 4:24 (C.O. 23.102).

70. Calvin to Grynaeus (C.O. 10.402–3).

71. Comm. Pss., pref. (C.O. 31.33, 35). See also Comm. Dan. 11:36, where Calvin suggests that there is little utility and no end to the articulation of differing interpretations. He cannot, however, totally ignore them because "they occupy the minds of many and thus close the door to the correct interpretation" (C.O. 41.265).

72. Comm. Ps. 110:3 (C.O. 32.163). Torrance correctly notes that Calvin preferred not to adopt extrinsic arguments for his positions, preferring to "lay bare the truth inherent in the subject-matter and to let it have its own force in convincing people," in *The Hermeneutics of John Calvin*, 107; see also 162.

73. Comm. Isa. 8:20 (C.O. 36.185). Also Comm. Isa. 27:4 (C.O. 36.451); Comm. Jer. 1:13, 14 (C.O. 37.486).

74. Comm. Jer. 22:6 (C.O. 38.376). Calvin sometimes mentions differing interpretations without bothering to refute them. In his exposition of Genesis 16:13 he presents several interpretation options and rejects them without offering any reason. "Although I have no intention to pause for the purpose of refuting each of these expositions, I yet freely declare that not one of these interpreters has apprehended the meaning of Moses." He apparently believes the deficiencies in the other interpretations will be sufficiently evident to the reader because of the superior clarity of his own explanation. Comm. Gen. 16:13 (C.O. 23.231).

75. Kraus, "Calvin's Exegetical Principles," 11. Chapter 3 of this study shows that Calvin's view of Augustine's exegesis was not so elevated as Kraus suggests.

76. Calvin to Grynaeus (C.O. 10.402–3).

77. Ibid.

78. David Steinmetz attempts to determine which commentators Calvin may have used in "John Calvin on Isaiah 6: A Problem in the History of Exegesis," *Interpretation* 36 (April 1982): 160–63. The tentativeness of his conclusions suggests that it is very difficult to determine with any confidence who the "some" of Calvin's commentaries is. Pieter Verhoef, in "Luther's and Calvin's Exegetical Library" (*Calvin Theological Journal* 3 [April 1968]: 9), lists some of the commentaries on Malachi that Calvin "could have used." Calvin cites by name Africanus, Hippolytus, Origin, Cyprian, Lactantius, Eusebius, Hilary, Ambrose, Chrysostom,

Jerome, Augustine, Theodoret, Gregory, Dionysius, Luther, Bucer, Oecolampadius, Musculus. It is not the goal of the present study to attempt to determine Calvin's sources. It appears to me that Calvin often lumps Christian exegetes together. Thus, I will refer to the "Christian exegetical tradition." Although Calvin does occasionally make explicit reference to the Targums and Rabbi David Kimchi, usually he does not name his Jewish sources. He simply refers to them as "Jews" or "rabbis."

79. Calvin to Francis Burkhard, Mar. 3, 1555 (C.O. 15.454). In light of this statement, perhaps what Calvin means in saying he does not like to refute others is that he does not choose to refute them by name, or perhaps he actually believes that the tone of his comments is nonpolemical.

80. Comm. Dan. 9:25 (C.O. 41.175–76).

81. William J. Bouwsma, *John Calvin: A Sixteenth Century Portrait* (New York: Oxford University Press, 1988), 2–3.

82. Anthony Baxter, "John Calvin's Use and Hermeneutics of the Old Testament" (Ph.D. diss., University of Sheffield, 1987), 330.

83. Comm. Dan. 7:27 (C.O. 41.82).

84. Comm. Isa. 43:19 (C.O. 37.94).

85. Comm. Isa. 52:10 (C.O. 37.249–50).

86. Comm. Ps. 87:4 (C.O. 31.802). He expresses similar reservations about Jewish and Christian interpretive traditions in his exposition of Isa. 16:1 (C.O. 36.300); 26:19 (C.O. 36.441); 45:15 (C.O. 37.141–42); 52:4 (C.O. 37.245); Jer. 30:4–6 (C.O. 38.614); 32:41 (C.O. 39.45–46); Dan. 7:7 (C.O. 41.46); 7:27 (C.O. 41.82); 11:36 (C.O. 41.265).

87. Comm. Hos. 6:2 (C.O. 42.320).

88. Ford Lewis Battles argues that Calvin's attempt to find a "middle way" between opposing extremes is a prominent characteristic of the structure of his theology; see Battles's *Calculus Fidei: Some Ruminations on the Structure of the Theology of John Calvin* (Grand Rapids: Calvin Theological Seminary, 1978). The extremes Calvin most often opposes in the *Institutes* are, according to Battles, those of Romanism and Anabaptism.

2

TWO PRESUPPOSITIONS
OF CALVIN'S EXEGESIS

Scripture, Calvin believed, was published by human authors who wished to be read and understood by their contemporaries. However, if one looks only at the human side of scripture, one gets only half the picture of what scripture is—and, in Calvin's view, the less important half. Scripture is not simply a collection of ancient writings authored by human beings; it also has the Spirit of God for its author (*Scripturarum author est*).[1] For many early Christian writers, the divine authorship of scripture had very definite hermeneutical implications. It allowed—or necessitated—interpretation that went beyond the letter.[2] In this study of Calvin's method of exegetical reasoning the issue of the hermeneutical significance of his view of the divine authorship of scripture is unavoidable. Before examining that issue, it will be helpful to highlight some of the components of his view of scripture.

Though scripture is, in Calvin's view, a collection of writings composed by many individuals over many centuries, its divine authorship gives it a unity possessed by no other collection of writings. In his commentary on the Gospel of John, Calvin draws out one of the implications of the unity of scripture: "The scriptures should be read with the aim of finding Christ in them. . . . By the scriptures, of course, is here meant the Old Testament."[3] Yet Calvin can be very critical of those who interpret the Old Testament christologically. On what basis does he reject such exegesis? What role should the unity of scripture play in one's exegesis? How does one find Christ in the Old Testament? These questions will be addressed in chapters 3 through 5. But before answers can be given, it is necessary to examine Calvin's view of the unity of the Bible. The final section of this chapter will be devoted to that task.

THE DUAL AUTHORSHIP
OF SCRIPTURE

If the human writer is understood to be the author of scripture, and if at the same time the Holy Spirit is regarded as the author of scripture, a host of questions arise. Who is responsible for the content of scripture? Who is responsible for the arrangement of the content? Who is responsible for the wording of the text? And most importantly, whose intention is the interpreter to be concerned with—the Holy Spirit's or the human writer's? In this section I examine what Calvin has to say in answer to each of these questions.

The Divine Side of Scripture

The *locus classicus* for Calvin's view of the divine inspiration of scripture is his exposition of 2 Timothy 3:16 ("All Scripture is inspired by God"):

> To assert its authority he [Paul] teaches that it is inspired by God, for if that is so, it is beyond all question that men should receive it with reverence. This is the principle that distinguishes our religion from all others, that we know that God has spoken to us and are fully convinced that the prophets did not speak of themselves, but as organs of the Holy Spirit [*spiritus sancti organa*] uttered only that which they had been commissioned from heaven to declare. All those who wish to profit from the scriptures must first accept this as a settled principle, that the Law and the prophets are not teachings handed on at the pleasure of men or produced by men's minds as their source, but are dictated by the Holy Spirit [*spiritu sancto dictatam*]. . . . Moses and the prophets did not utter rashly and at random what we have received from them, but, speaking by God's impulse [*Dei impulsu loquerentur*], they boldly and fearlessly testified the truth that it was the mouth of the Lord that spoke through them. . . . [W]e owe to the scripture the same reverence as we owe to God, since it has its only source in Him and has nothing of human origin mixed with it [*nec quidquam humani habet admistum* (sic)].[4]

Scripture is authoritative because it has its source in God. Calvin makes this point in the strongest possible way. Scripture came from prophets who were instruments of the Holy Spirit; it was "dictated by the Holy Spirit"; it "has nothing of human origin mixed with it."[5]

The term Calvin most often uses to emphasize God's role in the production of the biblical text is *dictare*. In his commentary on John, he writes that God "so dictated [*dictavit*] to the four Evangelists what they should write that, while each had his own part, the whole formed one complete body."[6] The same is true of the Old Testament. "Histories were added to these, also the labor of the prophets, but composed under the Holy Spirit's dictation [*dictante spiritu sancto compositae*]."[7] "Daniel did not speak from his own discretion, but whatever he uttered was dictated by the Holy Spirit [*sed dictatum fuisse a spiritu sancto quidquid protulit*]."[8] Moses did not have "any intention of boastfully celebrating his own virtues, but that the Spirit dictated what would be useful to us [*sed quod nobis utile erat dictavit spiritus*], and, as it were, suggested it to his mouth."[9] "The words which God dictated [*dictavit Deus*] to his servant were called the words of Jeremiah; yet properly speaking, they were not the words of man [*iterea proprie loquendo non sunt hominis sermones*], for they did not proceed from a mortal man, but from the only true God."[10]

Calvin uses other expressions to convey essentially the same idea. Of the apostles and prophets he writes, "their lips are the mouth of the one true God [*illorum ora os unius Dei esse*]."[11] He calls the apostles "sure and genuine scribes of the Holy Spirit [*certi et authentici spiritus sancti amanuenses*]."[12] He has the Holy Spirit so involved in the production of the biblical text that Forstman is led to conclude that "it is as easy—one should probably say easier—for Calvin to speak of the scriptures as the writings of the Spirit as to think of them as the product of the men who actually moved the pens."[13] Again and again, using varying terminology, Calvin insists that the Spirit of God is to be regarded as the author of the Bible.[14]

The Human Side of Scripture

Although Calvin never articulates precisely how he conceives of the process of inspiration, this much is certain: the inspiration of scripture did not occur at the expense of the personalities of the human writers. The inspiration process he envisions is far from mechanical. In his discussion of God's revelation to the patriarchs, he clearly suggests that they received their revelation as thinking people. "There is no doubt that firm certainty of doctrine was engraved in their hearts, so that they were convinced and understood that what they had learned proceeded from God."[15] He believes that the writers of scripture kept their mental faculties intact as they arranged and wrote scripture. He writes of the psalmists "laying open all their inmost thoughts and affections,"[16] clearly suggesting the involvement of the human mind.

Calvin's comments on the literary style of the biblical text reflect his belief that the human authors' minds remained active in the production of scripture. He attributes stylistic variations to the fact that various writers were responsible for different portions of the Bible. He rejects Pauline authorship of the epistle to the Hebrews because he finds stylistic differences between it and the epistles he believes to be genuinely Pauline. "The manner of teaching and style sufficiently show that Paul was not the author."[17] He doubts that the apostle Peter wrote 2 Peter because he does not recognize in it "the genuine language of Peter."[18]

Calvin occasionally notes very significant stylistic differences among the prophets.

> I admit that some of the prophets had an elegant and clear, even brilliant, manner of speaking, so that their eloquence yields nothing to secular writers; and by such examples the Holy Spirit wished to show that he did not lack eloquence while he elsewhere used a rude and unrefined style [*voluit ostendere spiritus sanctus non sibi defuisse eloquentiam dum rudi et crasso stylo alibi usus est*]. But whether you read David, Isaiah, and the like, whose speech flows sweet and pleasing, or Amos the herdsman, Jeremiah, and Zechariah, whose harsher style savors of rusticity, that majesty of the Spirit of which I have spoken will be evident everywhere.[19]

He might also have mentioned the prophet Ezekiel, whose wordy style, he believes, is not as appealing as that of the other prophets. He attributes Ezekiel's lack of refinement to his background. "His language has evidently a foreign tinge, since those who are in exile naturally contract many faults of language, and the prophet was never anxious about elegance and polish, but, as he had been accustomed to a homely language, so he spoke himself."[20] Elsewhere he reaffirms his view that Ezekiel's verbosity should be understood in part as the result of the region where he lived; during the exile the purity of the people's language was lost and foreign elements were mixed into it. Furthermore, Ezekiel's coarse style was appropriate to the slowness and stupidity of the people.[21] So it is clear that Calvin understands stylistic peculiarities as in large part the natural product of the writer's training, the times in which he lived, and the needs of the people. Whatever the inspiration of the scripture involves, it cannot mean that the individual writer's peculiar literary style is negated.[22]

The imprint of the human writers of scripture is not limited to stylistic matters. Calvin finds evidence that the total personalities of these writers were involved. In his introductory comments on Paul's letter to Philemon, he writes that "the sublime quality of Paul's spirit, although seen better in his more important writings, is also apparent in this epistle."[23] Such a statement would be meaningless if the impact of the writer's personality was negated by the Spirit's inspiration.[24]

Calvin does not find the same sublime spirit in all the biblical writers. Some of the emotional outbursts of the psalmist stretch his considerable exegetical skill as he tries to find an acceptable explanation for how such sentiment could be in scripture. He sees improper emotions expressed in Psalm 88:14 ("O LORD, why dost thou cast me off? Why dost thou hide thy face from me?") and Psalm 89:46 ("How long, O LORD? Wilt thou hide thyself forever? How long will thy wrath burn like fire?"). In both instances he tentatively condones the psalmist's outbursts—in Psalm 88 because it contains tacit prayers,[25] in Psalm 89 because it is accompanied by faith.[26] He has greater difficulty, however, explaining David's bitter complaint against God in Psalm 39:13 ("Look away from me, that I may know gladness, before I depart and be no more"). "This concluding verse of the psalm relates to the disquietude and sinful emotions which he had experienced according to the flesh." Calvin finds it difficult to explain this text in an acceptable way. David's complaint was "not well seasoned with the sweetness of faith." However, David's outburst may not be as bad as it at first appears, for he is not entirely negative. He speaks "in a becoming manner, in acknowledging that there is no hope of his being restored to health, until God ceases to manifest his displeasure."[27] Calvin does not seem very satisfied with his explanation. Forstman suggests that if pressed on this point, Calvin had an answer available in a principle of multiple causation, "worked out mainly in his discussion of the problem of evil but equally applicable here." This, Forstman believes, would allow Calvin to say that "although David's words were unbecoming, the Spirit, speaking through David and using David's excess, intended something entirely acceptable."[28] Forstman's explanation derives some support from the immediate context, where Calvin suggests that God may have intended to communicate something useful for his people through David's intemperate speech.

> David spoke under the influence of a distempered and troubled state of mind, but there is included in his language this very profitable lesson, that there is no remedy better fitted for enabling us to rise above all necessary cares than the recollection that the brief period of our life is only, as it were, a hand-breadth.[29]

Is Calvin suggesting here the idea of two distinct purposes or intentions in the passage—one human and one divine? If so, it raises an important hermeneutical question. Whose intention is the interpreter of scripture concerned with—that of the human writer or that of the Holy Spirit? This is a question Calvin never systematically addresses. Thus far, this much is clear: Calvin believes the style and personality of the human writers left their mark on scripture.

The Selection and Arrangement of Content

Calvin believes the Holy Spirit's involvement in the production of scripture extends to the actual selection of what to include in the biblical text. This is evident throughout his treatment of the Pentateuch. In his exposition of Genesis 5, the selection of material—or more correctly, the decision not to select material—is attributed to a divine decision. It is the intention of the Holy Spirit (*consilium spiritus*) that accounts for the fact that great and memorable events were left unrecorded.[30] He notes that Moses, in Genesis 17, omits any record of over thirteen years of Abram's life. This omission should not be understood to imply that nothing worth remembering occurred, but rather "because the Spirit of God, according to his own will, selects those things which are most necessary to be known [*sed quia spiritus Dei arbitrio delegit quae cognitu maxime necessaria erant*]."[31] That there is no record of over a decade of Abram's life is not the result of Moses' decision alone. The Holy Spirit did not deem it necessary that posterity know what happened during those years. In his treatment of Genesis 24 he suggests that the Spirit of God was responsible for the recording of details of the courtship and marriage of Isaac—information that seems trivial.[32] In his *Harmony of the Last Four Books of Moses* Calvin addresses the issue of the Holy Spirit's responsibility for the arrangement of the material. He responds to the charge that he is trying to improve on the arrangement of the Holy Spirit by altering "the order which the Holy Spirit himself has prescribed to us [*spiritus sanctus nobis praescribit*]." In defending himself, he argues that he is not trying to improve on the excellent arrangement dictated to Moses—that would be "an act of audacity akin to sacrilege."[33] This is a meaningful statement only if Calvin considers the Holy Spirit to be responsible for the arrangement of the contents of Exodus through Deuteronomy.

The Wording of the Text

The Holy Spirit's involvement in the production of scripture extends beyond the selection and arrangement of material to the choice of the very wording of the text. The Holy Spirit is "the best master of language." So Calvin writes in his commentary on Daniel 4:35. Here the prophet recounts the confession of Nebuchadnezzar that "God does what he pleases with the powers of heaven and the peoples of earth." Calvin admits that this statement may seem overly harsh, since God is said to act in any way he wills—"as if there were no moderation, or equity, or rule of justice with him." He insists, however, that the choice of the precise language involved more than a human decision.

> From this sentence we gather that nothing happens by chance, but every event in the world depends on God's secret purpose. We ought not to admit any distinction between God's permission and his wish. For we see the Holy Spirit—the best master of language [*optimus loquendi magister*]—here expresses two things: first, what God does; and next, what he does by his own will.[34]

In his attempt to justify God against the charge that according to his absolute power God may act unjustly (that he may even be the author of sin), Calvin expresses his belief that the language of this verse is exactly what the Holy Spirit wished to use to convey his message.[35]

He adopts a similar line of reasoning in his exposition of Psalm 105, where the psalmist writes that God turned the hearts of the Egyptians to hate his people. He objects to those who think the active form is too harsh and so choose to adopt a passive interpretation of the verb.

> If the delicate ears of some are offended at such doctrine, let it be observed that the Holy Spirit unequivocally affirms in other places as well as here that the minds of men are driven here and there by a secret impulse (Prov. 21:1), so that they can neither will nor do any thing except as God pleases. . . . The Holy Spirit, we see, affirms that the Egyptians were so wicked that God turned their hearts to hate his people. The middle-scheme men seek to evade and qualify this statement by saying that his turning their hearts denotes his permitting this; or, that when the Egyptians were so wicked, that when the Egyptians set their hearts upon hating the Israelites, he made use of their malice, as what, so to speak, came accidentally in his way; as if the Holy Spirit, from being defective in the power of language, spoke one thing when he meant another.[36]

Two points may be noted here. First, the Holy Spirit is viewed as affirming something very specific—"that the Egyptians were so wicked that God turned their hearts to hate his people." Second, although the idea that God actively turns the hearts of men to do evil may seem offensive to some, Calvin insists that the meaning of the text must not be diluted by treating the verb as though it were in the passive voice. The Holy Spirit is able to use any language he likes in order to communicate precisely what he wishes. If the Holy Spirit had wanted to communicate a passive idea here, he certainly could have provided the passive verb.

Calvin's observations elsewhere confirm that, in his view, the Holy Spirit is deeply involved in the production of the very wording of the text. In his commentary on Psalm 129:3 ("The plowers plowed upon my back; they made long their furrows") he attributes a very specific figure of speech to the agency of the Holy Spirit. "The Holy Spirit not unfitly compares us to an arable field."[37] The Holy Spirit is also responsible for the form of many of the prayers found in the Bible. In his exposition of Psalm 44:19 Calvin writes: "In these words the Holy Spirit dictates to us a form of prayer [*in his verbis dictari nobis a spiritu sancto precandi formam*]."[38] In his discussion of the Lord's Prayer in the *Institutes* he is emphatic concerning the Holy Spirit's authorship of the prayers found in the Bible. "Here and there in Scripture one reads many prayers, far different from it in words, yet composed by the same Spirit [*eodem tamen spiritu conscrip-*

tae]."[39] The Holy Spirit was thus involved in the form and composition of the prayers of scripture; it is as if he had composed them himself. In his exposition of Genesis 39:6 Calvin attributes the language (the "form of speech") to both Moses and the Holy Spirit. He finds in the account of the attempted seduction of Joseph by Potiphar's wife the words "his master's wife cast her eyes upon Joseph." He observes that the Holy Spirit by this form of speech admonishes all women that their demeanor should reflect a pure heart. Yet he also attributes the words to Moses. "Moses here describes an impure and dissolute look."[40] Calvin further highlights the close connection of the human and divine roles in the writing of scripture in his exposition of Obadiah. "Jeremiah and this prophet made use of the same thoughts and nearly the same words, as we shall hereafter see." This is not simply a matter of two prophets who happen to use similar language, for Calvin explains that the Holy Spirit was in some way responsible for the language of these parallel passages. "The Holy Spirit could, no doubt, have expressed the same things in different words, but he was pleased to join together these two testimonies that they might obtain more credit."[41]

The Holy Spirit's Intention
as an Exegetical Concern

Since Calvin wants to understand the genuine meaning of the text, and since he views scripture as having both a divine side and a human side, the question naturally arises, Is the genuine meaning that of the human writer or that of the Holy Spirit? McNeill argues that Calvin "habitually keeps in view the human writer of each book, his purpose and intent in each passage."[42] Jean Crispin, Calvin's printer, indicates that the genuine meaning for Calvin is that which conforms to the intent of the Holy Spirit. "He everywhere so unfolds the intention of the Holy Spirit [*spiritus sancti consilium*], so gives his genuine meaning. . . ."[43]

Some of Calvin's comments indicate that Crispin's statement accurately reflects Calvin's goal as an exegete—one does not truly understand the text until one discovers the meaning intended by the Holy Spirit. In defense of Paul's use of Psalm 5 ("their throat is an open grave") in Romans 3:13, Calvin argues that the apostle is correct in extending the reference beyond the Jews to include all humankind. Paul's interpretation is justifiable because it does not go beyond the mind or intention of the Spirit (*praeter mentem spiritus*).[44] In his commentary on Daniel 12:4 Calvin rejects an interpretation with the statement "I think the Holy Spirit has a different intention here [*consilium spiritus sancti*]."[45] In his comments on Numbers 14:11 he approves of the Vulgate reading because Jerome's word choice in this translation comes near the genuine sense of the text—the sense of God. "Let us be contented with the genuine sense of God [*genuina Dei sententia*]."[46]

The task of biblical interpretation involves asking what God's purpose may have been in giving the information recorded in scripture. In his interpretation of Leviticus 11:13 Calvin indicates that the exegete must always consider the intention of God (*Dei consilium*). By this he means that the interpreter must keep in mind God's purpose in giving the law to his people.[47] The intention of God in this case extends beyond the literal meaning of the words.

> We must, I say, inquire how far interpretation ought to overstep the limits of the words themselves so that it may be seen to be, not an appendix to the divine law from men's glosses, but the Lawgiver's pure and authentic meaning faithfully rendered. . . . Now, I think this would be the best rule, if attention be directed to the reason of the commandment; that is, in each commandment to ponder why it was given to us.[48]

In introducing his lecture on Daniel 7, Calvin offers instruction to his young students who wish to understand the visions described in the chapter. They must "try to understand the intention of the Holy Spirit [*spiritus sancti consilium*]." The Holy Spirit's intention in this passage was to hold out the hope of deliverance to God's people who were captive in Babylon.[49] In his exposition of Daniel 11 Calvin insists that "we must always strive to ascertain the intention of the Holy Spirit [*consilium spiritus sancti*]." Here the intention of the Holy Spirit was to provide encouragement for God's people under the heavy afflictions they were to encounter.[50] In his commentary on Jeremiah 10, he argues: "If we desire to read what has been written with profit, we must consider the meaning intended by the Holy Spirit [*consilium spiritus sancti*]."[51] Correct application of the text in each of these instances depends upon understanding the intention of the Spirit.

The Human Writer's Intention
as an Exegetical Concern

Calvin's concern with the intention of the Holy Spirit does not lead him to ignore that of the human writer. Throughout his Old Testament commentaries he affirms that the role of an interpreter is to expound the intention of the prophet. In his commentary on Psalm 8 he writes, "I have now discharged the duty of a faithful interpreter in opening up the mind of the prophet [*ad explicandam prophetae mentem*]."[52] In his letter to Simon Grynaeus he writes that it is almost the only task of an interpreter "to unfold the mind of the writer [*mentem scriptoris*] he has undertaken to expound." The interpreter "misses his mark, or at least strays outside his limits, by the extent to which he leads his readers away from the purpose [a scopo] of his author."[53] Calvin frequently charges other interpreters with failing to consider the human author's intention. He reviews two interpretations of Amos 6:10, rejecting both, because, as he says, "it seems to me that the Prophet's intention [consilium prophetae] is another, which interpreters have not sufficiently weighed."[54] He argues that the clause "affliction shall not rise up the second time" in Nahum 1:9 has been wrongly understood to mean that "God does not punish men twice, nor exceed moderation in his wrath." This is an unacceptable interpretation, he argues, because it is "wholly foreign to the mind of the prophet [a mente prophetae]."[55]

Calvin's desire to interpret the text according to the intention of the writer is probably most clearly reflected in his lectures on Hosea. He indicates that he cannot follow previous interpreters because they do not come to grips with the intention of the prophet who produced the work. Hosea 6:3 ("we shall know, and shall pursue on to know Jehovah") was sometimes explained as a prophecy of "that doctrine, which is now by the Gospel set forth to us in its full brightness, because God has manifested himself in his Son as in a living image." This, Calvin believes, is too subtle (arguta). "It is enough for us to keep close to the intention of the prophet [prophetae consilium]."[56] Two chapters later, in Hosea 8, interpreters once again are wrong in their exegesis, because they have not sufficiently considered "the intention of the prophet [consilium prophetae]." They do not, he writes, "attend sufficiently to the mind of the prophet [prophetae mentem]."[57] In Hosea 10:1 he is unable to accept an interpretation because "these interpreters do not seem to understand the mind of the Prophet [prophetae mentem]."[58] In his lecture on Hosea 13 he chastises exegetes who depart "from the mind of the prophet [a prophetae mente]."[59]

Calvin's concern for the intention of the human writer is not limited to the book of Hosea. It extends from the first book of the Pentateuch to the last of the Old Testament prophets. He questions an overly subtle Christian interpretation of Genesis 28, in which Jacob's act of pouring oil on a stone memorial is allegorized. The stone became "a symbol of Christ, on whom all the graces of the Spirit were poured out, that all might draw out of his fullness." Calvin questions whether any such thing "entered the mind [mentem] of Moses or of Jacob."[60] He rejects an interpretation of Psalm 75:3 that would never have entered the mind of the prophet (prophetae in mentem).[61] He rejects an interpretation of Psalm 89:11 that "seems too much removed from the mind of the prophet [a prophetae mente]."[62] In his exposition of Amos 5, the intention of the prophet becomes the controlling factor in determining the meaning of the Hebrew word   . Some interpreters took the word to mean a cake; others regarded it as a proper name; still others rendered the word literally.

Against the first view he argues that those who hold it have not attended to "the intention of the prophet [*prophetae consilium*]."[63] Malachi 4 has not been clearly and fully explained, "because interpreters did not know the intention of Malachi [*consilium Malachiae*] or consider the circumstances of the time [*temporis circumstantiam*]."[64] The true meaning is the one intended by the prophet.

The Relation of Divine Intention
and Human Intention

Calvin believes the intention of the Holy Spirit and that of the human writer are very closely related. In his commentary on Zechariah he says that he knows of no reason to seek "other meanings at variance with the mind and intention of the prophet [*mente et consilio prophetae*]."[65] Yet, he insists in his comments on Leviticus 11:13 that the exegete must always consider the intention of God (*Dei consilium*).[66] He acknowledges no tension between such affirmations. He is reluctant to allow any division between human and divine intentionality. There appears to be no *sensus plenior* intended by God that is very different from the intention of the prophet.[67]

Calvin's comments on Joel 2:28 provide an example of the link between the intention of the prophet and that of the Holy Spirit. This passage ("I shall afterwards pour my spirit out on all flesh") is quoted in Peter's sermon (Acts 2) as a prophecy fulfilled in the coming of the Holy Spirit on the day of Pentecost. Calvin believes this must be understood as hyperbole, because everyone ("all flesh") did not actually partake of the gift. In the process of defending his interpretation he attributes the hyperbole first to the prophet—then to the Spirit of God.

> We must also remember that the Prophet hyperbolically [*hyperbolice*] extols the grace of God; for such is our stupidity and dullness that we can never sufficiently comprehend the grace of God, except it is set forth to us in hyperbolical language; nor is there indeed any excess in the thing itself, if we take a right view of it: but as we hardly understand the hundredth part of God's gifts, when he presents them before our eyes, it was needful to add a commendation, calculated to elevate our thoughts. The Spirit of God is then constrained to speak hyperbolically [*hyperbolice*] on account of our torpidity or rather carelessness.[68]

In his commentary on Isaiah 34 Calvin uses language that suggests that there is little difference between attributing words to the prophet or to the Holy Spirit. "What Isaiah threatens in this passage against the Edomites, the Spirit elsewhere declares as to the house of Ahab [*Quod autem minatur hoc loco Idumaeis Isaias, alibi pronuntiat spiritus de domo Achab*]." He sees the threat in one passage as originating with the Holy Spirit, while the almost identical threat in another passage is the work of the prophet.[69]

In his discussion of Jacob's rejection of Leah in favor of Rachel in Genesis 29 Calvin highlights the close connection between the work of the Spirit and that of the human writer in the production of scripture. He states that "Moses asserts that Leah was hated," only to indicate a few lines later that "the Holy Spirit pronounced those as hated who are not sufficiently loved." Calvin here seems to indicate that the pronouncement of Moses can be looked at as either his own assertion or as that of the Holy Spirit.[70] Clearer still is his comment on Jeremiah 17:12, in which he appears to equate the intention of the prophet with that of the Holy Spirit. "We must understand the intention of the prophet [*prophetae consilium*]; for the Holy Spirit sometimes commemorates the blessings of God [*Aliquando enim spiritus sanctus commemorat Dei beneficia*] to raise the minds of men to confidence, or to rouse them to make sacrifices of praise."[71]

The most interesting examples of the intimate connection between the human and divine sides of scripture are found in several instances where Calvin attributes a statement to the human writer, then appears to correct himself and attribute it to the Holy Spirit. In his interpretation of Psalm 87 he writes, "we must consider the intention of the prophet, or rather the object of the Spirit of God, speaking by the mouth of the prophet [*Spectandum est prophetae consilium, vel potius quo spectet Dei spiritus per os prophetae ipsius loquens*]." This passage is most significant because here he seems to suggest that the intention of the prophet and the Holy Spirit are so closely related as to be virtually interchangeable.[72] His choice of words seems deliberate, for he uses similar phraseology in other commentaries. In the Genesis commentary he upbraids impious men who "wonder that Moses, or rather the Spirit of God [*in rebus tam minutis occupari Mosen, vel potius Dei spiritum*]," should be employed in matters so minute as the courtship and marriage of Isaac.[73] In his exposition of Ezekiel 16:4, 5, he attributes an idea to the prophet, then corrects himself. "Now, therefore, we understand the intention of the prophet, or rather of the Holy Spirit [*Nunc ergo tenemus consilium prophetae, vel potius spiritus sancti*]."[74] He uses almost identical phraseology in his comments on Ezekiel 18:1–4: "We now understand the intention of the prophet, or rather of the Holy Spirit [*Nunc tenemus consilium prophetae, vel spiritus sancti potius*]."[75] He rebukes those who criticize Isaiah for being too verbose: "They who suppose that the Prophet, or rather the Spirit of God, uses too many words are not well acquainted with themselves." Here he attributes to the Holy Spirit the very wording of the text.

It is apparent that Calvin is unwilling to divorce the intention of the human writer from the meaning of the Holy Spirit. It is difficult to escape the conclusion that for him, the intention, thoughts, and words of the prophet and of the Holy Spirit in the production of scripture are so closely related there is no practical way to distinguish them.[76]

THE UNITY OF SCRIPTURE

"The covenant made with all the patriarchs is so much like ours in substance and reality [substantia et re ipsa] that the two are actually one and the same [unum prorsus et idem]."[77] Calvin could hardly have chosen stronger words to describe how the dispensation of the patriarchs is related to the New Testament dispensation. The people of God are one and God's revelation to his people as recorded in scripture is one. The differences between the revelation under the old and new covenants pale when compared with that which remains the same. So strong is his view of the unity of the two testaments that Kraeling is led to conclude that Calvin is guilty of Christianizing the Old Testament; he adopts an approach that is historically inadmissible; he "practically closes his eyes to the new moral values in the preaching of Jesus and reduces Him to the level of a correct interpreter of Moses."[78]

In setting forth such a strong view of the unity of the Bible, Calvin is not breaking new ground. In fact, the more novel approach was to argue for the discontinuity of the two testaments, as some of the Anabaptists did. The remainder of this chapter will consist of an examination of the prominent role the unity of scripture played in Calvin's thought.

The Relation of the
Old and the New Testaments

A serious challenge was posed to Calvin's understanding of biblical unity by a view commonly held among Anabaptists that the Old Testament is fundamentally different from the New.[79] The Old Testament dispensation was fleshly and temporary, with a different hope and faith than that which Christians share. The hope of people of the Old Testament was directed toward earthly prosperity. Their relationship to God was regulated by their own good works. They knew little of Christ. The Old Testament is a Jewish book, vastly inferior to the New, and obviously of much less value to God's people in the Christian era.[80]

Calvin objects to each of these conclusions. He insists that "carnal prosperity and happiness did not constitute the goal set before the Jews to which they were to aspire." The Jews, like Christians of the present age, "were adopted into the hope of immortality." While it is true that the promises of the Old Testament appear to have been directed to the present earthly life, they actually offered eternal life. We know this because the writers of the New Testament make it abundantly clear that the hope they offer is no different from that offered in the Old Testament. Does not the apostle Paul identify his preaching with the message of the Old Testament in Romans 1:2 when he ties his own apostolic status to the gospel that God had promised through his prophets long beforehand? Does he not also write in Romans 3:21 that the Law and Prophets bear witness to the very same righteousness taught by himself—a righteousness of faith, apart from the Law? Calvin draws the conclusion: "If the doctrine of the gospel is spiritual, and gives us access to the possession of incorruptible life, let us not think that those to whom it had been promised and announced omitted and neglected the care of the soul, and sought after fleshly pleasures like stupid beasts."[81]

In his Old Testament commentaries Calvin reaffirms his view that the people of that period were not limited to an earthly, carnal knowledge; they did have a hope of immortality. The Old Testament promises appear earthly because they are repeated with much more clarity in the New Testament. God used the earthly promises to direct the minds of his people upward to the heavenly reality. The perceptive reader, Calvin believes, will realize that the Old Testament saints saw beyond the earthly promise to the spiritual reality. For example, though Isaac in blessing Jacob in Genesis 27 appears to confine his remarks to earthly prosperity, he actually saw much farther. "The Lord did not formerly set the hope of the future inheritance plainly before the eyes of the fathers (as he now calls and raises us directly towards heaven), but he led them by a circuitous course." God appointed the land of Canaan "as a mirror and pledge to them of the celestial inheritance. . . . Therefore, although Isaac makes the temporal favors of God prominent, nothing is further from his mind than to confine the hope of his son to this world."[82] Isaac understood that the blessing he gave to Jacob was not limited to an earthly inheritance. From Genesis to Malachi the hope of God's people was spiritual, not earthly. "Under the law we know that the groaning and the sighings of the godly were towards Christ."[83]

Just as it was never the will of God for the minds of God's people to be centered on the promises of earthly prosperity, it was not his will that the physical ceremonies of the Old Testament cult be the object of their faith. "It was not the will of God that the minds of his people should be entirely engrossed with the magnificence of the building, or with the pomp of outward ceremonies, but that they should be elevated to Christ, in whom the truth of the figure of the former economy was exhibited."[84] The basis of salvation is exactly the same in both the Old Testament and the New—the unmerited favor of God. The condition of salvation is also the same—faith in the Mediator. God's people in both ages are one people, for all have freely received eternal life through faith in Christ. Believers in the later dispensation have no grounds for adopting an attitude of superiority toward God's people in the Old Testament, for "Christ the Lord promises to his followers today no other 'Kingdom of Heaven' than that in which they may sit at the table with Abraham, Isaac, and Jacob."[85] Although the Old Testament law appears to be carnal when viewed in the fuller light of the New Testament, in fact the messages are no different. This is because the ceremonies of the law were intended, not as ends in themselves, but as means to point the Jews to the spiritual reality that they symbolized. An example of this may be seen in the necessity of ceremonially cleansing anyone who touched the unclean scapegoat on the Day of Atonement. When the people of Old Testament times reflected on the fact that a man was forbidden to enter the camp if he had been ceremonially polluted by touching the goat, they were necessarily directed to the spiritual lesson: "How much wider was the alienation between God and themselves, when they bore upon them an uncleanness not contracted elsewhere, but procured by their own sin."[86] Calvin insists that it was never God's intent for the people of the Old Testament simply to hear the Word of God and participate in the ceremonies. The value of the ceremonies depended upon the people elevating their minds above the outward things and rendering to God spiritual worship. The external ceremonies were to serve as "ladders, by which the faithful might ascend to heaven."[87] The message they were to receive under the old economy was never anything other than God's gracious provision for salvation through Christ. The ceremonies were meant to be "a most unmistakable sign of that atonement, whereby, in the fullness of time, they were to be reconciled to God." The eulogy of Moses recorded in Leviticus 16 "exalts the grace of the coming Mediator, so that He may direct the minds of believers to him alone."[88]

The Old Testament believer was as closely tied to the intercessory work of Christ as the believer of the New Testament.

> Who, then, dares to separate the Jews from Christ, since with them, we hear, was made the covenant of the gospel, the sole foundation of which is Christ? Who dares to estrange from the gift of free salvation those to whom we hear the doctrine of the righteousness of faith was imparted?[89]

Had not the Lord himself said that Abraham had rejoiced to see his day? Knowledge of Christ had been central to God's people since the time of Abraham. This view, Calvin recognizes, could be challenged, since Christ did not actually appear bodily until New Testament times. He argues, however, that in words of the Abrahamic covenant, Christ was truly promised.

> It may be objected, "Why is Christ appointed to a covenant which was ratified long before? For, more than two thousand years before, God had adopted Abraham, and thus the origin of the distinction was long before

the coming of Christ." I reply, the covenant which was made with Abraham and his posterity had its foundation in Christ; for the words of the covenant are these, "In thy seed shall all nations be blessed" (Gen. 22:18). And the covenant was ratified in no other manner than in the seed of Abraham, that is, in Christ, by whose coming, though it had been previously made, it was confirmed and actually sanctioned.[90]

Did the people of the Old Testament really understand that the basis of their relationship with God was to be found in Christ? Calvin insists that they did and that this explains why the prophets often attached prophecies of Christ's kingdom to their messages. When the people of the Old Testament were overwhelmed with sorrow and near despair, the prophets placed Christ before them to give them hope. It was necessary that the people know of Christ in order to endure their hardships. Otherwise, neither the love of God nor the testimony of his kindness and paternal favor could be confirmed. The godly have always directed their minds to Christ.[91] Whatever assurance of God's favor the people of the Old Testament had came through faith in him. This is how Calvin explains a stylistic peculiarity of the prophets. They abruptly break into whatever they were writing in order to speak of Christ, "for in him are ratified all the promises which would otherwise have been doubtful and uncertain."[92] Thus, the major issue of life for the people of the Old Testament was no different than in the New Testament—faith in Christ.

Calvin does recognize several differences between the Old and New Testaments, differences that he insists in no way detract from the Bible's unity.[93] First, the mode of training is higher in the new dispensation than it was in the old. God trained his people in Old Testament times by displaying the gospel "under earthly benefits." He gave earthly promises to help them direct their thoughts upward to the heavenly reality. The Lord, "in testifying his benevolence toward believers by present good things, then foreshadowed spiritual happiness by such types and symbols, so on the other hand he gave, in physical punishments, proofs of his coming judgment against the wicked."[94] The people of the old covenant were not blind to the fact that the Lord accommodated his message to their weakness in using earthly means to train them. They were attracted all the more to the goodness of God who would stoop to speak to them through such means.

A second difference between the Old and New Testaments is that, in earlier times God used figures, images, or shadows of divine truth in place of the reality itself. The New Testament, however, "reveals the very substance of truth as present."[95] Calvin finds this teaching developed most fully in the epistle to the Hebrews.[96] There, he observes, the apostle was arguing against those who believed the abolition of Mosaic ceremonies meant the ruin of the religion associated with them. But, according to Hebrews 10:1, in the law there was " 'the shadow of good things to come' and not 'the living likeness of the things themselves.' Therefore, its sole function was to be an introduction to the better hope that is manifested in the gospel."[97] It was God's will to train Old Testament believers as children, using external observances, until Christ came bringing the possibility of fuller knowledge and maturity. Immaturity characterized not only the average believer of the Old Testament but the prophets themselves who, for all their remarkable knowledge, were still to be classed as children. Not one of them "possessed discernment so clear as to be unaffected by the obscurity of the time."[98] In his commentary on Daniel, Calvin notes the clear inferiority of the Old Testament economy and warns that "whoever desires to copy them in all their actions, would rather become an ape than the imitator of antiquity."[99]

This is just the mistake that supporters of the papacy made in their use of instrumental music in their churches. Calvin believes this defect of papal practice is rooted in a failure to recognize the superiority of the mode of training in the New Testament. Supporters of the papacy were seeking to imitate people of the ancient dispensation. He launches into a very sharp critique of their use of instrumental music as "a silly delight in that worship of the Old Testament which was figurative and terminated with the gospel." The outward worship of God in the ceremonies of the Old Testament was never the essential part of worship. It was necessary to lead people who were weak and defective in knowledge into a true spiritual worship of God. Now that Christ has appeared and the church reached maturity, to return to the shadowy dispensation as the supporters of the papacy do is to bury the light of the gospel.[100] Calvin argues that the injunction of Psalm 81 to use musical instruments in the worship of God provides no support for the use of such instruments in the new dispensation. One must recognize the shadowy nature of worship before the advent of Christ.

> The Levites, under the law, were justified in making use of instrumental music in the worship of God, it having been his will to train his people, while they were as yet tender and like children, by such rudiments, until the coming of Christ. But now when the clear light of the gospel has dissipated the shadows of the law, and taught us that God is to be served in a simpler form, it would be to act a foolish and mistaken part to imitate that which the prophet enjoined only upon those of his own time. From this, it is apparent that the Papists have shown themselves to be very apes in transferring this to themselves.[101]

Supporters of the papacy also make the mistake of slavishly following other ceremonial rites of the old dispensation. They do not see that the outward rites of the old dispensation are done away because of the superior clarity of the new. "It appears how foolishly the popish bishops, as it were, ape Moses, when, in imitation of him, they sprinkle their priests and altars and other rubbish with stinking oil, since it is abundantly clear that this ceremony of anointing, belonging as it did to the ancient shadows of the Law, ceased at the coming of Christ."[102] According to Calvin, there was no efficacy in the anointing with oil "except insofar as it was a figure of the Holy Spirit [spiritus figura]."[103] In view of the clear New Testament teaching concerning the Holy Spirit, there remains no purpose in observing the outward rite.

The relative obscurity of Old Testament teaching is a frequent theme in Calvin's commentaries. He contrasts the obscure teaching of the law with the open light of the gospel.[104] It is on the matter of clarity that Calvin most often finds differences between the two economies. The law given to Moses was clothed in ceremonies and earthly elements that very much resembled those of neighboring peoples. Nevertheless it did instruct the Jews in the spiritual worship of God and directed them in a figurative, shadowy way to a true understanding of God. Later God sent his prophets, who taught the people more about the substance of the ancient shadows by drawing their attention to the kingdom of Christ. Finally the apostles came, preaching the very same message as the Old Testament prophets, yet in a clearer form. It is the apostles who teach that Christ alone is the fulfillment of the promises. It is they who show that Christ abolished all typical ceremonies by fulfilling them. In the apostolic message we see that the rites of the Old Testament apart from Christ "are mere farces, since neither the blood of animals, nor the sweetness of fat, nor aromatic odors, nor candles, nor anything of that sort, have any power to propitiate God." Yet since the promises of God accompanied the legal sacrifices and ceremonies of the Old Testament, "we are reminded that all the ancient figures were sure testimonies of God's grace and of eternal salvation."[105]

The third difference between the Old and New Testaments is related to the message of 2 Corinthians 3, where the apostle contrasts the New Covenant with the Old. The Old Testament, he notices, "is of the letter, for it was published without the working of the Spirit. The New is spiritual because the Lord has engraved it spiritually upon men's hearts." The Old brought cursing, accusation, and condemnation; the New brings freedom and life, justification and righteousness. Since the ceremonial law "bore the image of things absent, it had to die and vanish with time." The gospel, on the other hand, "because it reveals the very substance, stands fast forever."[106] We should not conclude, however, that the giving of the law was totally fruitless. It is only through a comparison with the clear preaching of the New Testament that the deficiencies of the Old Covenant become so evident.

The fourth difference arises out of the third. The Old Testament, which is characterized by bondage producing fear, is contrasted in Romans 5 with the New Testament, which produces freedom and lifts one to trust and assurance. The people of the Old Testament were compelled to observe all of the ceremonies—symbols of God's tutelage. While it was true that those who were reborn of God obeyed out of faith working through love and thus belonged to the New Covenant,[107] even the most spiritually mature Old Testament believer was not totally exempt from the bondage and fear produced by the law. "For, however much they enjoyed the privilege that they had received through the grace of the gospel, they were still subject to the same bonds and burdens of ceremonial observances as the common people."[108]

The fifth difference is that following the incarnation, God extends to all nations his salvation, which was earlier confined largely to the Jews. That this difference is almost an afterthought is suggested by Calvin's introduction to the chapter. "Those chief differences, as far as I can note or remember, are four in number. If anyone wants to add a fifth difference, I shall not object at all."[109]

Calvin cannot fully explain why God made the change in administration. It is not thinkable, however, that one could charge God with changeableness because he chose to work in different ways in different ages. The best answer Calvin can provide is to say that God graciously accommodated his methods to the immaturity of the Old Testament people.[110] Such accommodation, it would seem, is no longer necessary; the apostle Paul compares Christians to young men rather than children in Galatians 4. The incarnation was the turning point. "It was necessary," writes Calvin, "with one kind of sign to represent Christ absent and to proclaim him about to come; but it is fitting that, now revealed, he be represented in another." Calvin's final appeal, for those who find such an explanation unconvincing, is directly to the sovereign will of God. "Who then, I pray, will say it is not fitting that God should have in his own hand and will the free disposing of his graces, and should illuminate such nations as he chooses."[111]

Some have suggested that Calvin's theology of the unity of scripture as stated in the *Institutes* is betrayed by his exegetical practice as expressed in his expository writings. Fullerton maintains that while Calvin emphasizes the unity of scripture very strongly in the *Institutes*, in his commentaries he overcomes his dogmatic orientation and interprets the text historically.[112] This, however, is an oversimplification of Calvin's approach. While he does attempt to interpret the text historically, he does not do this at the expense of the unity of scripture. His strong belief in this unity is as apparent in his expository writings as it is in the *Institutes*. His statements in the commentaries confirm what he says in the *Institutes*. The Old

Testament is obscure, figurative, and full of shadows, yet the substance of its teaching is identical with that of the New Testament.

> It was necessary that all the ancient ceremonies should be abolished, and that a new form of teaching should be introduced, though the substance of the doctrine continue to be the same; for the law formerly proceeded out of Mount Sinai (Ex. 19:20), but now it proceeded out of Zion, and therefore it assumed a new form. Two things, therefore, must be observed: first, that the doctrine of God is the same, and always agrees with itself, that no one may now charge God with changeableness, as if he were inconsistent, and though the law of the Lord be now the same that it ever was, yet it came out of Zion with a new garment; secondly, when ceremonies and shadows had been abolished, Christ was revealed, in whom the reality of them is perceived.[113]

In the same context he confirms what he writes in the *Institutes* about the excellence of the New Testament. In it God's grace is extended to those who were excluded under the old economy. "The Prophet shows that the boundaries of his kingdom will be enlarged, that he may rule over various nations. He likewise notices indirectly the difference between the kingdom of David, which was but a shadow, and this other kingdom, which would be far more excellent."[114] In his commentary on Psalm 47:7 ("For God is the king of all the earth"), he expresses the same view. "By these words he intimates that the kingdom of God would be much more magnificent and glorious at the coming of the Messiah than it was under the shadowy dispensation of the Law, inasmuch as it would be extended to the utmost boundaries of the earth."[115]

The Relation of the
Law and the Prophets

As Calvin emphasizes the unity of Old and New Testaments, so he emphasizes the unity of the law and the prophets. He develops his view in a very substantial way in the preface to his Isaiah commentary.[116] The prophets derive their doctrine from the law "like streams from a fountain; for they placed it before them as their rule, so that they may be justly held and declared to be its interpreters, who utter nothing but what is connected with the law." The law, he notes, may be divided into three chief parts: first, the doctrine of life; second, threatenings and promises; third, "the covenant of grace, which being founded on Christ, contains within itself all the special promises." It is the purpose of the prophets to be precise in their elaboration and application of each of these areas so that the people of their day might derive maximum benefit from the law. First, they illustrate more fully what is stated briefly in the two tables of the law;

second, they apply Moses' general threatenings in very specific ways to their own time; third, they explain more fully what Moses stated obscurely about Christ. The prophets add nothing to the law; they simply interpret it. In calling the people to their moral duties, they "bring forward nothing new, but only explain those parts of the law which had been misunderstood."[117] It may seem that the prophets' visions of future events are something new; however, this is not the case. These are intended to show the people how the promises and threatenings of the law apply to them.

> Moses says, "If thou keep the commandments, the Lord will bless thee," and then gives a general description of blessings. But the prophets enter into detail. "This is the blessing which the Lord will bestow upon thee." Again, by Moses the Lord promises in this manner—"Though thou be scattered and driven to the utmost parts of the world, yet will I bring thee back" (Deut. 30:4). But by the prophets he says, "Though I drive thee into Babylon, yet after seventy years will I restore thee."[118]

God established a free covenant with the patriarchs that was based upon the mediation of Christ. The prophets strengthen the people's attachment to that covenant by reminding them of Christ, "who was both the foundation of the covenant and the bond of mutual relation between God and the people, and to whom therefore the whole extent of the promises must be understood to refer."[119]

Calvin's belief in the dual authorship of scripture and his views of the unity and diversity of scripture deeply impacts his approach to exegesis. Belief in the human authorship of scripture is foundational to his historical interpretation—the Bible must be interpreted as a product of human writers speaking to an audience of contemporaries. Calvin's historical approach to exegesis will be examined in chapter 3. Calvin's recognition of the divine authorship of scripture in conjunction with his strong sense of the unity of scripture also have a massive impact on his exegesis. This will be explored in chapter 4.

NOTES

1. *Inst.* I.ix.2 (O.S. 3.83).
2. Robert M. Grant explores the link between early views of the inspiration of scripture and allegorical exegesis in *The Letter and the Spirit* (London: SPCK, 1957).
3. Comm. John 5:39 (C.O. 47.125).
4. Comm. 2 Tim. 3:16 (C.O. 52.382).
5. In none of his writings did Calvin articulate a doctrine of the inspiration of the Bible. One must study the matter inductively, piecing together clues from throughout his writings, particularly from his biblical commentaries. Perhaps this

explains the divergent views on precisely what his position was. Roger Nicole, in "John Calvin and Inerrancy," *Journal of the Evangelical Theological Society* 25 (December 1982): 427, lists over thirty authors who are said to affirm that Calvin believed in the verbal inspiration (and therefore inerrancy) of the Bible. He lists almost that number who believe Calvin did not have a doctrine of verbal inspiration. At least three views of Calvin's teaching on inspiration have won support. (1) Some have argued that Calvin's language describing the Holy Spirit's role as the source of scripture is so strong and so precise that he must be viewed as affirming that the very words of scripture are inspired. Most proponents of this position would not believe that Calvin held to a mechanical dictation view. Warfield, in the classic argument for this position, suggests that Calvin was "somewhat addicted" to the traditional language of dictation, but what he really had in mind was not the mode of inspiration but "that the result of inspiration was as if it were by dictation." See Benjamin B. Warfield, "Calvin's Doctrine of the Knowledge of God," *Princeton Theological Review* 7 (1909): 255. (2) Others have argued—often basing their opinion upon the seeming incompatibility of statements Calvin makes in his exegetical writings with the first view—that he has a freer view in which the doctrines or ideas are inspired, but not the very words. The major modern proponent of this view is John T. McNeill. Seeking to prove that *dictare* does not have to be understood with reference to "the form of words" in which ideas are expressed, McNeill argues that "Calvin, like the rest of us, is familiar with the use of the word 'dictate' in a context which has reference to ideas." He makes a case for Calvin's use of "dictate" with reference to "doctrines" rather than "words." See John T. McNeill, "The Significance of the Word of God for Calvin," *Church History* 28 (June 1959): 140–43. McNeill is correct in insisting that Calvin was interested primarily "in teaching rather than in the form of expression." His opinion that Calvin nowhere taught the verbal inspiration of scripture is less certain. See John T. McNeill, ed., *Calvin: The Institutes of the Christian Religion*, Library of Christian Classics (Philadelphia: Westminster Press, 1960), vol. 2: 1157, n. 9. (3) A third interpretation offers to synthesize the strengths—and avoid the weaknesses—of the first two. While Calvin's language does suggest verbal inspiration, his lack of concern about some of the apparent errors in the text he had received suggests that verbal inspiration did not function for him as it did for later Reformed theologians. His was not the mechanical view of inspiration found in later Reformed orthodoxy. The Holy Spirit rules the choice of words, but only in order that these words may faithfully communicate the subject matter. Calvin was more concerned with the function (or more correctly the "matter"—*Sache*) than with the form of scripture. See Werner Krusche, *Das Wirken des Heiligen Geistes nach Calvin* (Göttingen: Vandenhoeck & Ruprecht, 1957), 183. This thesis seems to be favored by B. A. Gerrish; see his "The Word of God and the Words of Scripture: Luther and Calvin on Biblical Authority," in idem, *The Old Protestantism and the New: Essays on the Reformation Heritage* (Chicago: University of Chicago Press, 1982), 63. Edward A. Dowey Jr.'s recantations in *The Knowledge of God in Calvin's Theology*, 2d ed. (New York: Columbia University Press, 1965), suggest that he too is persuaded of Krusche's position— almost. He believes that Krusche may be overstating the case in suggesting that the seventeenth century offered an "absolute *novum*." He quite properly wonders how Krusche's view may be harmonized with Calvin's treatment of Jer. 36:28 (C.O. 39.133), where God is seemingly very concerned that the prophet not omit a syllable of what is dictated. The evidence I cite in this chapter is difficult to harmonize with the second interpretation. While the differences between the first and third interpretations are minor, the third may be nearer to the spirit of many of Calvin's comments.

6. Comm. John, theme (C.O. 47.viii).

7. *Inst.* IV.viii.6 (O.S. 5.138).

8. Comm. Dan., pref. (C.O. 40.530).

9. Comm. Ex. 3:1 (C.O. 24.34).

10. Comm. Jer. 36:8 (C.O. 39.121).

11. Comm. 1 Peter 1:25 (C.O. 55.230).

12. *Inst.* IV.viii.9 (O.S. 5.141).

13. H. Jackson Forstman, *Word and Spirit: Calvin's Doctrine of Biblical Authority* (Stanford, Calif.: Stanford University Press, 1962), 50.

14. *Inst.* I.ix.2 (O.S. 3.83). Against the exaltation of the Spirit over scripture by the Libertines, Calvin argues that the Holy Spirit has stamped his image upon the scriptures.

15. *Inst.* I.vi.2 (O.S. 3.62).

16. Comm. Pss., pref. (C.O. 31.17).

17. Comm. Heb., theme (C.O. 55.6).

18. Comm. 2 Peter, theme (C.O. 55.441).

19. *Inst.* I.viii.2 (O.S. 3.72–73).

20. Comm. Ezek. 2:3 (C.O. 40.63).

21. Comm. Ezek. 12:4–6 (C.O. 40.256).

22. Calvin recognizes that the Hebrew of Amos is not on the same level as that of Isaiah, Jeremiah, or David. This should not lead one to conclude, however, that Amos is of less authority than the others. The authority of Amos comes from the fact that in his writings the Spirit uses popular, unpretentious language. See John Calvin, *Des Scandales*, ed. Olivier Fatio (Geneva: Librairie Droz, 1984), 64–65.

23. Comm. Philemon, theme (C.O. 52.441).

24. It is one thing to say, as Calvin does, that the Holy Spirit is author of scripture; it is quite another to describe the process by which this takes place. It is risky to try to describe in a coherent way how he may have envisioned that process, and whatever is said must be tentative, since he never systematically treated the matter. It does seem possible, however, to isolate several elements that would likely have formed a part of his understanding of the subject. His preferred figure for describing the relationship of the biblical writers to the Holy Spirit in the production of scripture is that of instrumentality. The human writer is the instrument of the Spirit of God. This fact, in large measure, accounts for the absolute authority of the Bible. The prophet brought forth nothing from his own brain. The authority of the prophets depended on their faithfully delivering what God commanded without adding anything of their own (Comm. Hos. 1:2 [C.O. 42.203]). Calvin explicitly denies that the prophets received revelation while in ecstatic states in which their rational faculties were bypassed. Their minds were sedate and composed. They were not mere channels through whom the Spirit flowed. They left their mark on the revelation they mediated, but not in such a way that the product was tainted by the human element (Comm. Ezek. 3:14 [C.O. 40.86–87]). "God himself raised up the prophets, and employed their labor; and, at the same time, guided them by his Spirit, that they might not announce anything but what had been received from him, but faithfully deliver what had proceeded

from him alone" (Comm. Amos 1:1 [C.O. 43:1–2]). His analysis of Jer. 36:4–6 (C.O. 39.118) indicates that the Spirit operated as a guarantor of the prophet's message by actually suggesting to the memory of the prophet things he might otherwise have forgotten. The Holy Spirit presided over and guided the mind and tongue of the prophet. The Holy Spirit worked in the mental processes of the prophet, aiding both his comprehension and then his articulation of God's message. The result is a message that may be understood to be "all of God." Beyond this, how Calvin may have understood the process remains unclear. In some places he seems to suggest that the actual words are given to the prophet by God; this may be what he means by God presiding over the mind and tongue of the prophet. Is this a mechanical process? The analogy from Amos 3 suggests cooperation. The prophets were mentally active, yet they were God's chosen vessels and were in submission to God in such a way that their speech may be understood to be his. This is what Amos means when he says "God is the author of what I teach" (Comm. Amos 3:3–8 [C.O. 43:40]). See also Comm. Jer. 36:8 (C.O. 39.170).

25. Comm. Ps. 88:14 (C.O. 31.810).
26. Comm. Ps. 89:46 (C.O. 31.828).
27. Comm. Ps. 39:13 (C.O. 31.404).
28. Forstman, *Word and Spirit*, 52.
29. Comm. Ps. 39:6 (C.O. 31.400).
30. Comm. Gen. 5:1 (C.O. 23.105).
31. Comm. Gen. 17:1 (C.O. 23.233).
32. Comm. Gen. 24:1 (C.O. 23.330).
33. *Harmony of the Last Four Books of Moses*, pref. (C.O. 24.5–6).
34. Comm. Dan. 4:35 (C.O. 40.687).
35. For a discussion of the exegetical implications of Calvin's consideration of the "absolute power" of God in sermons on Job, see Susan E. Schreiner, "Exegesis and Double Justice in Calvin's Sermons on Job," *Church History* 58 (September 1989): 322–38.
36. Comm. Ps. 105:25 (C.O. 32.109).
37. Comm. Ps. 129:3 (C.O. 32.331).
38. Comm. Ps. 44:19 (C.O. 31.445).
39. *Inst.* III.xx.49 (O.S. 4.365).
40. Comm. Gen. 39:6 (C.O. 23.504).
41. Comm. Obad., pref. (C.O. 43.178).
42. McNeill, "Significance of the Word of God for Calvin," 139.
43. Comm. Minor Prophets, Jean Crispen's pref. (C.O. 42.190).
44. Comm. Ps. 5:9 (C.O. 31.70).
45. Comm. Dan. 12:4 (C.O. 41.293).
46. Comm. Num. 14:11 (C.O. 25.198).
47. Comm. Lev. 11:13 (C.O. 24.350). This principle is critical to a proper understanding of the moral law. If the reader does not inquire concerning God's purpose in giving each of the commandments, misunderstanding is inevitable. "In each commandment we must investigate what it is concerned with; then we must seek out its purpose, until we find what the Lawgiver testifies there to be pleasing or displeasing to himself" (*Inst.* II.viii.8 [O.S. 3.350]).
48. *Inst.* II.viii.8 (O.S. 3.350).
49. Comm. Dan. 7:1, 2 (C.O. 41.36).
50. Comm. Dan. 11:6 (C.O. 41.225).

51. Comm. Jer. 10:23 (C.O. 38.88).
52. Comm. Ps. 8:2 (C.O. 31.90).
53. Calvin to Grynaeus (C.O. 10.403). The Greek σκοπός in patristic times meant "end, aim, object" or "purport, meaning, significance." G.W.H. Lampe, *A Patristic Greek Lexicon* (Oxford: Clarendon Press, 1961), s.v. σκοπός.
54. Comm. Amos 6:10 (C.O. 43.113).
55. Comm. Nahum 1:9 (C.O. 43.448).
56. Comm. Hos. 6:3 (C.O. 42.323).
57. Comm. Hos. 8:4 (C.O. 42.364).
58. Comm. Hos. 10:1 (C.O. 42.409).
59. Comm. Hos. 13:1 (C.O. 42.474).
60. Comm. Gen. 28:18 (C.O. 23.395).
61. Comm. Ps. 75:3 (C.O. 31.702).
62. Comm. Ps. 89:11 (C.O. 31.815–16).
63. Comm. Amos. 5:25, 26 (C.O. 43.99).
64. Comm. Mal. 4:4 (C.O. 44.493). The necessity of determining the intention of the human author is emphasized in the following sequence: "There is . . . nothing better than to attend to the intention of the prophet [*consilium prophetae*], and then to regard the circumstances of the time [*circumstantias temporis*], and thirdly to follow the analogy between the signs and the things signified [*tertio analogiam sequi inter signa et res signatas*]."
65. Comm. Zech. 7:14 (C.O. 44.231).
66. Comm. Lev. 11:13 (C.O. 24.250). Calvin is referring here to God's intention in giving the law to his people.
67. See G. R. Evans, "Sensus Plenior," in *The Westminster Dictionary of Christian Theology*, ed. Alan Richardson and John Bowden (Philadelphia: Westminster Press, 1983), 538.
68. Comm. Joel 2:28 (C.O. 42.567–68).
69. Comm. Isa. 34:11 (C.O. 36.585).
70. Comm. Gen. 29:31 (C.O. 23.405).
71. Comm. Jer. 17:12 (C.O. 38.274).
72. Comm. Ps. 87:3 (C.O. 31.801).
73. Comm. Gen. 24:1 (C.O. 23.330). There is nothing superfluous here, according to Calvin. It is all to be read with reverence, because it is all the work of the Spirit of God.
74. Comm. Ezek. 16:4, 5 (C.O. 40.336).
75. Comm. Ezek. 18:1–4 (C.O. 40.423). See also Comm. Jer. 36:30 (C.O. 39.137). The citation from Isaiah that follows is from Comm. Isa. 14:26 (C.O. 36.288).
76. Calvin's reluctance to distinguish divine intention from human intention is evident throughout his commentaries. This will be especially important in his understanding of typology. In chapter 5 I examine Calvin's approach to typology.
77. *Inst.* II.x.2 (O.S. 3.404).
78. Emil G. Kraeling, *The Old Testament since the Reformation* (London: Lutterworth Press, 1955), 25.
79. Willem Balke elaborates on some of the hermeneutical differences between Calvin and the Anabaptists, especially the problem of the relationship between the Testaments, in *Calvin and the Anabaptist Radicals*, trans. William J. Heynen (Grand Rapids: Wm. B. Eerdmans Publishing Co., 1981), 309–27. He suggests (p. 95) that the Anabaptist threat in Geneva has been greatly underestimated. Klassen argues

that the two major areas of disagreement between Pilgrim Marpeck and Martin Bucer, Calvin's mentor, were the problem of old and new convenants and the problem of the spirit and the letter. "Marpeck resolved these problems by viewing the Old Testament as being secondary to the New and superseded by the full revelation of the Son of God": William Klassen, *Covenant and Community: The Life, Writings, and Hermeneutics of Pilgrim Marpeck* (Grand Rapids: Wm. B. Eerdmans Publishing Co., 1968), 157, 181.

80. For Calvin's view of the relationship between the convenants, see Hans Heinrich Wolf, *Die Einheit des Bundes: Das Verhältnis von Altem und Neuem Testament bei Calvin*, Beiträge zur Geschichte und Lehre der reformierten Kirche, no. 10 (Neukirchen: Verlag der Buchhandlung des Erziehungsvereins, 1958).

81. *Inst.* II.x.3 (O.S. 3.405).

82. Comm. Gen. 27:27 (C.O. 23.378).

83. Comm. Mal. 3:1 (C.O. 44.462).

84. Comm. Ps. 78:69 (C.O. 31.745).

85. *Inst.* II.x.23 (O.S. 3.422).

86. Comm. Lev. 16:26 (C.O. 24.505).

87. Comm. Ps. 9:12 (C.O. 31.102).

88. Comm. Lev. 16:29 (C.O. 24.505).

89. *Inst.* II.x.4 (O.S. 3.405).

90. Comm. Isa. 42:6 (C.O. 37.64).

91. Comm. Jer. 31:31, 32 (C.O. 38.687).

92. Comm. Isa. 42:1 (C.O. 37.57).

93. *Inst.* II.xi.1 (O.S. 3.423). Parker argues very cogently that the differences should not be viewed as balancing the similarities and that the chapter setting forth the differences should be regarded as an appendix rather than as part of the main argument. See T.H.L. Parker, *Calvin's Old Testament Commentaries* (Edinburgh: T. & T. Clark, 1986), 50–51.

94. *Inst.* II.xi.3 (O.S. 3.425).

95. *Inst.* II.xi.4 (O.S. 3.426).

96. Kraeling charges that one of Calvin's major flaws as an exegete was "his yielding to the influence of the Epistle to the Hebrews and its Christianizing allegorical use of the Old Testament law and institutions" (*Old Testament since the Reformation*, 31).

97. Ibid.

98. *Inst.* II.xi.6 (O.S. 3.428).

99. Comm. Dan. 9:1–3 (C.O. 41.127).

100. Comm. Ps. 92:3 (C.O. 32.11).

101. Comm. Ps. 81:3 (C.O. 31.760).

102. Comm. Ex. 40:12 (C.O. 25.125).

103. Comm. Ex. 40:9 (C.O. 25.12). Calvin uses *figura* and *typus* interchangeably.

104. Comm. Dan. 9:25 (C.O. 41.180–81).

105. Comm. Ex. 25:8 (C.O. 24.403).

106. *Inst.* II.xi.8 (O.S. 3.421). As Wendel observes, "too much accentuation of the divergences between the Law and Gospel would not . . . be in harmony with Calvin's conception as a whole. So he hastens to return to the defense of the Law." François Wendel, *Calvin: Origins and Development of His Religious Thought*, trans. Philip Mairet (New York: Harper & Row, 1963), 213.

107. *Inst.* II.xi.10 (O.S. 3.433).

108. *Inst.* II.xi.9 (O.S. 3.432).

109. *Inst.* II.xi.1 (O.S. 3.423).

110. Battles writes that Calvin explicitly refers to *accommodatio* or *attemperatio* at least forty-one times in the *Institutes*, "and it is implicit in many other passages." Ford Lewis Battles, "The Future of Calviniana," in *Renaissance, Reformation, Resurgence*, ed. Peter De Klerk (Grand Rapids: Calvin Theological Seminary, 1976), 144. Battles argues that "any study of Calvin as scriptural exegete would be incomplete which failed to examine his frequent appeal to the principle of accommodation," in "God Was Accommodating Himself to Human Capacity," *Interpretation* 31 (January 1977): 19. The central role of accommodation in Calvin's doctrine of scripture is now generally recognized. References to the principle of accommodation are found throughout Calvin's commentaries on the Old Testament. Accommodation is an important part of his explanation of the rationale for typology.

111. *Inst.* II.xi.14 (O.S. 3.437).

112. Kemper Fullerton, *Prophecy and Authority: A Study in the History of the Doctrine and Interpretation of Scripture* (New York: Macmillan, 1919), 133–64. McKee argues against the bifurcation of the *Institutes* and the commentaries. "It is apparent that Calvin's statements that the *Institutes* and the commentaries were intended to complement each other express a symbiotic relationship which should be taken more seriously than has been common, and that this mutuality deserves more attention. It is also clear that at least *some* of the development in the comprehensive theology was brought about by the struggle with the biblical texts themselves." Elsie Anne McKee, "Exegesis, Theology, and Development in Calvin's *Institutio*," in *Probing the Reformed Tradition: Historical Studies in Honor of Edward A. Dowey, Jr.*, ed. Elsie Anne McKee and Brian G. Armstrong (Louisville, Ky.: Westminster/John Knox Press, 1989).

113. Comm. Isa. 2:3 (C.O. 36.64).

114. Comm. Isa. 2:4 (C.O. 36.64).

115. Comm. Ps. 47:7 (C.O. 31.470).

116. Comm. Isa., pref. (C.O. 36.19–24). He reiterates the point in his comments on Isa. 1:10 (C.O. 36.38) and Isa. 9:7 (C.O. 36.200).

117. Ibid. (C.O. 36.21).

118. Ibid. (C.O. 36.22).

119. Ibid.

3

THE "JEWISH" APPEARANCE
OF CALVIN'S EXEGESIS

From the earliest days of the church many Christian interpreters have felt free to read the Old Testament nonhistorically. According to Greer, in the first century "the only method used is that of claiming that the interpretation given is the clear meaning of the text, that is, proof texting."[1] Justin Martyr, the leading Apologist of the second century, carried on the tradition of proof texting. According to Shotwell, "only rarely did Justin interpret the Old Testament to mean exactly what it said. . . . He uses the Old Testament as one great mass of proof texts."[2] While it would be erroneous to suggest that all Christian exegetes prior to the sixteenth century lacked interest in the historical meaning of the Old Testament,[3] it is clear that many Christian thinkers were not seriously concerned with interpreting the text historically. The popularity of proof texting bears eloquent witness to the perceived dispensability of historical exegesis—especially when it did not appear to support established Christian belief.

Calvin actively participated in a sixteenth-century reorientation in biblical studies—one that was serious about historical interpretation. His historical approach to interpretation did not begin with his biblical commentaries. Long before he wrote on the Old Testament, he published a commentary on Seneca's *De clementia*. His approach to Seneca was very much what one might expect of a humanist interpreting an ancient writer. He corrected the text; analyzed the structure, vocabulary, idioms; and sought to understand the text in its original historical and cultural context. In short, he studied the text historically.[4] His comments demonstrated his awareness of the historical distance that separated the world of the sixteenth century from the world of antiquity. If Seneca's *De clementia* was to be understood, it must be understood as a work by an author who intended his words to have meaning for his contemporaries. When Calvin later took up the work of biblical interpretation, he did not depart from his early historical approach. Scripture, like the corpus of classical literature, is a collection of ancient human writings and demands to be interpreted as such. His historical sensitivity deeply affected his approach to the Old Testament.[5]

It was Calvin's insistence on the necessity and adequacy of historical interpretation which Hunnius found so offensive, and which led him to accuse Calvin of "Judaizing." That Calvin was often critical of Christian exegesis and sometimes favorable toward Jewish exegesis could only have made him appear more guilty in Hunnius's eyes. He frequently appealed to Jewish interpreters in matters of lexicology and grammar, and he occasionally consulted them in other matters.[6] In his exposition of Hosea he announces his approval of the "Jewish" view that the prophet did not actually take a harlot as his wife "but was bidden to do so in a vision."[7] He insists that the Jewish interpretation is correct in his treatment of Jeremiah 3:17–18 ("At that time Jerusalem shall be called the throne of the LORD, and all nations shall gather to it, to the presence of the LORD in Jerusalem, and they shall no more stubbornly follow their own evil heart"). The text "can be explained in no other way than by referring it to the kingdom of Messiah."[8] He indicates that the Jews are also correct in taking Lamech's statement in Genesis 5 ("Out of the ground which the LORD has cursed this one shall bring us relief from our work and from the toil of our hands") as a prophecy of Messiah.[9]

Two elements of Calvin's approach made Christian interpreters such as Hunnius very uncomfortable: first, his criticism of some types of Christian exegesis, and second, his use of historical and literary reasoning in interpretation.

CRITICISM OF CHRISTIAN EXEGESIS

Christian exegesis, in Calvin's view, regrettably too often gave Jewish critics a very large target to take aim at. He sometimes finds Jewish criticism of Christian exegesis to be compelling. He rejects a christological interpretation of Psalm 72, noting that to adopt it would be to do violence to the words (*nimis violenter torquere verba*). "We must always beware of giving the Jews occasion of making an outcry, as if it were our purpose, sophistically, to apply to Christ those things which do not directly refer to him."[10] He confesses that the traditional Christian interpretation of Jeremiah 31:22 is "deservedly laughed at by the Jews."[11] He notes that both the Greek and Latin Fathers have strained the words of Psalm 16. "It is better to adhere to the natural simplicity [*genuina illa simplicitate*] of the interpretation which I have given, that we may not make ourselves objects of ridicule to the Jews."[12]

Calvin faults Christian interpreters for disregarding the language and context of the Old Testament and finding only what they want to find in the text. He differentiates among earlier exegetes, favoring the tradition represented by Chrysostom over the tradition of Origen and his followers and the Latin tradition of Augustine. He appreciates the exegetical approach of Chrysostom because Chrysostom did not succumb to the temptation of twisting the words of the text to unnatural meanings.[13] He offers an extremely negative evaluation of Origen because of Origen's excessive allegorization at the expense of the literal meaning. "He searches everywhere for allegories" and "corrupts the whole scripture."[14]

Calvin's critique of the exegesis of Augustine, one of his theological heroes, illustrates the lack of solidity he finds in much Christian exegesis.[15] He has profound appreciation for Augustine's theological contributions, but this does not blind him to Augustine's exegetical deficiencies. Sometimes he finds Augustine guilty of using the wrong text to prove a useful doctrine.[16] He observes one such instance in the exposition of Psalm 85:11 ("Faithfulness will spring up from the ground, and righteousness will look down from the sky"). Here, Calvin observes, Augustine presents a beautiful thought that should prove very consoling to God's people: "that the mercy of God is the origin and source of all his promises, from which issues the righteousness which is offered to us by the gospel, while from that righteousness proceeds the peace which we obtain by faith, when God justifies us freely." Augustine believes that the psalmist's picture of "righteousness looking down from heaven" teaches that righteousness is not acquired by one's own merit. This interpretation, Calvin believes, must be rejected because it is subtle rather than solid. "Let us remain content with the genuine sense of the prophet [*genuino prophetae sensu*]."[17] In Calvin's interpretation of Psalm 111:2 he notes that Augustine, following the Septuagint, has speculated in such a way that, while what he says is appealing, it has nothing to do with the text. "Augustine has therefore taken occasion, with philosophical subtlety, to ask, how can there be, or, at least, appear to be, a plurality of wills in God?" This issue, Calvin admits, deserves some thought, but it has no relation to the text in question.[18] In interpreting Psalm 59:10, Augustine again follows the Septuagint in a grammatical point and "too ingeniously, though with good intent, has repeatedly quoted the passage against the Pelagians, in proof that the grace of God is antecedent to all human merit." While Calvin enthusiastically endorses Augustine's anti-Pelagian teaching, he believes that here Augustine argues too subtly. He cautions that we must always be on guard lest we twist the meaning of scripture.[19] He observes that Augustine uses Psalm 71:16 more than a hundred times in his writings to overthrow the merit of works. While agreeing with the truth of this doctrine, he points out that Augustine twists the words of David to something other than their real meaning.[20]

The exegesis of Luther is also found to be lacking. "The speculation of Luther here, as in other places, has no solidity."[21] This, and other comments like it, suggests that Calvin may have more reservations about Luther the exegete than Luther the theologian. He is correct in recognizing that Luther's approach to the Old Testament differs from his own—a truth that also did not go unnoticed by Luther's follower Hunnius. Luther accepts the idea that a biblical text should be interpreted according to its historical context and is critical of those who allegorize excessively, yet he often seems quite ready to ignore the historical context in his effort to find Christ in the Old Testament.[22] Bornkamm states that "any research which thinks historically will have to give up, without hesitation or reservation, Luther's scheme of Christological prediction in the Old Testament."[23] One following Luther's approach "is forced to carry the concepts of the New Testament revelation into the Old Testament and put them in the mouths of the patriarchs and writers."[24] Luther argues that those interpreters who are overly concerned with the history apart from the christological message are like Jewish rabbis.[25] He criticizes the humanist cardinal Jacopo Sadoleto for failing to show any understanding of Psalm 51. Sadoleto's interpretation of the psalm is defective christologically.[26] This, of course, is precisely the charge Luther's disciple Hunnius later levels against Calvin.[27]

Calvin believes that the interpreter must understand the function of the biblical writings in the setting in which they were originally given. The prophets were speaking first to their contemporaries. The interpreter must take into account the language, culture, and history of Old Testament times. Calvin is not willing to base Christian doctrine on scripture texts that he deems inconclusive. He dares to adopt interpretations that do not provide the strongest support for Christian dogma.[28] He argues in the *Institutes* against several patristic proofs for the deity of the Holy Spirit drawn from the Old Testament on the grounds that they do not take into account Hebrew poetic style (synonymous parallelism) nor the usage of the same Hebrew words elsewhere in the Old Testament.

> I deliberately omit many testimonies that the church fathers used. They thought it justifiable to cite from David, "By the word of the Lord the heavens were established, and all their power by the spirit of his mouth" [Ps. 33:6], to prove that the universe was no less the work of the Holy Spirit than of the Son. But since it is common practice in the Psalms to repeat the same thing twice, and since in Isaiah "spirit of the mouth" means the same thing as "the word" [Isa. 11:4], that was a weak reason.[29]

Godly minds, he insists, need something more secure upon which to rest. In his commentary on Psalm 33:6 ("By the word of the LORD the heavens were made, and all their host by the breath of his mouth"), his argument is the same. Earlier Christian interpreters have been overly subtle in using the second colon of the verse as a proof of the deity of the Holy Spirit. Calvin disputes their interpretation on two grounds. First, the psalmist was adopting a commonly used Hebrew rhetorical device—synonymous parallelism. Second, the phrase "spirit of the mouth" is used in Isaiah 11:4 and other passages figuratively for speech. It should be taken the same way in this passage. It would, therefore, be unwise to press the text against the Sabellians as a proof of the eternal deity of the Holy Spirit.[30]

Calvin frequently appeals to linguistic considerations or context to justify his interpretations. The context of Isaiah 64:6 ("We have all become unclean") invalidates the view of some that the passage provides a proof that our works are not meritorious and are downright rotten in God's sight. Though he agrees with the theology, the interpretation is foreign to the sense intended by the prophet. In this context, Isaiah was not speaking of the whole human race, but was simply describing the complaint of Jews who were in captivity. As they experienced the wrath of God against them, they were led to confess that they and their righteousness were like a filthy garment.[31]

Such caution in the use of Old Testament texts is characteristic of Calvin's approach. His view that language and context are weighty matters in exegesis and his reluctance to depart from historical interpretation—even for good theological reasons—lead Hunnius to view him as a Judaizer.

HISTORICAL EXEGESIS

The qualities of Calvin's exegesis that provoked Hunnius's charge are the same qualities that led Philip Schaff three centuries later to designate him the "founder of modern historical-grammatical exegesis."[32] In Schaff's judgment Calvin's exegesis was more oriented to matters of grammar and history than was the exegesis of those who preceded him.

Use of Hebrew

In Calvin's century there was an explosion of interest in Hebrew studies among Christians. Yet many questions were raised about the value of such studies—some by leading humanists. Erasmus in a letter to the Strassburg Reformer and Hebraist Wolfgang Capito expressed the fear that the revival of Hebrew studies might lead to a revival of

Judaism.[33] Sadoleto explained in a letter to his friend Federigo Fregoso that he was not opposed to the study of Hebrew; he simply questioned its usefulness, comparing its value to that of the Cabala.[34] He offered two reasons for his reservations. First, since the New Testament was clearly superior to the Old, it followed that the knowledge of Hebrew, the language of the Old Testament, should be regarded as only of secondary value.[35] Second, since the apostle Paul always quoted from the Septuagint, it must be regarded as an authoritative version of scripture.[36] To the arguments of Erasmus and Sadoleto may be added the widely held belief that the Jews had deliberately corrupted the Hebrew text in order to undermine the Old Testament foundation for Christian claims about Christ.[37]

Friedman, in his study of sixteenth-century Christian Hebraica, has categorized non-Catholic approaches to Hebrew studies in four basic types, demonstrating that there was little agreement on what use to make of Hebrew in the period of the Reformation.[38] First was the radical approach of Servetus, who used Jewish sources for far more than philological guidance as he tried to get his anti-Trinitarian message across. Not surprisingly, orthodox Catholics and Protestants were unhappy with the radical Judaizing of Servetus. Second was "the Strassburg-Basel-Zurich school of Hebraica." This school favored a relatively restrained use of rabbinic sources to clarify the meaning of the Old Testament. Oecolampadius's comments reflect the importance of a knowledge of Hebrew and a familiarity with rabbinic commentators for some Christian scholars: "For my part I am compelled to confess that I have been unable to grasp the mind of the prophet . . . [and] except that I had the ability to read Hebrew and consult the commentaries of the Hebrews, I would not have dared to undertake this [scriptural study]."[39] A third approach to Hebraica, one which reflected Luther's concerns, was developed in Wittenberg. It may have emerged out of the sharp law-gospel distinction and *loci* method of exposition, each of which may have facilitated the reading of the theology of the New Testament into the Old. The historical context of the Old Testament was not very important. Knowledge of the Hebrew language may be useful, but rabbinic sources are virtually worthless. A fourth approach was adopted by Paul Fagius, who believed that the New Testament was written from a Hebrew point of view; thus a knowledge of rabbinics was needed to discover its riches. Fagius's method, which seemed to place Christians at the mercy of unbelieving Jewish commentators, made Protestants so uncomfortable that it was stillborn.

According to Friedman, in the 1540s "a climate of tension" arose between the Lutheran and Reformed Hebraists. The parties became polarized over the issue of the use of Jewish commentators. The Reformed were much less restrained in their use of rabbinics than were the Lutherans.[40] Sebastian Münster, the Basel Hebraist and leading defender of the Reformed approach, published Latin translations of the Old Testament in parallel columns with the Hebrew text. His annotations following each chapter were full of rabbinic citations intended to clarify the meaning of obscure and ambiguous texts. In a preface entitled "Hebrew Commentaries are not to be Condemned," Münster defends his use of Jewish exegesis. He refutes arguments against Hebrew studies and the use of rabbinics, reasoning that the example of Jerome, who was not reluctant to consult knowledgeable rabbis, should make the value of Jewish exegesis abundantly clear.[41] Largely through the efforts of scholars like Münster, Oecolampadius, Bucer, Capito, and Jud, Hebrew studies flourished in the Reformed triangle of Strassburg, Basel, and Zurich.[42] Kraus indicates that "there is scarcely a Reformed exegete of the sixteenth century who did not have a good knowledge of Hebrew and was passionately concerned to establish the *hebraica veritas*."[43]

It is not surprising that Calvin would adopt the Strassburg-Basel-Zurich approach; he lived in Basel for a little over a year (1535–36) and in Strassburg for three years (1538–1541), studying Hebrew in both cities, perhaps drawing upon the expertise of Münster in Basel and Capito in Strassburg.[44] How well Calvin learned his lessons has long been disputed. He probably should not be regarded as a expert Hebraist, as was Münster, but he did know the language a great deal better than the seventeenth-century Roman Catholic scholar Richard Simon believed. Simon charged that Calvin knew little more than the Hebrew letters.[45] Tholuck was certainly closer to the truth in suggesting that Calvin had a thorough knowledge of the Hebrew language.[46] Better still is the balanced judgment of Hall that Calvin was "competent in Hebrew without being a distinguished Hebraist"; although he made mistakes, he was an "*homme trilingue,* a worthy representative of French humanism."[47]

An indication of Calvin's reliance on the Hebrew text and his competence in using it may be gathered from his translation and commentary on Psalm 51. Out of the twenty-one verses of the psalm, his translation is identical to the Vulgate in only one verse.[48] Though some of his changes may simply reflect stylistic preferences, others are better understood as a reflection of his desire to be faithful to the Hebrew text. An examination of his corrections indicates that he tries to get behind the Greek version upon which the Psalms portion of the Vulgate was based. He translates the Hebrew, not the Greek, text.[49] He is not satisfied with the Vulgate's *tibi soli peccavi* in verse 6, which is an accurate translation of the Septuagint's σοὶ μόνῳ ἥμαρτον. He prefers *tibi, tibi soli peccavi* which agrees with the Hebrew לְךָ לְבַדְּךָ חָטָאתִי. In the same verse he changes the Vulgate reading *et malum coram te feci* to *et malum coram oculis tuis patriavi,* which is a more literal translation of וְהָרַע בְּעֵינֶיךָ עָשִׂיתִי.[50]

Calvin's confidence in the superiority of the Hebrew text over the Greek is also apparent in his commentary on the psalm. He explicitly rejects the Septuagint translation of וּבְסָתֻם in verse 8. The Septuagint reading suggests that God has revealed secret mysteries. Calvin believes that the Hebrew word should be understood, not as the object of God's revelation, but as the manner in which the revelation is made. Thus he understands the verse to mean that wisdom has been revealed to the psalmist in a secret, hidden manner.[51] He also rejects the Septuagint rendering of נְדִיבָה in verse 14. Instead of a "princely" or "royal" spirit (the Septuagint reads ἡγεμονικῷ), he prefers a "free" or "liberal" spirit.[52]

That Calvin was competent as a Hebraist is seen in a number of his practices. First, his method of conducting lectures reflects a much greater familiarity with the Hebrew language than Simon acknowledged. His normal practice was to read the text in Hebrew, offer a very literal translation into Latin, then follow with a smoother translation along with his commentary.[53] Second, he was competent enough to attempt rather extensive word studies. Third, he often based his interpretations on points of Hebrew grammar. Fourth, he showed a sensitivity to peculiarities of Hebrew style,[54] often comparing or contrasting Hebrew idioms with Latin or Greek idioms.[55]

Lexicology and Grammar

"A marked trait of Calvin's Commentary is the care he lavished upon the meaning of words and phrases of the text."[56] Battles so describes, not one of Calvin's biblical commentaries, but the *Commentary on Seneca's De Clementia*, a work that Battles views as "the apprenticeship of a consummate Scriptural exegete."[57] Parker, in his meticulously detailed study of Calvin's New Testament commentaries, notes the similarity in Calvin's method of presenting his New Testament exegesis to that of his early commentary on Seneca. "Anyone who knows Calvin's biblical commentaries will find himself in familiar country as he travels through this commentary. Here is the same form, the same approach to problems of thought and language, the same style, the same diction."[58] Parker is correct in suggesting that Calvin did not fundamentally alter his approach from the commentary on Seneca's work to the New Testament commentaries. The same may be said of his Old Testament commentaries. In his early work on *De clementia*, written when he was barely in his twenties, Calvin offers a sample of the method he will still be using three decades later in interpreting the Old Testament. In the early work he exhibits a concern for explaining the meaning of words and clarifying the significance of Latin grammar and syntax. This will carry over to his later analysis of the Hebrew words, grammar, and syntax of the Old Testament. His interest in philology as a tool for understanding the biblical text, and his resulting deviation from the opinions of earlier Christian exegetes, may be rooted in his training as a humanist.

Calvin believes that many exegetical mistakes result from not knowing the meaning of words; accordingly, the most basic level of exegetical reasoning he offers in his Old Testament commentaries consists of simple lexicological observations. Sometimes he simply states a preference for one meaning over another and gives no justification for his choice. Other times he discusses the options, then adds that the choice is unimportant. When he does bother to defend a lexicological decision, he usually appeals to one of the following (in a generally ascending order of importance): (1) the opinion of Jewish commentators, (2) etymology, (3) biblical usage, and (4) context.

In his commentary on Isaiah 65:11 Calvin appeals to etymology, usage, and context to justify his translation. He notes that the usage of a form of לַגַד in this passage has been explained by interpreters in different ways—some taking it to mean Jupiter or the star of Jupiter; others taking it to mean fortune. Jerome, he notes, thinks the word means prosperity. Calvin, however, believes it probably means a large number—a band, a troop, or an army of false gods. First, this translation agrees well with the etymology of the word (he simply makes the assertion; he doesn't explain the etymology); second, it agrees with the context; third, it seems to fit well with the usage of the word elsewhere in scripture, specifically in Genesis 30:11. There, he reasons, Leah uses the word בְּגָד in rejoicing that she has plenty—or a large number—of children, and accordingly names her fifth son גָּד, which Calvin takes to mean a troop or an army. Calvin therefore concludes that גָּד ought to be taken to mean a large number or army in this passage as well.[59]

Jewish Commentators

Calvin frequently makes use of Jewish commentators because of their lexicological expertise; he recognizes their technical skill and is reluctant to break with their opinion on lexical matters.[60] In his interpretation of Jeremiah 30:18 he defers to them: "Some think that אַרְמוֹן means the temple; and this sense I do not reject, but as the Hebrews for the most part understand by this term a splendid, large, or high building, I prefer the former sense, that is, that he speaks of a royal palace."[61] He embraces their lexicological work on the meaning of אִכָּר in Amos 5:16: "But, as all the Hebrews agree as to the meaning of this word, I am unwilling without authority to make any change."[62] Yet, while acknowledging the linguistic expertise of the Jewish interpreters, he cautions that depending on them even in lexicological matters is not without risk. They do not hesitate to deceive their readers if it serves to undermine Christianity in any way. Even in seemingly benign areas of interpretation, he counsels caution. In his exposition of Psalm 29:1 he follows the Jewish commentators, who are all agreed that the meaning of אֵלִים is "mighty." However, when they begin to explain what the word refers to, "they pervert and obscure the genuine meaning [genuinum sensum] with their frigid comments."[63] They often demonstrate little understanding beyond their knowledge of the technical meaning of words.[64]

Etymology

Calvin sometimes bases his translation of Hebrew words on etymology alone. In his interpretation of Psalm 3:2 he discusses the meaning of Selah, noting that some interpreters take it as a term of affirmation (equivalent to "truly" or "amen"). Others think it means "forever." He argues that the word is derived from סָלַל ("to lift up") and probably refers to "the lifting up of the voice in harmony in the exercise of singing."[65]

In his exegesis of Psalm 144:13 he uses etymology to justify his interpretation. He indicates that he does not totally reject the view of those who translate מְזָוֵינוּ as "storehouses," but he argues that the word comes from the same root as the word translated "corner" in the previous verse, thus "it seems more agreeable to the etymology to translate the words as I have done—that the recesses or corners were full."[66]

In his interpretation of Isaiah 59 he rejects the etymological reasoning of the rabbis, who he believes mistakenly derive אֲשֵׁמִים from the wrong word. "The Jews, who choose to derive it from שָׁמֵן, 'to be fat,' appear to me to argue childishly and to have no solid ground for their opinion. They think that it denotes men, because שֶׁמֶן denotes 'ointment,' and say that this word is used for describing the Gentiles." He favors the view of Jerome, who derives the word from אָשַׁם.[67]

He appeals to the etymology of the tetragrammaton to show the absurdity of the Jewish refusal to speak the name Yahweh. "It is certainly a foul superstition of the Jews that they dare not speak, or write it, but substitute the name Adonai." Yahweh, he argues, is the essential name of God and is clearly derived from הָוָה ("to be"). It suggests that he is the self-existent One and the upholder of all things; other names of God are simply epithets. "Nor do I agree with the grammarians, who will not have it pronounced, because its inflection is irregular; because its etymology, of which all confess that God is the author, is more to me than a hundred rules [quando pluris mihi est etymologia, cuius omnes fatentur Deum esse autorem, quam centum regulae]."[68]

Usage

The etymology of a word, though of some use, can only guide the interpreter so far. Of much greater importance is the usage of a term elsewhere in scripture.[69] In his commentary on Jeremiah 25:30 Calvin finds that etymology is of little use in trying to decide between two options for the meaning of הֵידָד. He is, however, able to make a choice because of the normal usage of the word. He reasons that since the word is only used for sailors in the Old Testament, "I prefer to adopt the word 'sound' or 'a loud noise.' "[70]

In his commentary on Psalm 55:22 he rejects what he considers to be an edifying interpretation of the Hebrew יְהָבְךָ because he believes it demands an unprecedented use of the term.

> The Hebrew term יָהַב signifies "to give," and יְהָבְךָ, according to the ordinary rules of grammar, should be translated "your giving," or "your gift." Most interpreters, however, have translated it "your burden," but they can give no reason for their view. There is absolutely no precedent for supposing that the word might be translated "burden" ("Cast your burden upon YHWH"). They have evidently felt themselves compelled to invent that meaning from the harshness and apparent absurdity of the stricter translation, "Cast your gift upon Jehovah."

Calvin grants that the sentiment they wish to express is a pious one; nevertheless he rejects it because he finds it used in this way nowhere else in scripture. "I find no example of such a translation of the word, and adhere therefore to the other."[71]

Frequently Calvin justifies a translation by appealing to the ordinary usage of the word in the Old Testament, yet often without specifying the texts upon which he bases his judgment. In his interpretation of Isaiah 44:25 he states that he is governed by usage elsewhere. "Some take the word בַּדִּים to mean 'lies,' as if he had said that the divinations to which the astrologers pretend are nothing but absolute delusions, but I choose rather to interpret it 'diviners,' as we frequently find it used in that sense."[72] In his commentary on Psalm 26:8 he writes that the Hebrew word מָעוֹן is sometimes understood to be derived from a word that signifies an eye and is thus translated as "beauty" or "appearance." "But as the word is almost everywhere used to signify a dwelling-place, which is more simple [simplicius], I prefer to retain it."[73]

He is sometimes more specific about the location of the biblical texts he is allowing to guide his interpretation. In his interpretation of Psalm 57:3 he reasons, "The Hebrew word גֹּמֵר, here employed, would seem to be used in the same sense as in Psalm 138:8."[74] He reasons that קַו, a line, and

מִשְׁקָלֶת, a plumbline, probably mean the same thing in Isaiah 28:17, based upon a similar usage in 2 Kings 21:13.[75] He takes the Hebrew word קַוָּם in Psalm 19:4 as a line of writing, basing his judgment on the use of the word in Isaiah 28:10.[76] He argues from the usage of the word (in Psalm 5) that צִנָּה in Psalm 35:2 probably does not mean a "dart" or some other kind of weapon, as some understood it. "As we have already seen, in the fifth psalm, that it properly signifies 'a buckler,' I see no reason why it should be differently interpreted in this place."[77] In each of these examples Calvin allows his lexicological reasoning to be governed by what he regards as the usage of the Hebrew word elsewhere in scripture.

Context

Although he appeals to rabbinic expertise, etymology, and biblical usage to justify his lexicological judgments, a more important exegetical consideration is the immediate literary context in which a word is found. He appeals to context often, in many instances presenting it as the decisive reason for adopting or rejecting a translation. One such instance is found in his commentary on Isaiah 41:14. "Some translate מְתֵי, 'men,' which does not at all agree with the context [*contextui*]. We are therefore constrained by obvious argument to translate it 'dead.' "[78] In Jeremiah 4:6 he again reasons contextually. "The words אַל־תַּעֲמֹדוּ may be explained in two ways. . . . The first exposition appears to me the best, as it is more suitable to the context [*ad contextum aptior*]."[79]

Calvin's view of the relation of context to etymology is clear in his comment on Jeremiah 20:3 ("The LORD does not call your name Pashur, but Terror on every side"), where he engages in an elaborate defense of his interpretation of the name "Pashur." He argues that the word should be understood to mean "one who breaks open the light." He offers a detailed defense of his proposed etymology for the word, but it is finally the context that leads him to adopt his interpretation. "The words which follow—'terror on every side'—lead me to give this interpretation."[80]

Calvin's commitment to contextual interpretation is even more striking in those texts where the translation that is most consistent with the etymology or normal biblical usage of a word does not fit the context. In his comments on Numbers 32:14, he writes, "With the Hebrews, תַּרְבּוּת is literally an increase, or multiplication, and thus is applied to usury." The context, however, will not allow that translation, so it must be rejected.[81] In his interpretation of Psalm 31:10, context has priority over the biblical usage of a word in establishing meaning. He acknowledges that either of two meanings for בַּעֲוֹנִי is possible. He admits that his choice is the less common of the two, yet he prefers it nonetheless because it agrees best with the context.[82] In his interpretation of Psalm 81 Calvin questions the etymology of עֵדוּת because it does not suit the context. The word is "by some derived from עָדָה, which signifies 'to adorn', and they translate it the honor or ornament of Joseph. But it rather comes from the verb עוּד, 'to testify,' and the context [contextus] requires that it should be translated a testimony or covenant."[83]

Calvin's understanding of the interpretive process may be viewed as concentric circles, with lexicology, grammar, and normal usage constituting an outer circle that circumscribes a large field of possible meanings. Often, however, lexicology, grammar, and normal usage do not provide an adequate basis for determining a precise meaning of a text. Context forms the inner circle, allowing the exegete to eliminate lexicological[84] and grammatical[85] possibilities, often enabling him to arrive at a single "probable" interpretation. Lexical and grammatical considerations provide Calvin with the interpretive "possibilities"; context provides the key to determining the interpretive "probabilities".[86]

It is nothing new to claim Calvin as an advocate of contextual exegesis. Almost every study that discusses his principles of exegesis lists his concern for interpreting contextually as one of his primary exegetical virtues. In the remainder of this chapter, I will examine how he appeals to literary context and historical context to justify his exegetical decisions.

Literary Context

In larger textual units Calvin almost always favors the interpretation that he believes best suits the context. Any interpretation that cannot be justified contextually is, at best, improbable. His approach to justifying his interpretation of Zechariah 6:1–3 is characteristic; he adopts as the simpler (simplicior) interpretation the one he believes is most consistent with the context.[87]

Calvin is not normally inclined to state the principles governing his exegesis, but buried deep in his comments on the Pentateuch is a statement in which he clearly spells out one of his exegetical principles. "It is incongruous to twist into different senses declarations which are made in the same place, and in the same words [Neque enim convenit torquere in diversos sensus quae uno in loco iisdem verbis pronunciantur]."[88] He confirms this principle in his exegesis of Exodus 8:26, where he explains that under normal circumstances it is "harsh to interpret the same forms of expression differently within a few words of each other [Durum esset eandem loquendi formam paucis verbis interpositis varie interpretari]."[89]

Calvin rebukes the Jews and corrects his fellow Christians for failing to adopt interpretations that fit the literary context. He disputes the Jewish interpretation of Daniel 2:39, arguing that "the Jews are not ashamed to distort and twist [trahere et torquere] what relates to the King of Macedon to this Alexander the son of Mamea. But their wickedness and ignorance is easily refuted by the context [*ex contextu*]."[90] In his exposition of Deuteronomy 21:10 he accuses the rabbis of twisting the words (*verba torquent*) of the text and argues that "their gloss is refuted by the context [*ex contextu*]."[91]

In his interpretation of Jeremiah 30:4–6 he accuses Jews and Christians alike of perverting the passage and departing from the prophet's genuine meaning (*a genuino prophetae sensu*). Although Jews and Christians hardly ever agree on anything, they are united in wrongly applying this passage to the time of the Messiah. "They all consider this as a prophecy referring to the time of the Messiah; but were any one wisely to view the whole context [*totum contextum*], he would readily agree with me that the prophet includes here the sum of the doctrine which the people had previously heard from his mouth."[92]

It is far more common to find Calvin criticizing Christian than Jewish exegetes for failure to interpret the Old Testament contextually. He frequently dissents from christological interpretations of the Old Testament that derive no support from the context of the passage. In his exposition of Isaiah 4:2 ("In that day the branch of the LORD shall be beautiful and glorious") he rejects an otherwise plausible christological interpretation because it does not fit the context. He admits that the usage of the term "branch" for Christ in Zechariah 6:12 supports the common Christian interpretation. He acknowledges that the argument for a christological interpretation is further strengthened by the fact that the prophet speaks of the "branch" with great respect. But in the immediate literary context, the branch of God and the fruit of the earth must denote an unusual and abundant supply of grace.[93] He argues that a christological interpretation of Isaiah 42:19 ("Who is blind but my servant?") has nothing to do with the prophet's meaning (*sed nihil ad prophetae mentem*). This, he insists, is clear from the context.[94] A christological interpretation of Zechariah 13:6 ("And if one asks him, 'What are the wounds on your back?' he will say, 'The wounds I received in the house of my friends' ") is very frivolous (*nimis frivolum*) because it has nothing to do with the subject about which the prophet is writing.[95]

Calvin rejects the view that Jeremiah 16:16 is a prophecy of Christ's apostles ("Behold, I am sending for many fishers, says the LORD, and they shall catch them; and afterward I will send for many hunters, and they shall hunt them from every mountain and every hill, and out of the clefts of the rocks"). Some interpreters, he notes, relate the verse to Jesus' recruitment of Peter and Andrew with the promise that he would make them "fishers of men." But such an interpretation is wholly foreign to the subject matter (*prorsus alienum est*) and thus cannot be justified (*non est fundata in firma ratione*). According to Calvin, in this text God threatens the

Jews and withholds the promise of any relief. The prophet sets forth the judgment that God is about to bring upon the Jews. The Chaldeans (not Jesus' disciples) are pictured as fishers because they will empty the whole land of its inhabitants. They are hunters "because the Jews, having been scattered here and there, and become fugitives, would yet be found out in the recesses of hills and rocks." Calvin equates his contextual interpretation with the simple (*simplicius*) meaning of the passage.[96]

Augustine had taught that the primary test of exegesis was edification. Does the interpretation teach the double love of God and man?[97] Though Calvin is pleased if interpretations contain edifying teachings, that test in itself provides no adequate basis for determining their validity. He sometimes rejects pious and useful interpretations that are not firmly grounded in the context. One instance is found in his interpretation of Psalm 27:11 ("Teach me thy way, O Jehovah!").

> Many think that David here requests that God would guide him by his Spirit, lest he should surpass his enemies in acting violently and wickedly. This doctrine is, no doubt, very useful, but it does not seem to agree with the present passage [*sed praesenti loco quadrare non videtur*].[98]

In his exegesis of Psalm 5:8 he rejects a "pious and useful" interpretation because it does not fit the context (*contextu*).[99] In his exposition of Psalm 97:1 he offers the same critique. Previous interpreters have not considered the context in arriving at a very useful teaching, and Calvin is against all such subtle interpretations.[100] In his exposition of Jeremiah 51:17 he rejects a teaching that in itself is true and useful, yet from the context (*ex contextu*) it is evident that the meaning must be something different.[101]

Calvin's emphasis on the necessity of contextual exegesis arises from more than a concern for correctness. Failure to observe the context in which a statement or command is found can lead to the wrong application of scripture. The reader may draw improper generalizations if he simply lifts a text out of its context in order to apply it to himself. A proper contextual interpretation of Amos 6:5, for instance ("who sing idle songs to the sound of the harp"), protects one from wrongly taking it as a blanket condemnation of music. In its context, it must refer to the evildoers who were living lives of overindulgence. "If then any one thinks that music is in these words condemned, he is very deceived, as it appears from the circumstances [*ex circumstantia*]."[102] Likewise the context of Isaiah 1:2 ("Hear, O heavens, and give ear, O earth; for the LORD has spoken; 'Sons have I reared and brought up, but they have rebelled against me' ") helps the interpreter avoid unwarranted generalization. The first clause should not be taken as a general exhortation to hear the word of the Lord. It must be understood in connection with the second clause.[103]

Historical Context

Calvin rarely loses sight of the fact that before one can explain how a passage applies to the person of the sixteenth century he must determine what its meaning was for the original writer's contemporaries. This means that Calvin can neither uproot a text from its immediate literary context nor neglect the environment in which the document was originally produced.[104] The exegete may not neglect the audience to whom the writing was originally addressed. Calvin makes this point in rejecting the view that Psalm 50 predicts the kingdom of Christ. While there is no doubt that Christians are correct in their teaching that the cultic aspects of the law were abrogated in the renewal of the church after the advent of Christ, they are mistaken in finding a prophecy of that renewal in this text. Calvin believes it is evident from the context (*ex contextu*) that the prophet is speaking to contemporaries, showing them that the ceremonies were of no importance whatsoever unless they were connected with a higher meaning.[105] The passage is best understood as a condemnation of the abuse and corruption of the worship of Israel.

In interpreting the vision of Zechariah 1, Calvin stresses the need for historical interpretation against those "whose curiosity has done much harm in examining every syllable of the prophet." They have advanced childish interpretations, in part because of their interest in foolish speculation, but also because of their neglect of the historical context. "There is nothing better than to attend to the intention of the prophet [*consilium prophetae*], and then to regard the circumstances of the time [*circumstantias temporis*], and thirdly, to follow the analogy between the signs and things signified."[106] By "circumstances of the time" Calvin means the historical setting. The goal of understanding the intention of the human writer and historical exegesis are closely related. "That the intention of the prophet [*prophetae consilium*] may be more clear, we must especially bear in mind the history [*historia*] of the case."[107] The historical backdrop necessary to understand Zechariah's prophecy was twofold: first, the issuance of the edict of Cyrus and Darius that allowed the Jews to return to their own land; second, the fact that some of the Jews were content with their lifestyle among the Chaldeans and thus preferred to enjoy a comfortable life there rather than obeying God and returning to their former land. Only in light of these circumstances can the interpreter understand why the writer would so sharply rebuke his people.

Both correct interpretation and proper application depend on accurate historical interpretation. Calvin insists that the highly figurative language of the prophet's discourse in Ezekiel 17 "cannot be understood without a knowledge of the history."[108] He believes that Jeremiah's prophecy in Jeremiah 48:1 must be interpreted in its historical context. "This prophecy would be uninteresting, were we not to know the history [*historiam*] on which the applications and use of what is said depends."[109] In his preface to his commentary on Lamentations, Calvin ties the writer's purpose to the historical context. "We must inquire when the book was composed [*quando hic liber compositus*] and what was the intention of its author [*autoris consilium*]." The benefit to be derived from the text depends in large measure on careful historical inquiry.

> Some think that Jeremiah, before this calamity happened, historically described it, and that he thus prophesied of what was future and yet unknown. But this is by no means probable, for Jeremiah here sets before the eyes of all those things which they knew as facts, and we shall easily discover that his manner of stating things is wholly different from that used in prophetic writings. There is, then, no doubt but that Jeremiah, after the city was destroyed and the Temple burnt, bewailed the miserable state of his own nation, not after the manner of heathens, but that he might show that even in so disastrous a state of things some benefit might be derived from what he says. And this is what ought to be especially noticed, for except we bear this in mind, the book will lose its peculiar interest [*frigebit nobis totus hic liber*], but if we direct our minds to that desolation, which wholly dejected not only the people in general but also the prophet himself, so that he lost all hope, we may surely hence derive no small benefit.[110]

One of the benefits derived from historical interpretation is clarity regarding how a passage is to be applied to one's own day. If one is to know how to apply scripture, one must know something of the time and circumstances of its composition. It is important, for instance, to know that the prophet Micah was prophesying during the reign of the virtuous King Hezekiah. Although Hezekiah was a pious king, Micah did not soften his message on that account—God would judge Jerusalem and the temple. Micah "did not hesitate to threaten with such a judgment the temple and the city, though he saw that the king was endued with singular virtues." Calvin believes that the application of much of the Old Testament is through analogy. There is a danger of drawing the wrong analogy if the historical setting is disregarded. Specifically, failure to understand the prophet Micah in his historical context could lead the reader to miss some important lessons for magistrates: first, that righteous magistrates must work hard to prevent the church from degenerating; second, that such magistrates should appreciate God's ministers, who make their work easier by reproving the vices of the people. "It is a desirable thing for them, that the free reproofs of teachers should be added to the punishments and judgments of the law." Ministers of God can also learn a very important lesson from a historical understanding of this text. They are to preach God's truth faithfully, even when it seems overly severe.[111]

One of the more common mistakes Calvin finds among Christian interpreters is their failure to recognize that historical fulfillment of certain Old Testament prophecies did not have to wait until New Testament times. Many interpreters overlooked an earlier historical fulfillment in their desire to explain how the prophecies were fulfilled in the New Testament. He corrects this error in the interpretation of Zechariah 14:1, 2:

> Some apply this chapter to the time of Antichrist, some refer it to the last day, others explain it of the destruction of the city which happened in the reign of Vespasian, but I doubt not but that the prophet meant here to include the calamities which were near at hand, for the city had not yet been built, the Jews having been much harassed by their neighbors; and we also know how atrocious was the tyranny which Antiochus exercised: in short, there was a continued series of evils from the time the city and the empire began to be built till the coming of Christ.[112]

Calvin finds a glaring occurrence of this mistake by interpreters who pass by Antiochus to apply Daniel 8:24, 25 to the Antichrist. He expresses surprise "that men versed in the Scriptures should so pour forth clouds upon clear light." According to Calvin this is no harmless mistake. Twisting so clear a scripture in order to apply it to Antichrist robs it of all authority. "I desire the sacred oracles to be treated so reverently that no one may introduce any variety according to the will of man, but simply hold what is positively certain." He rejects any interpretation that takes the passage as a direct prophecy of the Antichrist; he even rejects the view that historical Antiochus should be understood as a figure or type of the Antichrist (*figuram Antichristi*). The verses are to be understood as a simple reference to Antiochus.

> It would please me better to see any one wishing to adapt this prophecy to the present use of the Church, to transfer to Antichrist by anagogy [*per anagogen*] what is said of Antiochus. . . . No doubt the Holy Spirit wished to teach us how to bear our cross by making use of this example."[113]

Calvin believes that we may rightly transfer to ourselves what happened to God's Old Testament people. "Whatever happened to the Church of old, belongs also to us, because we have fallen upon the fullness of times." The application, however, must be based upon the similarity of past and present circumstances. We may not disregard the history without running the risk of making an incorrect application. The distinction Calvin makes between application by anagogy and typology is that typology is truly prophetic—that is, the prophet knows he is speaking to a future age as well as to his own. Although this passage is not typological, it may be applied by way of anagogy, since all scripture is profitable.[114]

Historical interpretation involves determining the historical referent of a text. Calvin believes that unless the exegete correctly determines who the original addressees were, he is likely to misapply the text. He observes such a mistake in the explanation of Jeremiah 48:10 ("Cursed is he who does the work of the LORD with slackness, and cursed is he who keeps back his sword from bloodshed"), which was used to exhort Christian people to diligent obedience. "This passage has been very absurdly explained, and it is commonly quoted as though the prophet had said that special care ought to be taken by us, not to omit anything of what God commands." This misrepresents the genuine meaning (*genuinum sensum*) of the prophet. According to Calvin, if the reader considers history, this text is perfectly clear. It is a warning addressed to the wicked Chaldeans. It should not be applied to God's people.[115]

Concerning Isaiah 40:3 ("a voice crying in the wilderness, prepare the way of Jehovah"), a passage quoted and applied to John the Baptist in the Synoptic Gospels (Matt. 3:3; Mark 1:3; Luke 3:4), Calvin again argues for an interpretation that does justice to the historical context. "The words relate to the hard bondage which they should undergo in Babylon." Who are the addressees? "Is it to believers? No, but to Cyrus, to the Persians, and to the Medes, who held that people in captivity." It should be noted that Calvin does not believe in this instance that the deliverance from Babylon exhausts the meaning of this passage. It is a figure of the deliverance accomplished fully in Jesus Christ. Thus the New Testament writers are using this passage properly in applying it to John the Baptist, who had the highest rank among the messengers of our redemption.[116] Although the passage reaches its ultimate fulfillment only in the New Testament, Calvin gives considerable attention to the nearer historical fulfillment.

Calvin's sensitivity to history may also be seen in his rejection of the traditional dating of several psalms. He rejects the idea that David composed Psalm 9 on the occasion of his victory over Goliath. For one to maintain this view, he must say that David spoke "by the Spirit of prophecy" of the residence of the ark on Mount Zion, since this would have been a future event at the time. This seems "harsh [*durum*] and forced [*coactum*]." It is better to adopt an understanding that would place the psalm at the end of David's reign—after the ark had been taken to Mount Zion. Psalm 84 also speaks of the Mount Zion.[117] Calvin concludes that, though the psalm recounts David's persecution by Saul, it should be placed late in David's reign. "If we reflect that David recorded in psalms the persecutions he endured under Saul long after he was delivered from them, we will not be surprised to find him making mention of Zion in connection with them."[118] Calvin disagrees with a "predictive" interpretation of Psalm 74, arguing, contrary to the popular view, that the psalm should not be ascribed to David. The conditions depicted, "a wasted and calamitous condition of the Church," lead him to place it in the time of Antiochus or possibly the Babylonian captivity.[119]

Calvin further demonstrates his historical orientation to the Old Testament through his interest in the question of how prophetic writings were composed and preserved. Although the Old Testament is a divine book, its contents were composed by humans and collected by them following very natural processes. He displays an interest in the circumstances of the original publication of some of the prophets' writings and in their compilation in their canonical form. In his preface to his Isaiah commentary he raises the question of whether Isaiah himself or someone else wrote the inscription to the prophecy. The question, he believes, can only be properly considered when it is placed in the context of how the prophets communicated with the people.

> Not one of the commentators whose writings I have hitherto perused answers this question. For my own part, though I cannot fully satisfy my mind, yet I shall tell what I think. The prophets, after having publicly addressed the people, drew up a brief abstract of their discourse and placed it on the gates of the temple, that all might see and become more fully acquainted with the prophecy. When it had been exposed for a sufficient number of days, it was removed by the ministers of the temple and placed in the Treasury, that it might remain as a permanent record. In this way, it is probable, the books of the Prophets were compiled, and this may be inferred from the second chapter of the book of Habakkuk, if it be properly examined, and likewise from the eighth chapter of this prophecy.[120]

Priests, whose charge it was to transmit the prophecies to posterity, later arranged the books to meet the needs of their day. Without such a scenario, the irregular chronological order found in the prophetic writings is something of a puzzle; with it their organization becomes intelligible. The final product should be viewed as an attempt to meet the needs of the moment, not as an attempt to provide a strict chronological history.[121]

He finds the same process operating in Jeremiah 25:13. The prophet delivered his message, wrote a summary, and following the usual custom of the time, attached it to the doors of the temple. This is what Jeremiah refers to when he mentions a book composed from his public addresses.[122] Such a context allows one to make sense of God's command in Habakkuk 2:2 to write down the revelation and make it plain on tablets.

> But he afterwards comes to the discharge of the prophetic office; for he was bid to write the vision on tables, and to write it in large letters, that it might be read, and that any one, passing by quickly, might be able by one glance to see what was written: and by this second part he shows still more clearly that he treated of a common truth, which belonged to the whole body of the Church; for it was not for his own sake that he was bid to write, but for the edification of all.[123]

This setting also allows Calvin to make sense of Isaiah 30:8 ("And now, go, write it before them on a tablet, and inscribe it in a book, that it may be for the time to come as a witness for ever") and Isaiah 8:1 ("Then the LORD said to me, 'Take a large tablet and write upon it in common characters' "). The prophet's deliberate display of his message in very large letters could be missed by no one. "When any prediction was remarkable and peculiarly worthy of being remembered, then the Lord commanded that it should be written in larger characters, that the people might be induced to read it, and to examine it more attentively."[124]

The importance of historical context for Calvin's exegesis would be hard to overestimate. Passages cannot be torn from their context to prove whatever the Christian interpreter wishes. He makes this clear in his interpretation of Isaiah 14:12 ("How art thou fallen from heaven, O Lucifer, son of the dawn"). The common opinion that this text refers to the fall of Satan is a useless fable that has arisen from ignorance. The context clearly relates the text to the king of Babylon. This mistake and others like it have arisen because scripture texts have been taken at random, with little attention being given to the context.[125]

In his exposition of Isaiah 41:25 ("I have stirred one from the north and he has come"), Calvin finds himself again opposing erroneous interpretations on historical grounds—in this instance the wrong referent is Christ, not Satan. Calvin does not bother to refute the view; he simply offers his own. "I think that here the prophet denotes two things, for when he says 'from the north,' he means the Babylonians, and when he says 'from the east,' he means the Medes and the Persians." In place of the christological view, Calvin offers one firmly grounded in history.[126]

This chapter has dealt with the side of Calvin's exegesis that led him to adopt interpretations that troubled Hunnius. His strong historical orientation is reflected in the attention he pays to Hebrew lexicology and grammar, to the literary context, and to the historical circumstances in which the Old Testament text was produced. He insists that a failure to understand the text in its immediate literary and historical context will lead to erroneous interpretations. He is especially critical of Christian interpreters for not making a case for their interpretations on solid contextual grounds. But Calvin's approach to exegesis is not simply historical. The concern of the next chapter is with the balancing side of his method—his distinctively Christian approach to exegetical reasoning.

NOTES

1. James L. Kugel and Rowan A. Greer, *Early Biblical Interpretation*, Library of Early Christianity (Philadelphia: Westminster Press, 1986), 3:127.

2. Willis A. Shotwell, *The Biblical Exegesis of Justin Martyr* (London: SPCK, 1965), 29.

3. The renewal of biblical studies led by Erasmus and his humanist contemporaries in the sixteenth century did not represent a break with the entire medieval tradition of interpretation. Smalley has shown that the fortunes of literal interpretation were not always at a low ebb; see Beryl Smalley, *The Study of the Bible in the Middle Ages* (Notre Dame, Ind.: University of Notre Dame Press, 1964), 83–195. "The scholars of the period about 1100 to 1350 had tried to study the originals and to produce clean texts. The fifteenth century must have forgotten or disowned its ancestry": Beryl Smalley, "The Bible in the Medieval Schools," in *The Cambridge History of the Bible*, vol. 3: *The West from the Fathers to the Reformation*, ed. G.W.H. Lampe (Cambridge: Cambridge University Press, 1969), 219. De Lubac has also shown that many exegetes of the Middle Ages who were troubled by the excessive allegorization of some writers sought to ground their own exegesis firmly in the historical meaning of the text; see Henri de Lubac, *Exégèse médiévale: Les quatre sens de l'Ecriture* (Paris: Aubier, 1959–64), 2.1.287–359. See also G. R. Evans, *The Language and Logic of the Bible*, vol. 1: *The Earlier Middle Ages* (Cambridge: Cambridge University Press, 1984), 67–71.

4. Battles so describes Calvin's critical method; see Ford Lewis Battles and André Malan Hugo, eds., *Calvin's Commentary on Seneca's De Clementia*, Renaissance Text Series, 3 (Leiden: E. J. Brill, 1969), 74*. He investigates Calvin's sources as a literary critic and rhetorician and finds him especially dependent upon Cicero and Quintilian. "These works [Cicero's rhetorical treatises] and Cicero's other works undergird Calvin's whole sense of style and his rhetorical skill" (pp. 81*–84*). Calvin's technical vocabulary was borrowed from these writers and several minor rhetoricians. Torrance describes the considerable influence of the rhetorical views of Cicero on Calvin's hermeneutics in several areas; see Thomas F. Torrance, *The Hermeneutics of Calvin* (Edinburgh: Scottish Academic Press, 1988), 100–111. Not least, according to Torrance, was Cicero's influence on Calvin's rejection of the use of syllogistic reasoning in persuasion. "He relied upon what Cicero called intrinsic arguments which sought to lay bare the truth inherent in the subject matter and to let it have its own force in convincing people" (p. 107). "The positive task of the interpreter is to handle the written text in such a way that it is allowed to be *perspicuous* or self-revealing. . . . Interpretation will thus involve any operation which clears away the unrealities or ambiguities that distort the meaning of the text. . . . [W]e must also take care to uncover any equivocation in the text by clarifying the relation between the script itself and the manifest intentions of the author" (p. 111). Bouwsma suggests that Calvin was in the rhetorical tradition that went back through the Latin fathers who were rhetoricians to Cicero and Quintilian. The merger of *persuasio* with *eruditio* in Calvin has its roots here; see William J. Bouwsma, *John Calvin: A Sixteenth Century Portrait* (New York: Oxford University Press, 1988), 117–25. For Calvin's relation to the classical philosophical tradition, see Charles Partee, *Calvin and Classical Philosophy*, Studies in the History of Christian Thought, vol. 14 (Leiden: E. J. Brill, 1977).

5. For a description of the tensions present in sixteenth-century Protestant biblical interpretation, see Jerome Friedman, *The Most Ancient Testimony: Sixteenth-Century Christian-Hebraica in the Age of Renaissance Nostalgia* (Athens, Ohio: Ohio University Press, 1983).

6. Calvin's many explicit citations of the Targums provide further evidence

that he found the work of Jewish interpreters to be valuable. See Comm. Gen. 3:2 (C.O. 23.57); Comm. Ps. 78:25 (C.O. 31.730); 139:17 (C.O. 32.382); Comm. Isa. 11:5 (C.O. 36.241); 13:15 (C.O. 36.267); 38:1 (C.O. 36.646); Comm. Jer. 1:1–3 (C.O. 37.473); 10:15 (C.O. 38.80); 11:15 (C.O. 38.115); 12:5 (C.O. 38.135); 25:26 (C.O. 38.494); 44:17 (C.O. 39.263); Comm. Lam. 2:9 (C.O. 39.544); Comm. Ezek. 1:1–2 (C.O. 40.21); 13:20 (C.O. 40.294); Comm. Hos. 1:6 (C.O. 42.211); Comm. Zech. 11:1–3 (C.O. 44.300).

7. Comm. Hos. 1:2 (C.O. 42.204).

8. Comm. Jer. 3:17–18 (C.O. 37.563). He is unable, however, to give unqualified approval to their view because they fail to recognize that the fulfillment of the prophecy only begins with the return and restoration of the people, which was "a prelude of Christ's kingdom." Chapter 6 of this study discusses Calvin's view that the fulfillment of Old Testament prophecies must be extended to include Christ.

9. Comm. Gen. 5:29 (C.O. 23.108). He believes they are wrong, however, in restricting the fulfillment of the prophecy to agriculture.

10. Comm. Ps. 72, pref. (C.O. 31.664).

11. Comm. Jer. 31:22 (C.O. 38.680).

12. Comm. Ps. 16:10 (C.O. 31.157); see also Comm. Isa. 4:2 (C.O. 36.96). Bucer seems to have shared Calvin's sensitivity to Jewish criticism; see R. Gerald Hobbs, "Martin Bucer on Psalm 22: A Study in the Application of Rabbinic Exegesis by a Christian Hebraist," in Histoire de l'exégèse au XVI siècle, ed. Olivier Fatio and Pierre Fraenkel, Etudes de Philologie et d'Histoire, no. 34 (Geneva: Librairie Droz, 1978), 151.

13. John Walchenbach, "John Calvin as Biblical Commentator: An Investigation into Calvin's Use of John Chrysostom as an Exegetical Tutor" (Ph.D. diss., University of Pittsburgh, 1974). Since Chrysostom did not know Hebrew, he was of less help in interpreting the Old Testament. Calvin apparently found no suitable replacement for Chrysostom among Christian exegetes of the Old Testament.

14. Comm. Gen. 21:12 (C.O. 23.302). Calvin's view of allegorical exegesis is examined in chapter 5 of this study.

15. For a general treatment of Augustine's exegesis, see Gerald Bonner, "Augustine as Biblical Scholar," in The Cambridge History of the Bible, vol. 1: From the Beginnings to Jerome, ed. P. R. Ackroyd and C. F. Evans (Cambridge: Cambridge University Press, 1970), 541–63. For Augustine's hermeneutical views, but not his exegetical method, see James Samuel Preus, From Shadow to Promise: Old Testament Interpretation from Augustine to the Young Luther (Cambridge, Mass.: Harvard University Press, Belknap Press, 1969), 9–23. Bright argues that Augustine misused the rules of Tyconius in his influential hermeneutical work, De doctrina Christiana; see Pamela Bright, The Book of Rules of Tyconius: Its Purpose and Inner Logic (Notre Dame, Ind.: University of Notre Dame Press, 1988). For Calvin's use of Augustine, see Lucesius Smits, Saint Augustin dans l'oeuvre de Jean Calvin. 2 vols. (Assen: Van Gorcum, 1951–58).

16. Calvin evaluates Augustine's exegesis favorably in the following: Comm. Gen. 25:1 (C.O. 23.343); Comm. Ps. 115:3 (C.O. 32.184); Comm. Isa. 39:5 (C.O. 36.668); Comm. Dan. 9:20, 21 (C.O. 41.163); Comm. Hag. 2:11–15 (C.O. 44.113). In the following texts Calvin offers negative evaluations of Augustine's Old Testament exegesis (with no balancing expression of approval for the doctrine taught): Comm. Gen. 1:26 (C.O. 23.25–26); 21:8 (C.O. 23.299); 35.10 (C.O. 23.470); Comm. Ex. 7:22 (C.O. 24.95); Comm. Pss. 31:19 (C.O. 31.310); 63:4 (C.O. 31.595); 69:5 (C.O. 31.639); 88:5 (C.O. 31.807); 101:1 (C.O. 32.56); Comm. Jer. 28:7–9 (C.O. 38.571).

17. Comm. Ps. 85:11 (C.O. 31.789–90).

18. Comm. Ps. 111:2 (C.O. 32.168).

19. Comm. Ps. 59:10 (C.O. 31.569). See also Comm. Ps. 58:1 (C.O. 31.559).

20. Comm. Ps. 71:16 (C.O. 31.659). See also Comm. Ps. 99:5 (C.O. 32.51).

21. Comm. Gen. 13:14 (C.O. 23.193); see also Comm. Gen. 11:27 (C.O. 23.170) and Comm. Dan. 8:22–23 (C.O. 41.114).

22. This is especially true in Luther's earlier expositions. His early lectures on the Psalms exhibit a disregard for the historical circumstances of the psalmist. In his interpretation of the *Miserere* (Psalm 50 in the Vulgate), delivered as lectures between 1513 and 1515, he ignores the historical setting in David's life found in the heading and emphasizes the prophetic elements of the Psalm. In fact he mentions the historical setting only once—and then to say that the psalm was composed, strictly speaking, not about David but about the church: Martin Luther, *D. Martin Luthers Werke, Kritische Gesamtausgabe* (Weimar, 1883–), 3.291 (hereafter W.A.). His later (1532) lectures on the same psalm are more oriented to the circumstances in David's life, but the psalm is still used primarily as a vehicle for articulating his doctrine of justification (W.A. 40. 315–470).

23. Heinrich Bornkamm, *Luther and the Old Testament* (Philadelphia: Fortress Press, 1969), 262. C. Clifton Black II, in "Unity and Diversity in Luther's Biblical Exegesis: Psalm 51 as a Test-Case" (*Scottish Journal of Theology* 38 [1985]:344–45), writes that "Luther's Christocentric reading of Scripture does not permit him a truly literal-historical sense by our ineluctable, post-nineteenth century standards. . . . To put the question facetiously but pointedly: why does David—nay, even God—always end up sounding so much like Martin Luther?"

24. Bornkamm, *Luther and the Old Testament*, 263.

25. W.A. 3.11.

26. W.A., *Tischreden* (Weimar, 1916), 3.217 (see also 4.234). Jacopo Sadoleto attempted to interpret the psalm historically. He was concerned with understanding the meaning of the psalm in David's experience. Except for his approval of the Septuagint over the Hebrew text, his approach is similar to Calvin's.

27. Baumgartner believes the Lutheran tradition differs from the Reformed tradition at this point. He suggests that Lutherans generally followed their founder in stressing the priority of dogmatic over grammatical-historical interpretation. J. Baumgartner, *Calvin Hébraïsant et interprète de l'Ancien Testament* (Paris: Librairie Fischbacher, 1889), 27–28.

28. The nondogmatic character of Calvin's exegesis is what distinguishes his exegesis from that of Luther, according to Kemper Fullerton in *Prophecy and Authority: A Study in the History of the Doctrine and Interpretation of Scripture* (New York: Macmillan, 1919), 133.

29. *Inst.* I.xii.15 (O.S. 3.129). This is one of Calvin's interpretations that Hunnius views as worthy of refutation; see Aegidius Hunnius, *Calvin Iudaizans* (Wittenberg, 1595), 26.

30. Comm. Ps. 33:6 (C.O. 31.327).

31. Comm. Isa. 64:6 (C.O. 37.412).

32. Philip Schaff, "Calvin as a Commentator," *Presbyterian and Reformed Review* 3 (July 1892): 466.

33. "Renascentibus Hebraeorum literis, Judaïsmus meditetur per occasionem reviviscere . . ." A. L. Herminjard, ed., *Correspondance des Réformateurs dans les pays de la langue française,* 7 vols. (Geneva and Paris, 1866), 1:29–30. For Erasmus, this

worry may have been coupled with the concern that the Christian church was putting too much emphasis on the Old Testament. See Jerome Friedman, *The Most Ancient Testimony*, 178. That Erasmus may have been ambivalent about the advisability of pursuing Hebrew studies is suggested in his more positive comments in a letter to Martin Dorp: "How much better, instead of doing what they are doing—wounding others and being wounded, wasting their own time and that of others—to learn Greek or Hebrew, or at least Latin, which are so indispensable to the knowledge of Sacred Scripture that I think it extremely impudent for anyone ignoring them to usurp the name of theologian." *Christian Humanism and the Reformation: Selected Writings of Erasmus*, ed. John C. Olin (New York: Fordham University Press, 1975), 80.

34. *Jacobi Sadoleti S. R. E. Cardinalis Epistolae quotquot extant proprio nomine scriptae nunc primum duplo auctiores in lucem editae*, ed. U. A. Costanz, 3 vols. (Rome, 1760–64), 2:156–57.

35. *Jacobi Sadolet: Cardinalis et Episcopi Carpentoractensis viri disertissimi, Opera quae extant omnia*, 4 vols. (Verona, 1738), 1:186. Sadoleto's approach to Psalm 51 (3:262–93) is strikingly similar to that of Calvin in its concern for treating the Psalm in its proper historical setting in David's life.

36. Sadoleto, *Jacobi Sadoleti . . . Epistolae* (ed. Costanz), 2:155.

37. Werner Schwarz, *Principles and Problems of Biblical Translation: Some Reformation Controversies and Their Background* (Cambridge: Cambridge University Press, 1955), 63–64. Calvin believes the concern may be justified. Comm. Ps. 22:16 (C.O. 31.229).

38. Jerome Friedman, *The Most Ancient Testimony*, 134–35.

39. J. Oecolampadius, *In Iesaiam Prophetam Hypomnematon* (Basel, 1525), folio a3 verso, cited in Friedman, *The Most Ancient Testimony*, 127.

40. The characteristic Lutheran position is evident in the title of Johannes Forster's Hebrew dictionary: "New Hebrew Dictionary, Not Arranged Out of the Comments of the Rabbis Nor Out of the Foolish Imitations of Our Native Doctors But out of Our Own Treasures of Sacred Scripture and Developed by an Accurate Collation of Biblical Passages." The irony of Forster's position, according to Friedman, is that in the composition of his dictionary, "the only available sources were those composed by such 'foolish imitators' as Sebastian Münster and Paul Fagius, who were in turn dependent upon rabbinic sources as well as the work of their contemporary Elias Levita": Friedman, *The Most Ancient Testimony*, 170.

41. Sebastian Münster, *Mikdash YHWH: Hebraica Biblia* (Basel, 1534, 1546).

42. Friedman's *The Most Ancient Testimony* contains the fullest description of the state of Christian Hebrew studies during this period. The question of Bucer's "Judaizing" is addressed by R. Gerald Hobbs in "How Firm a Foundation: Martin Bucer's Historical Exegesis of the Psalms," *Church History* 53 (December 1984): 477–91, and "Martin Bucer on Psalm 22," 144–63, and by Johannes Müller, *Martin Bucers Hermeneutik*, Quellen und Forschungen zur Reformationsgeschichte, no. 32 (Gütersloh: Gerd Mohn, 1965).

43. Hans-Joachim Kraus, "Calvin's Exegetical Principles," *Interpretation* 31 (January 1977): 15.

44. Calvin probably began his study of Hebrew with François Vatable during his second stay in Paris (1531–33) and continued it later in Basel with Sebastian Münster and perhaps in Strassburg with Wolfgang Capito. Baumgartner, *Calvin Hébraïsant*, 15; Emile Doumergue, *Jean Calvin: Les hommes et les choses de son temps*,

vol. 1: *La jeunesse de Calvin* (Lausanne: G. Bridel, 1899), 505; Basil Hall, "Biblical Scholarship: Editions and Commentaries," *The Cambridge History of the Bible*, vol. 3: *The West from the Reformation to the Present Day*, ed. S. L. Greenslade (Cambridge: Cambridge University Press, 1976), 89. Hugo argues that it is probable "though not altogether certain" that Calvin attended the lectures of the Hebraist Vatable while in Paris. Battles and Hugo, *Calvin's Commentary on Seneca's De Clementia*, 5*.

45. Richard Simon, *Histoire critique du Vieux Testament* (Rotterdam, 1689), 435.

46. August Tholuck, "Die Verdienste Calvins als Ausleger der heiligen Schrift," in *Vermischte Schriften gröstentheils apologetischen Inhalts* (Hamburg: Friedrich Perthes, 1839), 2:332–33.

47. Hall, "Biblical Scholarship," 89. See also Wilhelm Vischer, "Calvin, exégète de l'Ancien Testament," *Etudes Théologiques et Religieuses* 40 (1965): 219–22.

48. A simple count of the words suggests that Calvin's translation differs from the Vulgate in well over one-third of its wording. (My count, using the *Psalmi iuxta Septuaginta emendati* in the *Biblia Sacra iuxta Vulgatam Versionem*, published by the Württemberg Bible Society in 1975, reveals agreement on 140 words, disagreement on 88 words.)

49. The version of the Psalter that Jerome translated from the Hebrew was not included in the Vulgate. Ernst Würthwein, *The Text of the Old Testament*, trans. Erroll F. Rhodes (Grand Rapids: Wm. B. Eerdmans Publishing Co., 1979), 95. Rodolphe Peter suggests that Calvin made use of textual notes made by Louis Budé, in Peter's "Calvin and Louis Budé's Translation of the Psalms," in *John Calvin: A Collection of Essays*, ed. Gervase E. Duffield, Courtenay Studies in Reformation Theology (Grand Rapids: Wm. B. Eerdmans Publishing Co., 1966), 1:196. For the question of which biblical text Calvin may have used in his commentary on Genesis, see H. F. van Rooy, "Calvin's Genesis Commentary—Which Bible Text Did He Use?" in *Our Reformational Tradition: A Rich Heritage and Lasting Vocation*, Institute for Reformation Studies, series F, no. 21 (Potchefstroom, South Africa: Potchefstroom University for Christian Higher Education, 1984), 203–16.

50. Comm. Ps. 51:6 (C.O. 31.509–10).

51. Comm. Ps. 51:6 (C.O. 31.514–15).

52. Comm. Ps. 51:14 (C.O. 31.519–20).

53. Comm. Dan., printer's pref. (C.O. 40.526).

54. Calvin is particularly aware of the Hebrew use of parallelism. Comm. Ps. 22:12 (C.O. 31.227); Comm. Dan. 4:27 (C.O. 40.674); Comm. Hos. 6:5 (C.O. 42.327); 13:14 (C.O. 42.493). Kugel entirely overlooks Calvin's use of synonymous parallelism in his study of the history of the recognition of parallelism; see James L. Kugel, *The Idea of Biblical Poetry: Parallelism and Its History* (New Haven, Conn.: Yale University Press), 1981.

55. Comm. Ps. 52:6 (C.O. 31.528); Comm. Isa. 5:27 (C.O. 36.122–23); 43:19 (C.O. 37.94); 51:19 (C.O. 37.240); Comm. Jer. 4:22 (C.O. 37.595); 24:6 (C.O. 38.461); 51:36 (C.O. 39.475); Comm. Lam. 4:11 (C.O. 39.614); Comm. Jonah 1:4 (C.O. 43.210); Comm. Hab. 2:7 (C.O. 43.543).

56. Battles and Hugo, *Calvin's Commentary on Seneca's De Clementia*, 85*.

57. Ibid., 87*.

58. T.H.L. Parker, *Calvin's New Testament Commentaries* (Grand Rapids: Wm. B. Eerdmans Publishing Co., 1971), 49.

59. Comm. Isa. 65:11 (C.O. 37.424).

60. Calvin makes use of Jewish interpreters less frequently for grammatical than for lexical help. He is more likely to differ with them on points of grammar. One instance in which he feels confident in rejecting their view is in the heading of Psalm 127. "There is no reason why the Jews should deny that this Psalm was composed by Solomon. They think the letter ל, which we translate 'of,' is equivalent to 'in behalf of Solomon,' which is at variance with common usage, for such a title in all cases designates the author. Accordingly, they absurdly devise a new sense, for which there is no necessity." Here Calvin bases his refutation of the Jewish view on what he understands to be the normal usage of ל as a prefix in the Psalms. Comm. Ps. 127:1 (C.O. 32.321).

61. Comm. Jer. 30:19 (C.O. 38.631).

62. Comm. Amos 5:16 (C.O. 43.88).

63. Comm. Psalm 29:1 (C.O. 31.286).

64. No substantial study has yet been published on Calvin's knowledge of Jewish exegesis. Calvin did not usually name his rabbinic sources. He usually attributed an interpretation to the "rabbis" and left it at that. Calvin's hesitance to name his sources is in marked contrast to the approach of one of his mentors, Martin Bucer. According to Hobbs, Bucer in his commentary on Psalm 22 explicitly invokes David Kimchi three times, Ibn Ezra seven times, and Rashi three times: Hobbs, "Martin Bucer on Psalm 22," 151. In his commentary on the same Psalm, Calvin explicitly rejects rabbinic interpretations, yet does not name his Jewish opponents. Baron observes that Calvin tends to lump all Jewish interpreters together. He usually drew "no distinction between the ancient homilists, who tried to deduce moral lessons from Scripture through imaginative hermeneutics, and his Jewish contemporaries, who were perfectly aware of the difference between addadic and allegorical interpretations, on the one hand, and the ordinary meaning of the biblical texts on the other" (Salo Baron, "John Calvin and the Jews," in *Ancient and Medieval Jewish History*, ed. Leon A. Feldman [New Brunswick, N.J.: Rutgers University Press, 1972], 343–44). According to Hobbs, Bucer found his rabbinic interpretations in the first and second editions of the "Rabbinic Bible" published by the Christian printer Daniel Bomberg. This four-volume work included the Hebrew text plus Targums and rabbinic glosses. Calvin could have used editions of the Rabbinic Bible that were published in 1517–18, 1523, 1546, or 1548. He may also have used Sebastian Münster's Hebrew Bible with Latin translation, *Mikdash YHWH: Hebraica Biblia*, which was published in Basel in 1534 and in a revised edition in 1546. Münster's work was full of citations from rabbinic sources. Münster also published David Kimchi's commentaries on Joel, Malachi, Amos, and Isaiah. Robert Estienne, who later settled in Geneva, published from 1539 to 1544 a Hebrew Old Testament, which included Kimchi's commentaries on the prophets. An investigation of the sources for Calvin's knowledge of Jewish exegesis would probably need to start with a comparison of his ubiquitous generic references to "the rabbis" with the various editions of the works of Bomberg, Münster, and Estienne.

65. Comm. Ps. 3:2 (C.O. 31.53–54).

66. Comm. Ps. 144:13 (C.O. 32.411).

67. Comm. Isa. 59:10 (C.O. 37.343).

68. Comm. Ex. 6:2 (C.O. 24.78).

69. Calvin reached the conclusion early in his career that usage has priority

over etymology. In an attempt to distinguish *tyrannus* and *rex* in his commentary on Seneca, he argues that it is "usage [*usus*] rather than etymology [*etymon*] or original meaning [*proprietas*]" that determines the meaning of words. Battles and Hugo, *Calvin's Commentary on Seneca's De Clementia*, 200.

70. Comm. Jer. 25:30 (C.O. 38.502).

71. Comm. Ps. 55:22 (C.O. 31.544–45).

72. Comm. Isa. 44:25 (C.O. 37.123). See also Comm. Isa. 19:19 (C.O. 36.343).

73. Comm. Ps. 26:8 (C.O. 31.268).

74. Comm. Ps. 57:1 (C.O. 31.555).

75. Comm. Isa. 28:17 (C.O. 38.476).

76. Comm. Ps. 19:4 (C.O. 31.197).

77. Comm. Ps. 35:2 (C.O. 31.346–47).

78. Comm. Isa. 41:14 (C.O. 37.43–44).

79. Comm. Jer. 4:6 (C.O. 37.580). See also Comm. Jer. 1:13–14 (C.O. 37.486).

80. Comm. Jer. 20:3 (C.O. 38.337).

81. Comm. Num. 32:14 (C.O. 25.326).

82. Comm. Ps. 31:10 (C.O. 31.306). In the following texts, Calvin rejects a translation that he admits is in accord with the normal biblical usage of a term because it does not fit the context. Comm. Gen. 30:9 (C.O. 23.411); Comm. Ps. 30:7 (C.O. 31.295–96); Comm. Ps. 88:6 (C.O. 31.808); Comm. Isa. 58:8 (C.O. 37.330); Comm. Jer. 5:18 (C.O. 37.628); Comm. Dan. 4:27 (C.O. 40.672); Comm. Hos. 3:2–5 (C.O. 42.265); Comm. Jonah 3:6–8 (C.O. 43.253); Comm. Zeph. 3:1, 2 (C.O. 44.46–47).

83. Comm. Ps. 81:5 (C.O. 31.760–61).

84. Calvin's view of the relative importance of lexicology and context in interpretation can be seen in the following instances. In each of these Calvin uses context as his basis for rejecting a translation of a Hebrew word. Comm. Gen. 26:12 (C.O. 23.36); Comm. Ex. 19:5 (C.O. 24.196); Comm. Lev. 22:28 (C.O. 24.543); Comm. Deut. 32:6 (C.O. 25.360); 32:7 (C.O. 25.361); Comm. Ps. 11:6 (C.O. 31.125); 37:1 (C.O. 31.366); 46:1 (C.O. 31.460); 73:6 (C.O. 31.677); 78:1 (C.O. 31.721); 90:8 (C.O. 31.836–37); 119:27 (C.O. 32.226); 119:149 (C.O. 32.282); Comm. Isa. 3:12 (C.O. 36.88); Comm. Joel 2:23 (C.O. 42.560); Comm. Micah 4:6, 7 (C.O. 43.353); Comm. Obad. 12—14 (C.O. 43.192); Comm. Zech. 7:14 (C.O. 44.231).

85. Grammatical considerations stand in precisely the same relationship to contextual considerations as do lexicological ones. The order of precedence is exactly the same. Calvin frequently begins with a comment on the grammar (much as he does with etymology), then he proceeds to point to the usage of the same grammatical structure elsewhere, and finally he adds that context—not grammar or usage elsewhere—is decisive. For Calvin's appeals to context in making grammatical decisions see: Comm. Ex. 5:20 (C.O. 24.74); 15:13 (C.O. 24.160); Comm. Lev. 6:1 (C.O. 24.528); Comm. Deut. 33:16 (C.O. 25.391); Comm. Ps. 37:3 (C.O. 31.367); 42:8 (C.O. 31.431); 75:1 (C.O. 31.701); 105:25 (C.O. 32.109); 122:1 (C.O. 32.303); 139:3 (C.O. 32.378); 139:6 (C.O. 32.378); Comm. Isa. 3:5 (C.O. 36.84); 3:6 (C.O. 36.84); 7:6 (C.O. 36.148); 11:3 (C.O. 36.237); 12:1 (C.O. 36.251); 16:8 (C.O. 36.308); 22:6 (C.O. 36.369); 63:1 (C.O. 37.393); Comm. Hos. 7:16 (C.O. 42.359); Comm. Hab. 1:12 (C.O. 43.508); 2:6 (C.O. 43.540); Comm. Zech. 7:14 (C.O. 44.231).

86. On occasion Calvin finds that more than one translation is possible on the basis of lexicology, grammar, and context (Comm. Isa. 22:5 [C.O. 36.369]). He

appears to reverse his normal approach in his comments on Ps. 80:13 (C.O. 31.757) where he rejects a translation that would fit the context because it is not the ordinary meaning of the word.

87. Comm. Zech. 6:1–3 (C.O. 44.202).

88. Comm. Lev. 18:16 (C.O. 24.663). See also Ex. 14:10 (C.O. 24.150).

89. Comm. Ex. 8:26 (C.O. 24.105).

90. Comm. Dan. 2:39 (C.O. 40.598).

91. Comm. Deut. 21:10 (C.O. 24.353).

92. Comm. Jer. 30:4–6 (C.O. 38.614).

93. Comm. Isa. 4:2 (C.O. 36.96).

94. Comm. Isa. 42:19 (C.O. 37.73).

95. Comm. Zech. 13:6 (C.O. 44.353).

96. Comm. Jer. 16:16 (C.O. 38.251).

97. Augustine, *De doctrina Christiana* I.xxxvi.40.

98. Comm. Ps. 27:11 (C.O. 31.278).

99. Comm. Ps. 5:8 (C.O. 31.69). See also Comm. Ps. 36:6 (C.O. 31.362).

100. Comm. Ps. 97:1 (C.O. 32.43).

101. Comm. Jer. 51:17 (C.O. 39.456).

102. Comm. Amos 6:5 (C.O. 43.108).

103. Comm. Isa. 1:2 (C.O. 36.28). Other passages that Calvin believes are applied too generally by interpreters because they do not consider the context are Deut. 32:4 (C.O. 25.358); Ps. 84:5 (C.O. 31.782); and Isa. 65:5 (C.O. 37.420).

104. Calvin's awareness of the cultic setting of the Psalms is evidence of his interest in how the writings of the Old Testament functioned for the people of the old covenant. Comm. Ps. 4:1 (31.58); 26:6 (31.267); 81:1 (31.760); 85:1 (31.785); 95:1 (32.29); 107:1 (32.135–36); 135:1 (32.357).

105. Comm. Ps. 50:1 (C.O. 31.495).

106. Comm. Zech. 1:7–10 (C.O. 44.138). In offering the advice that one should follow the "analogy between the signs and the things signified," Calvin intends the reader to understand that in the vision recorded in this passage God is accommodating his teaching to limited capacities of human beings. In this passage the sign is the vision of runners sent by God to run through the earth; the thing signified is God's providential care for the world.

107. Comm. Zech. 2:6 (C.O. 44.156).

108. Comm. Ezek. 17:1–2 (C.O. 40.402).

109. Comm. Jer. 48:1 (C.O. 39.314). See also Comm. Ps. 87, pref. (C.O. 31.799); Comm. Isa. 16:3 (C.O. 36.301); Comm. Jer. 37:1, 2 (C.O. 39.140); Comm. Jer. 50:19 (C.O. 39.410); Comm. Ezek., pref. (C.O. 40.21).

110. Comm. Lam., pref. (C.O. 39.505).

111. Comm. Micah 3:11, 12 (C.O. 43.332–38).

112. Comm. Zech. 14:1–2 (C.O. 44.360).

113. Comm. Dan. 8:24–25 (C.O. 41.121–22). Calvin's understanding of the proper use of typological or figural interpretation is addressed in chapter 5.

114. Calvin is not using the term *per anagogen* in the sense of the medieval theory of the four senses. He appears to be using it in the sense of analogy or similarity. See T.H.L. Parker, *Calvin's Old Testament Commentaries* (Edinburgh: T. & T. Clark, 1986), 72–73. The Edinburgh edition of Calvin's commentaries, while not strictly correct in translating it "by analogy," does appear to have the meaning right. In other passages Calvin uses "anagogy" in very close connection with

typology: Comm. Isa. 33:17 (C.O. 36.572); Comm. Zech. 9:16 (C.O. 44.283). For the meaning of the term in the early church, see Robert M. Grant, *The Letter and the Spirit* (London: SPCK, 1957), 124. For the latitude of the term's usage in the medieval period, see de Lubac, *Exégèse médiévale*, 1.2.418.

115. Comm. Jer. 48:10 (C.O. 39.320).

116. Comm. Isa. 40:3 (C.O. 37.7).

117. Comm. Ps. 9:12 (C.O. 31.102).

118. Comm. Ps. 84:1 (C.O. 31.779–80).

119. Comm. Ps. 74, pref. (C.O. 31.690). Other instances where Calvin draws attention to the historical referent: Comm. Ps. 140:1 (C.O. 32.387); Comm. Isa. 45:4 (C.O. 37.135); Comm. Isa. 65:15 (C.O. 37.427).

120. Comm. Isa., pref. (C.O. 36.24).

121. This may be one reason Calvin is not bothered by chronological inversions in the Old Testament. The authors were not writing history per se. They were addressing the needs of their day, and presumably the primary need was not for an account of their past. Calvin acknowledges chronological irregularities in the following: Comm. Gen. 3:20 (C.O. 23.77); 25:1 (C.O. 23.343); Comm. Ex. 16:32 (C.O. 24.174); 35:20 (C.O. 25.260); Comm. Deut. 1:27 (C.O. 25.196); Comm. Isa. 36:2 (C.O. 36.601); 38:7 (C.O. 36.652).

122. Comm. Jer. 25:13 (C.O. 38.483). See also Comm. Jer. 17:19–21 (C.O. 38.285).

123. Comm. Hab. 2:2 (C.O. 43.523). See also Comm. Isa. 8:1 (C.O. 36.165); Comm. Hos. 14:9 (C.O. 42.509).

124. Comm. Isa. 30:8 (C.O. 36.512).

125. Comm. Isa. 14:12 (C.O. 36.277).

126. Comm. Isa. 41:25 (C.O. 37.52).

4

THE "CHRISTIAN" CHARACTER
OF CALVIN'S EXEGESIS

For Calvin, the Old and New Testaments are one book. The Hebrew Bible must never be interpreted as though it stood alone—it can only be properly understood when its interpretation is informed by the superior clarity of the New Testament. While it is important for the interpreter to have strong philological skills, the possession of such skills does not guarantee proper understanding of the Old Testament. It is far more important that one read scripture with the proper goal—that of finding Christ. "Whoever turns aside from this object, even though he wears himself out with all his learning, will never reach the knowledge of the truth."[1] This chapter will examine the unambiguously Christian character of Calvin's exegesis as seen in his criticism of Jewish exegesis and his embrace of the New Testament as an exegetical guide.

CRITICISM OF JEWISH EXEGESIS

In his comments on Amos 9:11 ("In that day I will raise up the booth of David that is fallen and repair its breaches, and raise up its ruins, and rebuild it as in the days of old") Calvin distinguishes those Jewish interpreters who are more moderate from those who "pervert all Scripture without any distinction." He regards those as moderate who recognize that the prophet refers to the advent of the Messiah in this verse.[2] In his exegesis of Isaiah 49:2 ("He made my mouth like a sharp sword, in the shadow of his hand he hid me; he made me a polished arrow, in his quiver he hid me away") Calvin makes the same distinction: those Jews who show any soundness of understanding admit that this passage must be understood as relating to Christ.[3] In his commentary on Psalm 112:5 he expresses his approval for the exegesis of Rabbi David Kimchi, whom he labels "the most correct expositor among the rabbis." Even Kimchi, though, had a major blind spot—he did not understand that all of scripture is a witness to Christ.[4]

Although Calvin often makes use of Jewish linguistic expertise and sometimes approves of Jewish interpretations in other matters, most of his comments about Jewish exegesis are negative.[5] He appears to delight in bringing fanciful opinions of the Jews to light. He observes that Jewish writers are particularly fond of speculating about the world of nature when it is alluded to in the text. He rejects the strange story invented by the rabbis to explain Jeremiah 17:11 ("Like the partridge that gathers a brood which she did not hatch, so is he who gets riches but not by right"). "The rabbis, according to their practice, have devised fables; for they imagine that the partridge steals all the eggs of other birds which she can find, and gathers them in one heap, and then that the pullets, when hatched, fly away, as by certain hidden instinct, they understand that it is not their mother." This is an absurd fable for which there is confirmation in neither Aristotle nor Pliny, the ancient authorities on such matters.[6] As another example of the inventiveness of the Jews, he cites a rabbi named Zaadias who, exercising his imagination in making up stories about the eagle, "pretends that the eagle flies upward into the region that is near the sun, and approaches the sun so closely that its old wings are burned and other new ones grow in their place."[7] He scoffs at a Jewish fable that is used to explain Psalm 147:9 ("He gives the beasts their food, and to the young ravens who cry"). "That the ravens desert their young ones as soon as put forth, and that worms are bred in the bark of the trees to feed them, this is one of their customary stories." He observes that whenever the Jews find a difficulty in the biblical text they display no scruples or shame in inventing some unfounded explanation.[8]

The Jewish readiness to invent fables is in Calvin's view an indication that they despise the simple meaning of the text. The rabbinic explanation of the recovery of Hezekiah from his deathbed was one example of their fable making. "Here the Jews make fables according to their custom, and contrive a story, . . . but there is no history of this, and it is entirely destitute not only of evidence but of probability."[9] The rabbinic understanding of the golden calf story in Exodus 32 (that gold was thrown into the furnace and through a miracle came out looking like a calf) is a ridiculous fable and an example of the license with which the Jews invent their ideas.[10] In one of the sketchiest narratives in scripture, Genesis 4:23 ("I have slain a man for wounding me, a young man for striking me"), the rabbis do not find enough information to satisfy their curiosity, so they invent a fable. Cain was hiding in the woods when he was killed by the blind Lamech's arrow. The young boy who was helping him aim his arrows accidentally mistook Cain for a wild animal. Lamech then killed the boy for causing the death. Although there are absolutely no grounds for this story, the Jews invent it because they are too proud to admit that they do not know what the biblical text means. "Ignorance of the true state of the case has caused everyone to allow himself to conjecture what he pleased."[11]

Calvin's belief that all of scripture is a witness to Christ as the mediator between God and man is nowhere more evident than in his condemnation of Jewish exegesis. Baron points out that in his attitude toward the Jews Calvin is very much a man of his time. He argues "like a typical medieval polemist, raising the same arguments against Judaism that had been voiced by Christian thinkers since the patristic age."[12] Calvin's comments concerning the fruits of Jewish exegesis offer little basis for disputing Baron's evaluation. They are mostly negative and often harsh and sarcastic. He is not critical of the Jews because they fail to understand this or that passage. The problem is the ignorance and impudence that permeates their work. He offers a particularly scathing rebuke in his exposition of the "seventy weeks" of Daniel 9:24.

> I will begin with the Jews, because they not only pervert its sense through ignorance, but through shameful impudence. Whenever they are exposed to the light which shines in Christ, they instantly turn their backs in utter shamelessness and display a complete want of uprightness. They are like dogs who are satisfied with barking. In this passage especially they betray their petulance, because with brazen forehead they cannot elude the Prophet's meaning.[13]

The tone of Calvin's rebuke suggests that the problem goes deeper than the simple fact that the Jews have misunderstood the passage. His criticism is directed toward the spiritual rebellion that lies at the heart of their flawed exegesis. They fail to understand the true meaning because they willfully reject the truth.

The most serious problem in their exegesis results from their failure to recognize the christological orientation of the Old Testament.[14] Calvin's clearest analysis of this problem is found in his exposition of Daniel 7:27, where he explains the reason for the ignorance of a certain Rabbi Barnibal,[15] who has tried to demonstrate that the text in question contains no reference to Christ:

> We must not be surprised at the shameful ignorance of these rabbis, and at their blundering at the very rudiments, since they do not acknowledge the necessity of a Mediator, through whom alone the Church can obtain any favor before God. . . . [T]heir separating the Church from the Mediator is like leaving a mutilated body apart from its disjoined head.[16]

Jewish exegetes adopt perverted interpretations of many other Old Testament texts in an attempt to escape the claims of Christ. In Micah 5:4

("And he shall stand and feed his flock in the strength of the LORD, in the majesty of the name of the LORD his God. And they shall dwell secure, for now he shall be great to the ends of the earth") it is clear that the prophet is speaking of Christ. The Jews, even "though they shamelessly pervert the whole Scripture," cannot deny that it is the prophet's desire to call attention to the coming of the Messiah.[17] The vanity of their exegesis cannot be excused as though it resulted from ignorance alone. They deliberately try to obscure the true meaning of scripture. Concerning the identity of "Immanuel" in Isaiah 7:14, Calvin admits to some obscurity in the passage; however, the Jews are partly to blame for this because by their quibbling they "have labored, as far as possible, to pervert the true exposition." The Jews "are hard pressed by this passage, for it contains an illustrious prediction concerning the Messiah, who is here called Immanuel, and therefore they have labored, by all possible means, to twist [*torquere*] the Prophet's meaning to another sense."[18] Rabbinic deceitfulness is evident in their interpretation of Daniel 2:39, where they display "the grossest ignorance [*crassissimam inscitiam*] and dishonesty [*improbitatem*]" in rejecting the christological meaning of the text. "They do not err through simple ignorance, but they purposely desire to overthrow what Scripture here states clearly concerning the advent of Christ."[19] Calvin insists that their perverted and wicked interpretation is refuted by the context.

The dishonesty of the Jews is deeply rooted in malice. It is their intent to perplex Christians and discredit the Christian Bible. They contest the meaning of every Old Testament passage that points to Christ. They challenge New Testament interpretations of the Old Testament. One text that was consistently interpreted by Christians as a clear prophecy of the crucifixion of Christ was Psalm 22:16 ("Dogs have surrounded me; a band of evil men has encircled me, they have pierced my hands and my feet"). According to Calvin, the word כָּאֲרִי ("like a lion") is found in all of the Hebrew Bibles with which he is acquainted. The Septuagint, however, seems to have followed a different reading ("they have pierced"). The Jews follow the Hebrew reading and accuse Christians of rejecting the literal interpretation. Calvin, without any textual evidence, suggests that the Hebrew text must have been intentionally corrupted by the Jews. There are "strong grounds for conjecturing that this passage has been fraudulently corrupted by the Jews [*locum a Iudaeis fraude esse corruptum*]." There is every reason to be suspicious because "it is the uppermost desire of their hearts to despoil the crucified Jesus of his uniqueness, and to divest him of his character as the Messiah and Redeemer."[20] Calvin knows that he cannot hope to persuade the Jews of their errors; they are too obstinate and opinionated. He does, however, hope to show Christians that they need not be perplexed by the textual problem.[21] There is also good reason to believe that the Jewish writers are driven by impure motives in raising questions about the accuracy of a quotation from Psalm 109:11 by Peter. "What purpose can it serve to pervert the sense of a word, the meaning of which is so pointed and plain, unless that, under the influence of a malignant spirit, they endeavor so to obscure the passage, as to make it appear not to be properly quoted by Peter?"[22]

Calvin uses the metaphor of blindness to describe the Jewish failure to understand scripture. "The Lord so blinded them and delivered them up to a reprobate mind, when he wished them to be examples of horrible blindness and prodigious stupidity [*specula horrendae caecitatis, et prodigiosi stuporis*]."[23] Theirs is not an excusable blindness; it is God's judgment on them for their impiety. "I have had conversation with many Jews: I have never seen either a drop of piety or a grain of truth or uprightness—no, I have never found common sense in any Jew."[24] In his interpretation of Genesis 2:3, he rails against the Jews for teaching that God, like an ordinary craftsman limited by time constraints, left some of creation imperfect on the sixth evening. "Ravings so monstrous prove the authors to have been delivered over to a reprobate mind, as a dreadful example of the wrath of God."[25] The blindness of the Jewish exegetes is a reflection of God's judgment on them for their attempt to pervert sound doctrine, especially their denial of the christological referent of prophecy. "Since their object is the adulteration of sound doctrine, God also blinds them till they become utterly in the dark."[26]

Calvin believes that Jewish dishonesty in handling scripture finds its source not only in their obstinacy in rejecting Christ but also in their racial pride. An example of dishonesty motivated by racial pride is their interpretation of Jeremiah 28:16–17 ("Therefore thus says the LORD: 'Behold, I will remove you from the face of the earth. This very year you shall die, because you have uttered rebellion against the LORD.' In that same year, in the seventh month, the prophet Hananiah died"). The Jews contend that their forefathers, who persisted in their rebellion against God's prophet Jeremiah following the death of Hananiah, must have been unaware of the news that the false prophet had been judged by God. In order to conceal the reproach of their nation they have fabricated the story that the prophet's disciples secretly took away his body and that the people knew nothing of his death.[27]

Jewish pride is evident in their willingness to twist scripture if it serves to magnify the status and privileges of Jewish people. They eagerly sift through the testimonies of scripture searching for evidence of the glory of their people. They then boast of their privileges before the rest of the world.[28] This is their concern in their strained interpretation of Joshua 2:1, where they deny that Rahab, the woman in Jericho who saved the lives of two Jewish spies, was a harlot. At issue is the meaning of the word זוֹנָה .

Calvin indicates that some rabbis interpret it "one who keeps an inn." However, since the term in its normal biblical usage almost always means harlot, there is no reason to depart from that meaning in this passage. The rabbis are simply following their regular practice of creating a fiction because the truth does not bring honor to their nation.[29]

The pride of the Jews is further exposed in the lack of humility with which they approach the scriptures. They allow nothing to remain uncertain. They have an opinion on every subject. Again and again he condemns their rashness and presumption. They never hesitate to offer their conjectures. "We have elsewhere shown how bold the Jews are in their conjectures, whenever they have no certain guide."[30] Not only are these interpreters overly bold and presumptuous; they are "the most obstinate people in the world."[31] They are exasperating because they are so contentious; they refuse to keep their opinions to themselves. Calvin is reluctant to battle them over the meaning of a phrase in Zechariah 2:8 ("For thus says the LORD of hosts, after the glory he has sent me to the nations which spoiled you") because they are combative and "they are disposed to think that we insist on proofs that are not conclusive." But it is the rabbis who give the poor explanation of this verse. A careful look at the unusual wording—"The Lord seems to be both the sender and the one who is sent"—indicates that Christ is introduced here. The text must be twisted to be applied to anyone except Christ.[32]

Sometimes the absurd conjectures of the Jews do not result from ignorance, nor even impiety or pride; sometimes, Calvin argues, their conjectures are literally diabolic.

> The Psalmist speaks of divisions in the plural number, which has led some Jewish authors to conjecture that there must have been more passages [of the Red Sea] than one—an instance of their solemn trifling in things of which they know nothing and of their method of corrupting the Scriptures entirely with their vain fancies. We may well laugh at such fooleries, yet we are to hold them at the same time in detestation; for there can be no doubt that the rabbinical writers were led to this by Satan, as an artful way of discrediting the Scriptures.[33]

Calvin offers a number of other less-than-flattering descriptions of rabbinic exegetes. They are boastful. "We know that they are always prone to vain boastings."[34] They are impudent and ignorant. "On this passage the Jews display both their impudence and ignorance; as, according to their usual habit, they babble with audacity about what they do not understand."[35] They are rebellious. "How foolishly those Jewish reasoners make war with God, and furiously oppose the clear light of the Gospel."[36] They are sacrilegious. They ridiculously ascribe the work of creation partly to angels.[37] They are shameless. "All sound and sensible readers will be perfectly satisfied that they act without either judgment or shame, and vomit forth whatever comes into their thoughts."[38] They are unreasonable. "They blend things of no weight, when reasons sufficiently important present themselves to us."[39] They are subtle[40] and inflexible.[41] They are foolish and they bring their foolish superstitions over into their exegesis. "The supposition of some of the Jews, that the ineffable name of God was placed beneath its [the breastplate of the high priest] texture, is not free from foolish and dangerous superstition."[42] They are lazy. "The abhorrence for Christ which the Jews feel, who have the Law constantly in their hands, must be imputed to their laziness."[43]

All in all, Calvin's evaluation of the Jewish exegesis is extremely harsh. Though much of his sharpest criticism is directed at them for promoting strained interpretations that have little to do with the text, his critique is grounded in his belief that Jewish rejection of Christ makes it impossible for them to understand the Old Testament.

> The Jews thought that the Scriptures were in themselves life-giving, when they were in fact strangers to its real meaning and even quenched the light of life contained in them. For how can the Law bestow life without Christ, who alone quickens it.[44]

THE NEW TESTAMENT
AS AN EXEGETICAL GUIDE

For all his emphasis on historical interpretation, Calvin does not depart from the belief that scripture interprets scripture. The Prophets interpret the Law, and more importantly, the New Testament interprets the Old Testament. In a letter dedicating his commentary on Romans to his friend Simon Grynaeus, Calvin explains that by understanding this epistle, the way is opened to understand the whole of scripture.

The Use of the Old Testament
in the New Testament

In suggesting that the New Testament be used to interpret the Old Testament, Calvin is simply approving of what earlier Christian interpreters advocated. Origen, the earliest great exegete of the church, found support in the New Testament for allegorical exegesis against the historical exegesis of the Jews.

> You can see how different Paul's tradition is from the historical reading: what the Jews think is a crossing of the sea, Paul calls baptism; where they see a cloud, Paul puts the Holy Spirit; and it is in this way that he

wants us to understand what the Lord commanded in the gospels when he said: "Whoever is not born again of water and the Holy Spirit cannot enter into the kingdom of heaven" (cf. John 3:5). And the manna too, which the Jews think of as food for the stomach and satisfaction for hunger, Paul calls "spiritual food" (1 Cor. 10:3). And not just Paul, but the Lord too, says in the same gospel: "Your fathers ate the manna in the wilderness, and they died. Whoever eats of the bread which I give him will not die for ever" (cf. John 6:49–50). And right after that: "I am the bread which came down from heaven" (John 6:51). Hence Paul speaks quite openly about "the rock which followed them": "And the Rock was Christ" (1 Cor. 10:4).

Origen argued that God through the New Testament writers was instructing his church in the proper method of interpreting the Old Testament. God intended Christian expositors to imitate the New Testament writers by interpreting the Old Testament allegorically.

> How then are we to act, who have received such principles of interpretation from Paul, the teacher of the Church? Does it not seem right that such a method coming to us from the tradition should serve as a model in all other instances? Or shall we, as some would like, abandon what so great and holy an apostle has given us and turn back to "Jewish myths" (Tit. 1:14)?[45]

Calvin agrees with Origen that the New Testament is a reliable guide in interpreting the Old Testament.[46] Romans 1:2–3 teaches him that God promised the gospel in Old Testament times through the prophets;[47] John 8:56, that Abraham saw the day of Christ and was glad;[48] 1 Corinthians 10:3–4, that the Old Testament believer ate the same spiritual food and drank the same spiritual drink as the New Testament believer, that is, Christ;[49] Matthew 22:23–32 and Luke 20:27–38, that Moses testified to the resurrection of the dead;[50] and Hebrews 11, that the Old Testament patriarchs believed God's promises would be fulfilled in something other than their earthly lives.[51] Calvin concludes that he and the Old Testament believer are united with Christ as part of the same church with the same hope and the same faith.

Calvin finds in Christ the "surest interpreter [*certissimus interpres*]" of the Bible,[52] an interpreter "than whom no better interpreter can be found [*quo nullus interpres quaerendus est melior*]."[53] "We ought not to seek a better interpreter than Christ himself."[54] His deference to Jesus' interpretation of the Old Testament is perhaps most evident in his exposition of the Decalogue. His treatment of the Sixth Commandment is representative of his general approach. The commandment "Thou shalt not kill" includes much more than a prohibition of murder. The word "kill" is a synecdoche for all violence and aggression. Additionally, he finds confirmation in the teaching of Jesus for his belief that "negative precepts" or prohibitions in the Bible should be understood to include the opposite affirmations. While the Sixth Commandment may appear only to prohibit murder, it also instructs us that we are to defend the lives of our neighbors. Jesus' teaching in Matthew 5:22 that hateful thoughts and words deserve judgment is intended to be an exposition of the genuine sense of this commandment. "He does not there as some have ignorantly supposed, frame a new law, as if to cast blame on His Father, but shows the folly and perversity of those interpreters of the Law who only insist on the external appearance, and husk of things." The apostle John confirms this teaching in 1 John 3:15, where he writes that whoever hates his brother is a murderer.[55]

In his exposition of the Seventh Commandment Calvin again relies on the New Testament as an exegetical guide. Although the command explicitly prohibits only adultery, he understands it to include an exhortation to chastity, for "if the Law is a perfect rule of holy living, it would be more than absurd to give a license for fornication, adultery alone being excluded." His basis for taking the law to be "a perfect rule of holy living" is once again the New Testament interpretation of the Old Testament. When Christ and his apostles taught about a perfect life, they referred believers to the law. They insisted that fornication was a violation of this law. No other warrant is needed for interpreting the commandment as a synecdoche in which the genus (all kinds of sexual immorality) is presented under one species (adultery). "Now, if Christ and the Apostles, who are the most faithful interpreters of the Law [si Christus et apostoli fidelissimi legis interpretes], declare that God's Law is violated no less by fornication than by theft, we assuredly infer that in this commandment the whole genus is comprehended under a single species." Anyone who contests that other kinds of fornication are condemned in the prohibition against adultery is accusing the apostle Paul of error.[56]

Calvin's method of interpreting the Decalogue as he describes it in the *Institutes* agrees perfectly with his practice in the commentaries.

> We must, I say, inquire how far interpretation ought to overstep the limits of the words themselves so that it may be seen to be, not an appendix added to the divine law from men's glosses, but the Lawgiver's pure and authentic meaning faithfully rendered [*purum germanumque Legislatoris sensum fideliter redditum*]. Obviously, in almost all the commandments there are such manifest *synecdoches* that he who would confine his understanding of the law within the narrowness of the words deserves to be laughed at. Therefore, plainly a sober interpretation of the law goes beyond the words [*ultra verba*]. . . . In each commandment we must investigate what it is concerned with; then we must seek out its purpose, until we find what the Lawgiver testifies

there to be pleasing or displeasing to himself. Finally, from this same thing we must derive an argument on the other side, in this manner: if this pleases God, the opposite displeases him; if this displeases, the opposite pleases him; if he commands this, he forbids the opposite; if he forbids this, he enjoins the opposite."[57]

Sprinkled throughout his exposition of the law in the *Institutes* are New Testament citations coupled with emphatic denials that he is offering a new interpretation of the Old Testament law. "When we say that this is the meaning of the law, we are not thrusting forward a new interpretation of our own, but we are following Christ, its best interpreter [*optimum Legis interpretem*]."[58]

And why should the New Testament not be used as a guide in interpreting the Old Testament? After all, even though the setting of the books differs and the human authors differ, the Holy Spirit is responsible for all of scripture, and he is certainly able to interpret his own words. Calvin uses this line of reasoning to explain his handling of the difficulty posed in Paul's quotation of the Song from Moses of Deuteronomy 32. Paul in Romans 15:10 appears to misinterpret it. Calvin insists that there is really no problem. "If we admit that Paul took this sentence from Moses, the same Spirit, who spoke both by Moses and Paul, is the best interpreter of His own words." Who can better interpret the words of the Holy Spirit than the Holy Spirit himself?[59] While the Holy Spirit's authorship of scripture does not yield Calvin an unambiguous hermeneutic, it does have great hermeneutical significance. He cannot imagine sober historical interpretation operating apart from the context provided by the New Testament writings. Argumentation from the use of the Old Testament by the New Testament writers and historical reasoning both come into play in his treatment of allegory, typology, and predictive prophecy.[60]

Problems with the Use of the Old Testament in the New Testament

Calvin admits that the writers of the New Testament at times appear to be overly subtle and even to make mistakes in quoting the Old Testament. He acknowledges several kinds of difficulties: first, numerical discrepancies; second, apparent distortions of the meaning of the Old Testament; third, misquotations of the Old Testament. He addresses the first type of problem in his treatment of 1 Corinthians 10:8. Paul indicates that twenty-three thousand people were killed in a judgment of God, yet Numbers 25:9, the Old Testament text this verse obviously refers to, says twenty-four thousand people perished by the hand of God. Instead of handling the problem as a scribal error,[61] he denies there is any difficulty.

The actual number of people destroyed must have been somewhere between twenty-three and twenty-four thousand. Moses rounded to the higher figure; Paul to the lower. "There is really no discrepancy." He defends his explanation by pointing out that "it is not unheard of, when there is no intention of making an exact count of individuals, to give an approximate number."[62]

Several times Calvin admits that the New Testament writer appears to have changed the meaning of an Old Testament passage. He normally suggests that the change in meaning is in appearance only. He may handle such texts in one of two ways. First, he sometimes argues that the New Testament writer did not intend to give an accurate interpretation of the Old Testament passage. The writer may quite properly allude to the language of the Old Testament text "to embellish the case he is making."[63] Second, he sometimes suggests that the New Testament writer may shed light on the Old Testament passage through his seemingly distorted interpretation. Paul appears to interpret Psalm 8:6 in a different sense than the psalmist intended when he gives it a christological interpretation in 1 Corinthians 15:27. However, he is right to apply the passage to Christ since the psalm will not be perfectly fulfilled until Christ fulfills it in the future.[64]

More than once Calvin notices that a New Testament reference to the Old Testament contains an inaccurate translation of the Hebrew text. In his commentary on Hebrews he explains that the apostles "were not over scrupulous in quoting words."[65] He shows no apparent concern over Paul's decision to follow the Septuagint rather than the Hebrew text in Romans 3:4. Though Paul did follow an inferior text, he "quoted this passage in its proper and genuine sense [in proprio et genuino sensu]." Calvin notes that "the apostles often used freer language than the original, since they were content if what they quoted applied to their subject, and therefore they were not over-careful in their use of words."[66] In his treatment of Isaiah 28:16, he again faces the problem of the New Testament writer using an inferior translation. The apostles followed the Greek not the Hebrew version. They did not feel bound to quote the exact wording, yet they never changed the meaning. They gave the true and correct interpretation, taking care to apply the Old Testament properly. They used it in accord with the original purpose of the Old Testament text. The New Testament writer was simply using different wording to make the same point as the Old Testament writer. Thus there was no contradiction with the historical meaning of the Old Testament.[67]

Calvin confronts a similar, yet more serious, problem in his interpretation of Psalm 8:5 ("For you have made him a little lower than *Elohim*, and crowned him with glory and honor"). He notes that the Septuagint renders *Elohim* as angels. He does not argue that the translation is impossible, because the title may be properly given to angels, but he favors taking the word to refer to God, since it "seems more natural, and as it is almost universally adopted by the Jewish interpreters." This decision assumes importance in light of the fact that Hebrews 2:7 quotes this passage from the Septuagint. Calvin's solution to this problem is to argue that the substance or meaning, not the precise wording, of the passage is what is most important, and the New Testament writer faithfully preserves the substance. The freedom exhibited by the apostles in quoting from the Old Testament should not be construed as an attempt on their part to change the meaning of the text. They were only concerned to show that their teaching was sanctioned by God's Word.[68]

Calvin's skills at harmonization are severely tested by the use of Psalm 8:5 ("Thou didst make him for a little while lower than the angels") by the author of Hebrews. It seems that the apostle was clearly changing the meaning of the psalmist in applying what the psalmist has said of the excellency of men to the humiliation of Christ. Calvin's solution is one he adopts when it seems there is no other way to achieve harmony. The New Testament writer does not intend to explain the Old Testament passage. He applies the quotation for illustrative purposes to the death of Christ, accommodating it to the subject he is discussing. Here Calvin adopts a very different approach to handling a difficulty by insisting that the apostle was in this case interested not in the meaning, but in the wording of the psalm.[69] He observes that Paul in Romans 10:6 does exactly the same thing in quoting Deuteronomy 30:12 ("Who shall go up to heaven for us and bring it to us, that we may hear and do it?") in a different sense than Moses intended. "Paul seems to have not only distorted the proper sense of the passage, but also to have changed the words to a different meaning." What Moses said of the law, Paul applies to the promises of the gospel. The contradiction is only apparent, however, because Moses intended to include the "whole doctrine of God in general, which includes the Gospel."[70] A more difficult problem is Paul's apparent misquotation of Psalm 68:18 ("Thou didst ascend the high mount, leading captives in thy train, and receiving gifts among men") in Ephesians 4:8 ("Therefore it is said, 'When he ascended on high he led a host of captives, and he gave gifts to men'"). Calvin argues that Paul was not so concerned with explaining the text as he was with piously accommodating it to the person of Christ.

> To accommodate it to his argument, Paul has twisted this quotation somewhat from its true meaning. Wicked men charge him with having abused Scripture. The Jews go still further, and, to make their accusations more plausible, maliciously pervert the natural meaning of this passage. . . . Although Paul saw that David was hymning his triumph for all the victories which God had wrought for the salvation of His Church,

he very properly accommodated this verse about the ascension of God to the person of Christ. The greatest triumph which God ever won was when Christ, after subduing sin, conquering death, and putting Satan to flight, rose majestically to heaven, that he might exercise His glorious reign over the Church. So far there is no ground for the objection that Paul has twisted this quotation from the meaning of David.[71]

The greater difficulty is found in Paul's transforming of "receiving gifts among men" to "he gave gifts to men." Calvin faces the problem squarely. "Where the Psalm says that God has received gifts, Paul reverses it to gave, and thus seems to translate it into the opposite meaning." Then he disposes of the problem by insisting that there is no real contradiction, because Paul in this case as in others was content to give the substance of a passage rather than quoting the exact wording. "Paul has not at all departed from the substance, however much he may have changed the words." Calvin insists that Paul never intended in this verse to quote the psalmist's "receiving gifts among men." He "allowed himself the liberty of adding what is not in the Psalm, yet nevertheless is true of Christ."[72]

Calvin may follow one of two principles for handling difficulties posed by the seeming misuse of the Old Testament by the apostles. First, he may reason that the New Testament writer may legitimately change the wording of a passage provided he does not change the meaning. Second, he may argue that the New Testament writer may use a passage in a different sense than the Old Testament writer intended as long as it is not his object to interpret the passage. In this way Calvin believes he is able to preserve the historical meaning of the Old Testament while guarding the New Testament writer from any accusation of erroneous interpretation.

Throughout his commentaries Calvin rebukes interpreters for twisting the meaning of scripture, yet in several cases he has to admit that the New Testament writers appear to do just that. He observes in his commentary on Psalm 40 that the writer of Hebrews "seems to twist [torquere] this passage when he restricts what is said of all the elect to Christ alone."[73] He notices that Paul explains Isaiah 64:4 differently from what the prophet intended—"to twist it to a different meaning [in aliam sententiam torquere]."[74] In his exegesis of Isaiah 52 he admits that Paul seems to twist the prophet's words [torquere prophetae verba]."[75] Calvin, who normally opposes subtle interpretations, cannot help but notice that the writer of Hebrews seems to offer a subtle interpretation of Jeremiah 31:34.[76] He observes that Paul seems to twist [torquere] the words of Habakkuk 2:4"[77] and to have misapplied the prophet Joel's words found in Joel 2:32. "What Paul applies generally to all mankind seems beyond the mind of the prophet [praeter mentem prophetae]."[78]

In each of these instances, Calvin concludes that there is only the appearance of misinterpretation or misuse of the Old Testament by the

New Testament writer. Hebrews 10:5 ("When Christ came into the world, he said, 'sacrifices and offerings thou hast not desired, but a body hast thou prepared for me' ") appears to both misquote and misapply Psalm 40:6 ("Sacrifice and offering thou dost not desire; but thou hast given me an open ear. Burnt offering and sin offering thou hast not required"). First, he restricts to Christ what the prophet said of all the elect; second, he contends that the sacrifices of the law are abrogated (David's point was only that they were less important to God than obedience of the heart); third, he makes the mistake of following the Septuagint, an inferior translation.[79] Calvin has a solution for each difficulty. First, he argues that the apostle is correct in relating this passage to Christ. David was not speaking exclusively for himself in the psalm, but for all of God's children. He was speaking for the church as the body of Christ, so it was perfectly proper to relate this to the head of the body—Christ. If one objects that David could not be referring to Christ, because he claims responsibility for the sins which have lead to his misery, the answer is easy. "It is by no means an uncommon thing to find our errors, by a mode of expression not strictly correct, transferred to Christ." Calvin's solution to the first difficulty depends on his understanding of the function of typology. He would not view this as a rejection of historical exegesis. Typological interpretation is, in Calvin's judgment, a defensible and even necessary way to make sense of much of the Old Testament. The second problem is the leap from the message of the Old Testament text to the abrogation of the sacrificial system by the New Testament writer. In his defense, Calvin argues that the Old Testament passage was not simply condemning sacrifices offered unworthily; it suggested that God has no pleasure even in the sacrifices of one who worships him sincerely. God must have had some other purpose in view; the sacrifices were intended as "infantile instructions designed to prepare them for some higher state." Since the truth and substance of the sacrifices are contained in Christ, it makes sense for them to be abolished after his appearance in the flesh. The New Testament writer is therefore interpreting the Old Testament properly— by making explicit what was implicit in the Old Testament. In his commentary on Hebrews 10:5 Calvin elaborates.

> Since he was under the Law, David should certainly not have neglected the custom of sacrificing. He ought, I admit, to have worshipped God with inner sincerity of heart, but he was not allowed to pass by what God had commanded him. In common with all the rest he was commanded to sacrifice. From this we conclude that he looked further than the pattern of his own age when he said "sacrifice thou wouldest not." Even in the time of David it was proved to some extent that God cared nothing for sacrifices, but, because they were still held under the yoke of the schoolmaster, David could not perform the worship of God

completely except when it was (so to speak) clothed in this form. We must come to the kingdom of Christ for it to be completely true that God does not wish sacrifice.

The solution to the third difficulty is easy. The words of the psalmist according to the Hebrew text are "you have opened my ears"; the Septuagint reading followed by the New Testament writer was "you have prepared a body." Calvin insists that the New Testament writers are within their rights in using the Greek text, because they keep faithfully to the main purpose of the Old Testament passage.

> They were not over-scrupulous in quoting words provided that they did not misuse Scripture for their convenience. We must always look at the purpose for which quotations are made because they have careful regard for the main object so as not to turn Scripture to a false meaning, but as far as words are concerned, as in other things which are not relevant to the present purpose, they allow themselves some indulgence.[80]

According to Calvin, there is nothing wrong with this type of usage unless one wishes to make the New Testament writer a slavish expositor of the prophet's meaning in every point.[81] Calvin attempts to preserve the historical meaning through a recognition that the New Testament writer may quote the Old Testament very loosely, provided he does not misconstrue the purpose of the Old Testament writer.

Calvin acknowledges that the writer of Hebrews also gives a rather subtle interpretation of Jeremiah 31:34 ("I will forgive their iniquity, and I will remember their sin no more") by applying the words to the abrogation of the sacrificial system in the New Testament. There was, however, no real abuse of the passage. He did not twist (*torquet*) the words of the prophet; there is nothing in his treatment that is forced (*coactum*) or very subtle (*nimis argutum*); he "wisely accommodated it to the subject he was discussing." The Old Testament prophet, he admits, appeared to have in mind the wonderful manifestation of God's grace to come later. He speaks of "the grace of regeneration, of the gift of knowledge, and at the same time promises that God would be propitious to his people in a different and more perfect way than he had been in former times." In applying this to the abrogation of the Old Testament ceremonies, the apostle has "faithfully interpreted the intention of the prophet [*consilium prophetae*]." In Calvin's view, the New Testament writer is not interpreting the Old Testament passage; he is applying the message of the prophet to his own circumstances.[82]

In his interpretation of Romans 1:17 ("The just shall live by faith")—the text that proved so critical in the spiritual experience of Luther—Calvin candidly confesses that the apostle Paul seems to twist (*torquere*) the prophet Habakkuk's words ("The just shall live by his faith"), using them beyond the prophet's intention. Habakkuk clearly referred to the present life; nowhere in the context did he speak of eternal life. The Habakkuk passage is an exhortation to long-suffering and an encouragement that God will deliver his people from their trial. Yet Paul finds here the message that eternal salvation of the soul is not by works but by God's mercy alone. He appeared to use the passage with too much subtlety (*nimis argute*). Calvin will not accept such a conclusion. He offers a principle derived from the unity of the message of the Bible, his sense of the progressive nature of God's revelation, and his belief that the gospel message was delivered to the Old Testament saints under obscure but meaningful figures. "Whatever benefits the Lord confers on the faithful in this life, are intended to confirm them in the hope of the eternal inheritance; for however liberally God may deal with us, our condition would yet be indeed miserable, were our hope confined to this earthly life." Whenever God delivers us from troubles in this world, he intends to raise our minds to our future heavenly deliverance. "When the prophet says that the faithful shall live, he certainly does not confine this life to so narrow limits that God will only defend us for a day or two, or for a few years, but he proceeds much farther, and says that we shall be made really and truly happy; for though this whole world may perish or be exposed to various changes, yet the faithful shall continue in permanent and real safety."[83] The earthly promises were never intended to be restricted to this life. The pious Old Testament saint would certainly have understood this. Paul, therefore, is correct in applying the text to the eternal hope that comes through faith in Christ.

In Romans 10, another central gospel text, Paul appears to extend the application of Joel 2:32 ("And it shall come to pass that whosoever shall call on the name of the LORD shall be delivered") too far in applying it to the Gentiles; Joel seemed to address only the Jews. Calvin reasons from the context that Joel must have had in view the blessing God promised to all nations in the covenant he made with Abraham. "When he afterwards described the miserable state in which the whole world would be, he certainly meant to rouse even the Gentiles, who had been aliens from the Church, to seek God in common with his elect people." Calvin argues that there was no discord between Joel's statement and Paul's use of it. First, Joel's use of the general term "whosoever" suggests an extension of the promise beyond the Jews. Second, the context supports the extension of the promise. Not only was Joel prophesying of the kingdom of Christ, which included Gentiles as well as Jews, but having spoken of God's anger extending even to the Gentiles, it follows that the message of hope was applied to them so that they might flee to God. Calvin concludes that Paul appropriately accommodated this text to his argument—the kingdom of God is open to Gentiles and there is now no distinction between Jew and Gentile.[84]

In at least two instances in Romans 10 alone, Calvin admits that Paul seems careless in his use of the Old Testament. In quoting Isaiah 52:7 ("How beautiful upon the mountains are the feet of him who brings good tidings, who publishes peace; who brings good tidings of good, who publishes salvation; who says to Zion, 'Your God reigns' "), Paul seems to twist the prophet's meaning. He wanted to prove that the preaching of the gospel originated in God, not men, and that ministers who preached the gospel were sent by him. Isaiah did not directly say that God sent ministers, only that their presence was very desirable. Paul assumes that nothing is desirable except what comes from God. "But whence comes salvation? From men? No; for none but God can be the author of such a distinguished benefit. Justly, therefore, does he conclude that it proceeds from God, and not from man."[85] Thus, there is no tension between the two passages. What was implicit in the Old Testament prophet is simply spelled out clearly in the New Testament.

Calvin admits that Paul's use of Deuteronomy 30:12 in Romans 10:6 ("Who will go up for us to heaven, and bring it to us, that we may hear it and do it?") appears to distort the proper sense of the passage and change the words "to a different meaning [in alienum sensum]"; Paul's interpretation seems "too forced and subtle [nimis coactam et argutam]." Moses used the words to suggest places that are remote and difficult to reach; Paul applies the words to the death and resurrection of Christ. The difficulty may be solved by recognizing that the apostle was not trying to explain the passage. He is simply applying it to the subject he is discussing. Paul does not repeat what Moses said exactly; he adapts Moses' words to his own purpose. Moses was referring to inaccessible places; Paul uses Moses' words for places hidden from our eyes but not inaccessible to our faith. Calvin concludes that no violence has been done to the text.

> If, therefore, we take these statements of Paul as having been made by way of amplification or as a gloss [amplificationem vel expolitionem], we shall not be able to say that he has done violence to or distorted the words of Moses. We shall, rather, acknowledge that his allusion to the words heaven and abyss is elegant without any loss of meaning.[86]

Paul's universal extension of Psalm 5:10 ("For there is no truth in their mouth; their heart is destruction, their throat is an open sepulchre, they flatter with their tongue") in Romans 3:23 raises the question of whether he applies the text too broadly. Calvin denies that Paul is doing anything inappropriate. He does not extend the meaning beyond the intention of the Spirit; he does not distort these words from their genuine meaning (a genuino sensu) in applying them to all people. Calvin's defense of his position is tied to his view of David as a type not only of Christ but also of the church. "Under the person of David, there is here described to us the church, both in the person of Christ, who is the head, and in his members." All those who have not been regenerated by the Spirit of God are appropriately called the enemies of God, even if they are within the visible church. Given the representative character of David's role, it is perfectly appropriate for the apostle to apply what he says universally.[87]

Paul also seems to misuse Isaiah 64:3 [4 Eng.] ("No eye has seen a God besides thee"), twisting it to a different purpose and quoting it in different words (following the Septuagint). But Paul does not in fact misuse the text. "In this respect the apostles were not squeamish; for they paid more attention to the meaning than to the words." They considered it sufficient to draw the attention of the reader to a passage of scripture in which their teaching might be found. Paul's version ("What no eye has seen, nor ear heard, nor the heart of man conceived, what God has prepared for those who love him") not only differs from the Hebrew text; it includes an addition not found in any known passage. Calvin insists that everything Paul adds fully agrees with the teaching of the prophet. Paul's purpose, which is to elevate the grace that God bestows on his church, agrees with the purpose of the prophet, which was to celebrate God's goodness by relating the kindness he showered on his people in ancient times. The difficulty is not yet removed, however, for Paul relates to spiritual blessings what the prophet said of temporal blessings. Calvin argues that the two may be harmonized by considering the cause of the blessing— whether spiritual or temporal. "We do not merely observe those things which fall under the sense of men, but contemplate the cause itself." Temporal blessings in the Old Testament resulted from the very same cause as spiritual blessings in the New—the fatherly kindness of God. "Although therefore the prophet appears to speak of external deliverance and other benefits of this life, yet he rises higher." It is probable, Calvin reasons, that the mind of the prophet was elevated as he reflected on the goodness of God "to so high a pitch as to meditate on that infinite abundance of blessings which is laid up for believers in heaven." Thus Calvin does not believe that Paul misuses this passage in any way; he applies it admirably to his subject.[88] The historical meaning of the Old Testament is not violated because the mind of the Old Testament prophet was raised in fact to contemplate the spiritual meaning. Although it may seem at first glance that Paul twists this passage, in fact, Calvin views Pauline usage (or rather the Holy Spirit's usage) as the determinative consideration in deciding how the Old Testament passage should be understood. Grammar and context seem to suggest one interpretation, but Paul's meaning "ought to carry more weight with us than other reasons [cui magis fidendum est quam ullis rationibus]." Why should Paul, who lived centuries after Isaiah, be the authority for determining Isaiah's meaning? Calvin answers with a question: "Who better than the Spirit of God will be a sure and faithful interpreter of this prophetic declaration, which He Himself dictated to Isaiah, seeing it was He who explained it by the mouth of Paul? [*Quis enim spiritu Dei certior aut fidelior erit interpres huius oraculi quod ipse Iesaiae dictavit, sicut per os Pauli exposuit?*]." In order to escape the "unjust charges of wicked men" that Paul perverts the genuine meaning of the passage in favor of a strained interpretation, Calvin insists that, while there is ambiguity in the text, the nature of the Hebrew construction of the Isaiah text allows for his interpretation.[89] So Calvin is able to argue that the authoritative interpretation of the Old Testament that is provided by the apostle Paul in no way violates the historical sense.

This chapter has dealt with the unambiguously Christian character of Calvin's method of exegetical reasoning. He insists that the New Testament as the product of the Holy Spirit must be regarded as an authoritative guide to the meaning of the Old Testament, yet he concedes that the New Testament writers sometimes appear to twist the Old Testament to meanings that are foreign to the original writer's intention. He sometimes solves the difficulty by arguing that it is not always the intent of the New Testament writers to interpret the Old Testament texts that they cited. Sometimes they use the Old Testament for illustrative purposes. Since it is not their intent to offer a historical interpretation, they should not be regarded as misconstruing its meaning. Sometimes, however, Calvin does believe that, even in their seemingly forced use of the Old Testament, the New Testament writers do intend to interpret the Old Testament. In such cases he allows the New Testament to inform him about what the Old Testament writer may have understood and intended. Chapter 5 will be concerned with Calvin's method of exegetical reasoning as it relates to the delicate matters of allegory, typology, and predictive prophecy, where historical interpretation and the guidance of the New Testament sometimes appear to be incompatible.

NOTES

1. Comm. John 5:39 (C.O. 47.125).
2. Comm. Amos 9:11 (C.O. 43.170).
3. Comm. Isa. 49:2 (C.O. 37.190).
4. Comm. Ps. 112:5 (C.O. 32.174).
5. Salo Baron, "John Calvin and the Jews," in *Ancient and Medieval Jewish History*, ed. Leon A. Feldman (New Brunswick, N.J.: Rutgers University Press, 1972), 343–44. See also Jaques Courvoisier, "Calvin et les Juifs," *Judaica* 2 (1946): 203–8; Gottfried W. Locher, "Calvin spricht zu den Juden," *Theologische Zeitschrift*

23 (1967): 180–96; Wilhelm Niesel, "Calvins Stellungnahme zu den Juden," *Reformierte Kirchenzeitung* 120 (1979): 181–83.

6. Comm. Jer. 17:11 (C.O. 38.272).

7. Comm. Isa. 40:31 (C.O. 37.30). He finds misinformed fables regarding the eagle in the Jewish treatment of Deut. 32:10 (C.O. 25.363–64). Likewise he says the opinion that in Ex. 19:4 eagles are mentioned instead of other birds "because they alone bear up their young ones on their wings, is a foolish and truly rabbinical gloss" (C.O. 24.195). See also Comm. Ps. 103:4–5 (C.O. 32.76).

8. Comm. Ps. 147:9 (C.O. 32.429).

9. Comm. Isa. 38:8 (C.O. 36.653).

10. Comm. Ex. 32:4 (C.O. 25.82).

11. Comm. Gen. 4:23 (C.O. 23.100).

12. Salo Baron, "Medieval Heritage and Modern Realities in Protestant-Jewish Relations," in *Ancient and Medieval Jewish History*, ed. Leon A. Feldman (New Brunswick, N.J.: Rutgers University Press, 1972), 328. Baron suggests that Calvin's traditionalism in this area may be seen in his *Ad questiones et obiecta cuiusdam responso* (C.O. 9.653–74), which Baron believes may be the summary of a 1539 debate between Calvin and Josel of Rosheim, a prominent Jewish polemicist; see Baron's "John Calvin and the Jews," 343–44.

13. Comm. Dan 9:24 (C.O. 41.167). Calvin believes he can demonstrate that the interpretation of his Jewish opponents is demonstrably false: "We should condemn them to little purpose, unless we can convict them by reasons equally firm and certain."

14. Though the problems of Jewish exegesis start with an ignorance of Christ and a resulting failure to understand Old Testament prophecies, they do not end there. The Jews also know nothing of astronomy, botany, or zoology, yet they stubbornly pretend to be learned in these sciences. Comm. Amos 5:8 (C.O. 43.77). Their bold assertions betray their lack of knowledge of other matters as well. In his interpretation of Jer. 31:39, after admitting that he himself has difficulty determining the location of the hill Gareb, Calvin complains of the Jews that, although they offer no real assistance in understanding the text, they do not abstain from making conjectures: "Of these places I cannot say much, for we do not know the ancient situation of the city; and the Jews themselves, when they make conjectures about these uncertain things, show their own ignorance [*inscitiam*]." Comm. Jer. 31:39 (C.O. 36.269).

15. This appears to be a reference to Don Isaac Abrabanel (1437–1538), whose commentaries on the prophets had attracted some attention from Christian interpreters. A distinguishing characteristic of Abrabanel's work was its preoccupation with Christian biblical exegesis. He was especially concerned to dispute christological interpretations of the Old Testament. *Encyclopedia Judaica* (Jerusalem: Keter, 1971), s.v. "Abrabanel," by Avraham Grossmann.

16. Comm. Dan. 7:27 (C.O. 41.85).

17. Comm. Micah 5:4 (C.O. 43.370).

18. Comm. Isa. 7:14 (C.O. 36.154).

19. Comm. Dan 2:39 (C.O. 40.598).

20. Comm. Ps. 22:16 (C.O. 31.228). Schwarz argues that one of the obstacles to the study of Hebrew in the fifteenth century was the belief that the Jews had purposely falsified the text in those places where Christ was prophesied. Werner

Schwarz, *Principles and Problems of Biblical Translation: Some Reformation Controversies and Their Background* (Cambridge: Cambridge University Press, 1955), 63–64.

21. Comm. Ps. 22:16 (C.O. 31.229).

22. Comm. Ps. 109:11 (C.O. 32.150).

23. Comm. Dan. 4:10–16 (C.O. 40.658).

24. Comm. Dan. 2:44–45 (C.O. 40.605). A major theme of Book 1 of the *Institutes* is the critical role of "piety" in the knowledge of God. The principle of piety also applies to a true understanding of scripture—it is impossible to understand scripture apart from true piety—and piety is an area in which the Jews are impoverished.

25. Comm. Gen. 2:3 (C.O. 23.34).

26. Comm. Dan. 7:27 (C.O. 41.82).

27. Comm. Jer. 28:17 (C.O. 38.580).

28. Comm. Dan. 2:44 (C.O. 40.603).

29. Comm. Josh. 2:1 (C.O. 30.439). There were two opposing Jewish traditions concerning Rahab. According to the first, she was a prostitute who became a proselyte, married Joshua, and became the ancestress of eight prophets and priests, including the prophet Jeremiah. According to the second tradition, she was not a prostitute, but an innkeeper. This view (which was held by Rashi) had a great appeal because it avoided the shame of having a prostitute as the ancestress of very important figures in Jewish history. It was defended exegetically by an interpretation of the Targum. Kimchi disputed the interpretation, arguing that its adherents had simply misunderstood the Targum. *Encyclopedia Judaica* (Jerusalem: Keter, 1971), s.v. "Rahab," by Chayim Cohen.

30. Comm. Dan. 5:8–9 (C.O. 40.704).

31. Comm. Ps. 110, pref. (C.O. 32.159).

32. Comm. Zech. 2:8 (C.O. 44.159).

33. Comm. Ps. 136:13 (C.O. 32.365–66).

34. Comm. Jer. 1:1–3 (C.O. 37.472).

35. Comm. Dan. 5:30–31 (C.O. 40.721).

36. Comm. Dan. 2:44–45 (C.O. 40.607).

37. Comm. Gen. 1:26 (C.O. 23.25).

38. Comm. Dan. 9:25 (C.O. 41.174).

39. Comm. Jonah 1:3 (C.O. 43.206).

40. Comm. Gen. 24:33ff. (C.O. 23.338).

41. Comm. Dan. 7:13 (C.O. 41.59).

42. Comm. Ex. 28:4 (C.O. 24.430).

43. Comm. John 5:39 (C.O. 47.125).

44. Ibid.

45. Origen, *Origen: Spirit and Fire; A Thematic Anthology of His Writings*, ed. Hans Urs von Balthasar, trans. Robert J. Daly (Washington, D.C.: Catholic University Press of America, 1984), 100–101. This selection is from Origen's homily on Ex. 5:1 in the Berlin edition of Origen, *Die griechischen christlichen Schriftsteller der ersten drei Jahrhunderte*, vol. 6, 184. Gregory of Nyssa followed Origen in appealing to the New Testament writers to defend allegorical interpretation. Ronald Heine notes that "examples from Paul constituted his [Origen's] most authoritative defense for the allegorical interpretation of Scripture" ("Gregory of Nyssa's Apology for Allegory," *Vigiliae Christianae* 38 [1984]: 360–70).

46. The prominence of the principle of "scripture as its own interpreter" is

discussed in Hans Heinrich Wolf, *Die Einheit des Bundes: Das Verhältnis von Altem und Neuem Testament bei Calvin*, Beiträge zur Geschichte und Lehre der reformierten Kirche, no. 10 (Neukirchen: Verlag der Buchhandlung des Erziehungsvereins, 1958), 134–39.

47. *Inst.* II.x.3 (O.S. 3.404–5).

48. *Inst.* II.x.4 (O.S. 3.406).

49. *Inst.* II.x.5 (O.S. 3.406).

50. *Inst.* II.x.9 (O.S. 3.410).

51. *Inst.* II.x.13 (O.S. 3.414).

52. Comm. Ex. 22:28 (C.O. 24.610).

53. Comm. Mal. 3:1 (C.O. 44.461).

54. Comm. Isa. 29:13 (C.O. 36.493).

55. Comm. Ex. 20:13 (C.O. 24.613); Comm. Deut. 5:17 (C.O. 24.642).

56. Comm. Ex. 20:14 (C.O. 24.641–42); Comm. Deut. 5:18 (C.O. 24.642–43).

57. *Inst.* II.viii.8 (O.S. 3.350–51).

58. *Inst.* II.viii.7 (O.S. 3.349).

59. Comm. Deut. 32:43 (C.O. 25.379).

60. See chapter 5 for an examination of Calvin's exegetical method as it relates to allegory, typology, and prophecy.

61. Calvin is not at all reluctant to admit that there are errors in the biblical text. He sometimes attributes the error to a copyist. He believes that "some ignorant reader" added the word σκηνὴ to Heb. 9:1 (C.O. 54.105). He attributes a discrepancy between Acts 7:14 and Gen. 46:9 to a copyist's mistake (C.O. 47.137). He does not blame a copyist for a problem of Acts 7:16, but neither does he express or imply, as McNeill suggests, that "Luke has 'made a manifest error' " Calvin simply states that it is obvious that an error has been made and that the text must be emended accordingly. It is uncertain whether he intended to attribute the error to a copyist (C.O. 47.138). See John T. McNeill, "The Significance of the Word of God for Calvin," *Church History* 28 (June 1959): 143.

62. Comm. 1 Cor. 10:8 (C.O. 49.458).

63. Comm. Heb. 2:7 (C.O. 55.25).

64. Comm. 1 Cor. 15:27 (C.O. 49.548).

65. Comm. Heb. 10:5 (C.O. 55.124).

66. Comm. Rom. 3:4 (C.O. 49.49).

67. Comm. Isa. 28:16 (C.O. 36.474).

68. Comm. Ps. 8:5 (C.O. 31.92).

69. Comm. Ps. 8:5 (C.O. 31.91).

70. Comm. Rom. 10:6 (C.O. 49.198–99).

71. Comm. Eph. 4:8 (C.O. 51.193). See also Comm. Ps. 68:18 (C.O. 31.627–29).

72. Ibid.

73. Comm. Ps. 40:8 (C.O. 31.412).

74. Comm. Isa. 64:4 (C.O. 37.408–9).

75. Comm. Isa. 52:7 (C.O. 36.248).

76. Comm. Jer. 31:34 (C.O. 38.695).

77. Comm. Hab. 2:4 (C.O. 43.529).

78. Comm. Joel 2:32 (C.O. 42.576).

79. Comm. Ps. 40:6 (C.O. 31.412–13).

80. Comm. Heb. 10:5 (C.O. 55.124).

81. Comm. Ps. 40:6 (C.O. 31.413).

82. Comm. Jer. 31:34 (C.O. 38.695–96).
83. Comm. Hab. 2:4 (C.O. 43.529–30).
84. Comm. Joel 2:32 (C.O. 42.576); cf. Comm. Rom. 10:13 (C.O. 49.203).
85. Comm. Isa. 52:7 (C.O. 36.248).
86. Comm. Rom. 10:6 (C.O. 49.199).
87. Comm. Ps. 5:9 (C.O. 31.70).
88. Comm. Isa. 64:3 (C.O. 37.409).
89. Comm. 1 Cor. 2:9 (C.O. 49.339–40).

5

CALVIN'S EXEGETICAL
VIA MEDIA

Christian interpreters before Calvin generally believed that the New Testament served as a reliable exegetical guide to the Old Testament. But in answering the question "What kind of guidance does it provide?" they were far from being of one mind. Origen believed that the usage of the Old Testament by New Testament writers established precedent for nonhistorical exegesis. Paul's use of ἀλληγορούμενα in Galatians 4:22–24 justified (or even demanded) the use of allegorical exegesis throughout the Old Testament. The apostle Paul intended his words to be a reproach to those who did not understand the spiritual meaning of the law. "They who do not believe that there are allegories in the writings do not understand the law."[1] Theodore of Mopsuestia, on the other hand, argued that allegorists could draw no support for doing away with the historical meaning of the Old Testament from the apostle's use of ἀλληγορούμενα.

> There are people who take great pains to twist the senses of the divine Scriptures and make everything written therein serve their own ends. They dream up some silly fables in their own heads and give their folly the name of allegory. They (mis)use the apostle's term as a blank authorization to abolish all meanings of divine Scripture. They make it a point to use the same expression as the apostle, "by way of allegory," but fail to understand the great difference between that which they say and what the apostle says here. For the apostle neither does away with history nor elaborates on events that happened long ago.[2]

Calvin agreed with Theodore. In so doing, he placed himself in opposition to much of the Christian exegetical tradition. To Hunnius it seemed that Calvin was siding with Jews against Christians. In this chapter I will explore Calvin's exegetical reasoning in several areas in which Christian and Jewish traditions often opposed one another. He was unable to agree fully with either tradition concerning how best to handle allegory and allegorical interpretation, typology, and the interpretation of Old Testament prophecies.

ALLEGORY

Calvin believed that allegorical interpretation of scripture was superficially appealing. As it was practiced in the church, it appeared to offer a plausible explanation of scripture but could not stand up under scrutiny.

> I am aware of the plausible nature of allegories [*Scio allegorias esse plausibiles*], but when we reverently weigh the teachings of the Holy Spirit, those speculations which at first sight pleased us exceedingly vanish from our view. I am not captivated by these enticements myself, and I wish all my hearers to be persuaded of this—nothing can be better than a sober treatment of Scripture.[3]

The term *allegorical* has in modern times been commonly employed to designate an approach to interpreting the Bible that ignores the historical meaning of a text in favor of a higher or spiritual meaning. Some early Christian practitioners of allegorical interpretation do appear to have treated the literal meaning as little more than a husk that hides a spiritual kernel of truth. The task of exegesis necessitated going beyond the historical sense of the text. The basic characteristic of such allegorization, according to Greer, is that it was essentially nonhistorical. "When Gregory of Nyssa allegorizes the life of Moses into a sketch of the Christian's spiritual life, there is really nothing left of the historical events of Moses' life, even though the events are still a part of Gregory's exegesis."[4] Modern Old Testament scholars often rule out allegorical exegesis because it finds the historical meaning of the text "indifferent or even offensive" and pushes it aside to make room for the spiritual sense.[5]

Calvin appears to endorse such a negative evaluation of allegorical exegesis. He calls interpretations "allegorical" if they disregard the historical context or if they interpret the details of a biblical text apart from a consideration of the immediate literary context. Allegorical exegesis is the antithesis of historical exegesis. His severest criticism—apart from his criticism of Jewish interpreters—is reserved for those who allegorize scripture excessively. He contrasts his own method (which is concerned only with what is useful) with the allegorical approach of other interpreters (which serves simply as a display for their cleverness).[6] "Let those who choose to hunt for subtle allegories receive the praise they covet; my object is only to profit my readers."[7]

Calvin has little appreciation for the quality of Origen's exegesis, but he is fully aware that many others in the church have found Origen's approach to their liking. Origen, "by hunting everywhere for allegories, corrupts the whole of Scripture." Others have followed his example and "extracted smoke out of light." In all of this, "not only has the simplicity of Scripture [*scripturae simplicitas*] been vitiated, but the faith has been almost subverted, and the door opened to many foolish dotings."[8] In his comments on one of the most frequently used proof texts for allegorical interpretation, 2 Corinthians 3:6 ("The letter kills, but the spirit gives life"), Calvin lays the blame for the evils of allegorical interpretation at Origen's door.

> This passage has been distorted and wrongly interpreted first by Origen and then by others, and they have given rise to the most disastrous error that Scripture is not only useless but actually harmful unless it is allegorized. This error has been the source of many evils. Not only did it open the way for the adulteration of the natural meaning of Scripture [*germanum scripturae sensum adulterandi*] but also set up boldness in allegorizing as the chief exegetical virtue. Thus many of the ancients without any restraint played all sorts of games with the sacred Word of God, as if they were tossing a ball to and fro. It also gave heretics a chance to throw the Church into turmoil, for when it was an accepted practice for anybody to interpret any passage in any way he desired, any mad idea, however absurd or monstrous, could be introduced under the pretext of an allegory. Even good men were carried away by their mistaken fondness for allegories into formulating a great number of perverse opinions.[9]

Calvin does not regard allegorization as simply a foolish indulgence. It is literally diabolic. Allegorical interpretation originates with the devil (as does its polar opposite, Jewish interpretation). Allegorization is a means by which Satan attempts to undermine the certainty of biblical teaching. "We must, however, entirely reject the allegories [*allegoriae*] of Origen, and of others like him, which Satan, with the deepest subtlety, has endeavored to introduce into the Church, for the purpose of rendering the doctrine of Scripture ambiguous and destitute of all certainty and firmness."[10] The plan of Satan had been most successful.

> For many centuries no man was thought clever who lacked the cunning and daring to transfigure with subtlety the sacred Word of God. This was undoubtedly a trick of Satan to impair the authority of Scripture and remove any true advantage out of the reading of it.[11]

Calvin usually simply states that allegorical interpretations are neither solid, nor simple, nor genuine and offers no further refutation.[12] He rejects the "allegorical" application of Augustine, who made Noah's ark a figure of the body of Christ because he finds there "scarcely anything solid [*solidi*]."[13] He points out that Genesis 15:4 is often interpreted allegorically by others, "but we maintain what is more solid [*magis solidum*]."[14] In his exegesis of Daniel 7:9 he recognizes that "subtle allegories [*subtiles allegoriae*] are pleasing to many," yet he argues that one should be satisfied only with what is solid (*solidum*).[15] In his interpretation of Deuteronomy 12:4 he contrasts allegory with the solid scholarship that is needed in the interpretation of scripture.

> But my readers must now be requested not only to pardon me for abstaining from subtle speculations [*argutis speculationibus*], but also themselves willingly to keep within the bounds of simplicity [*simplicitatis*]. Many have itching ears, and in our natural vanity, most men are more delighted by foolish allegories [*inanes allegoriae*] than by solid erudition [*solida eruditio*]. But let those who shall desire to profit in God's school learn to restrain this perverse desire of knowing more than is good for them, although it may tickle their minds.[16]

Elsewhere he comments, "It seems to me far too frivolous [*nimis frivolum*] to search for allegories. We should be content with true simplicity [*simplicitate*]."[17] A simple exposition of the true sense of scripture (*simplex veri sensus expositio*) will dispose of all the subtle triflings (*futiles omnes argutias*) of those who delight in allegory.[18] He contrasts the genuine meaning (*genuino sensu*) with that of the allegorical interpreters whose chatter is entirely contrary to the prophet's meaning.[19] He declares that an allegorical interpretation is forced (*nimis coactum*) and offers in its place the genuine intention of the prophet (*genuinam prophetae mentem*) that is supported by the context.[20] Instead of embracing allegory, we "ought reverently and soberly to interpret the prophetic writings and not to fly in the clouds but ever to fix our foot on solid ground."[21]

Calvin's commentary on Galatians 4 is a pertinent text for his view of allegorical interpretation. He admits that Paul appears to interpret the story of Isaac and Ishmael allegorically, but he does not believe the passage provides any justification for Origen's method of allegorization.

> Origen, and many others along with him, have seized this occasion of twisting Scripture this way and that away from the genuine sense [*genuino sensu*]. For they inferred that the literal sense is too meagre and poor and that beneath the bark of the letter there lie deeper mysteries which cannot be extracted but by hammering out allegories. And this they did without difficulty, for the world always has and always will prefer speculations which seem ingenious, to solid doctrine. With such approbation the licence increased more and more, so that he who played this game of allegorizing Scripture not only was suffered to pass unpunished but even obtained the highest applause.[22]

When he indicates that the Old Testament story was an allegory, Paul is not suggesting that Moses intended to write it as such. He simply means that the story may be understood figuratively with no departure from the literal meaning.

> An anagoge [*anagoge*] of this sort is not foreign to the genuine and literal meaning [*genuino literae sensu*], when a comparison was drawn between the Church and the family of Abraham. For as the house of Abraham was then the true Church, so it is beyond doubt that the principal and most memorable events that happened in it are types [*typi*] for us. Therefore, as in circumcision, in sacrifices, in the whole Levitical priesthood there was an allegory [*allegoria*], as there is today in our sacraments, so was there likewise in the house of Abraham. But this did not involve a departure from the literal meaning [*a literali sensu*]. In a word, it is as if Paul says that there is depicted in the two wives of Abraham a figure of the two covenants, and in the two sons a figure of the two peoples.[23]

Paul uses the term ἀλληγορούμενα imprecisely in Galatians 4. He interprets the Old Testament narrative typologically;[24] he does nothing that would undermine contextual exegesis.

Calvin observes that allegorists have tried to use other New Testament passages to support their rejection of historical exegesis. He opposes their view that Paul establishes precedent for allegorical exegesis in Romans 10:18 by interpreting Psalm 19:4 allegorically ("Their voice goes out through all the earth, and their words to the end of the world. In them he has made a tent for the sun"). "Those who have imagined that Paul departed from the literal sense [*a literali sensu*] of David's words are grossly mistaken."[25] "Those who were more reverent and proceeded more modestly in their interpretation of Scripture are of the opinion that Paul has transferred to the apostles what the psalmist had properly said of the architecture of heaven."[26] He rejects the opinion of allegorists that the writer of Hebrews allegorized Psalm 104:4 ("who makes the winds thy messengers, fire and flame thy ministers").[27] He denies their contention that Matthew 2:18 ("Then was fulfilled what was spoken by the prophet Jeremiah. 'A voice was heard in Ramah, wailing and loud lamentation, Rachel weeping for her children; she refused to be consoled, because they were no more' ") interprets Jeremiah 31:15 allegorically in applying it to Herod's slaughter of the male children in Bethlehem.

> This passage is quoted by Matthew, where he gives an account of the infants under two years old who had been slain by the command of Herod: then he says that this prophecy was fulfilled, even that Rachel again wept for her children. But the explanation of this is attended with no difficulty; for Matthew meant no other thing than that the same thing happened at the coming of Christ as had taken place before, when the whole country was reduced to desolation. . . . To no purpose then do interpreters torture themselves by explaining this passage allegorically;

for Matthew did not intend to lessen the authority of ancient history, for he knew in what sense this had been formerly said, but his only object was to remind the Jews that there was no cause for them to be greatly astonished at that slaughter, for that region had formerly been laid waste and bereaved of all its inhabitants, as though a mother, having had a large family, were to lose all her children.[28]

In light of his often harsh critique of allegorical interpretation, it may come as a surprise that Calvin sometimes approves of what he clearly regards as an allegorical understanding of the text. One such instance is found in his commentary on Daniel 4:10–16.

There is no doubt at all of the whole discourse being metaphorical—nay, properly speaking, it is an allegory, since an allegory is only a continued metaphor [*continua metaphora*]. If Daniel had only represented the king under the figure of a tree, it would have been a metaphor, but when he pursues his own train of thought in a continuous tenor, his discourse becomes allegorical.[29]

Metaphor and allegory belong in the same class of figures; the writers of scripture use both.

Calvin believes that many of the Old Testament promises of a future kingdom were meant to be taken allegorically. He finds an allegory in Isaiah 30:25 ("And upon every lofty mountain and every high hill there will be brooks running with water, in the day of the great slaughter, when the towers fall").

When the prophets describe the kingdom of Christ, they commonly draw similitudes [*similitudines*] from the ordinary life of men; for the true happiness of the children of God cannot be described in any other way than by holding out an image of those things which fall under our bodily senses, and from which men form their ideas of a happy and prosperous condition. . . . But those expressions are allegorical and are accommodated by the prophet to our ignorance, that we may know, by means of those things which are perceived by our senses, those blessings which have so great and surpassing excellence that our minds cannot comprehend them.[30]

Old Testament texts that, if taken literally, promise a time of great earthly blessing for God's people, are usually given a spiritual (or allegorical) interpretation by Calvin. He usually demonstrates the validity of his spiritual exegesis by pointing out that the prophecy in question has not had a literal fulfillment. He takes the magnificent restoration of Jerusalem promised in Jeremiah 31 as a promise of the spiritual kingdom of Christ.

Though Jerusalem before Christ's coming was eminent and surrounded by a triple wall, and though it was celebrated through all the East, as even heathen writers say that it excelled every other city, yet it was never accomplished that the city flourished as under David and Solomon. We must necessarily come to the spiritual state of the city, and explain the promise as the grace that came through Christ.[31]

He insists that, in adopting this type of spiritual interpretation, he is not guilty of twisting scripture—something he charges that the allegorists do. He is forced to the interpretation because there has been no literal historical fulfillment. He observes that anyone who looks for a literal fulfillment of the prophecy recorded in Amos 9:15 ("And I will plant them on their land and they shall no more be pulled up out of their land which I have given them") will be disappointed. The prophecy, therefore, must be fulfilled in Christ.[32]

It is axiomatic for Calvin that "whatever is foretold of Christ's kingdom must correspond to its nature and character." And what is the nature of Christ's kingdom? It is spiritual. "When Scripture, as we have seen, promises a large produce of corn and wine, an abundance of all good things, tranquillity and peace, and bright days, it intends by all these things to set forth the character of Christ's kingdom."[33] When the prophet warns of the judgment of God in Joel 2 ("I will give portents in the heavens and on the earth, blood and fire and columns of smoke. The sun shall be turned to darkness, and the moon to blood, before the great and terrible day of the LORD comes"), he intends to warn God's people not to find their happiness in this world. "The prophet here checks vain imaginations, lest the faithful should think that Christ's kingdom would be earthly, and fix their minds on corn and wine, on pleasures and quietness, on the conveniences of the present life."[34] It was never God's intention that the coming kingdom of Christ be understood as earthly.

> We must again call to remembrance what is the nature of Christ's kingdom. As he does not wear a golden crown or employ earthly armor, so he does not rule over the world by the power of arms, or gain authority by gaudy and ostentatious display, or constrain his people by terror and dread; but the doctrine of the gospel is his royal banner, which assembles believers under his dominion. Wherever, therefore, the doctrine of the Gospel is preached in purity, there we are certain that Christ reigns, and where it is rejected, his government is also set aside.[35]

The language of Isaiah 11:6 ("The wolf shall dwell with the lamb, and the leopard shall lie down with the kid, and the calf and the lion and the fatling together, and a little child shall lead them") is to be understood spiritually. "By these modes of expression he means nothing else than that those who formerly were like savage beasts will be mild and gentle, for he compares violent and ravenous men to wolves and bears which live on prey and plunder, and declares that they will be tame and gentle, so that they will be satisfied with ordinary food, and will abstain from doing any injury or harm." In defense of his spiritual interpretation, Calvin appeals to the apostle Paul, who in Ephesians 1 and Colossians 1 teaches that "Christ came to gather together out of a state of disorder those things which are in heaven and on earth."[36] The text refers to the time when men are cleansed of their depraved natures by the Spirit of regeneration.[37]

In his interpretation of Amos 9:15 he again argues that "what is said here of the abundance of corn and wine must be explained with reference to the nature of Christ's kingdom." Since this kingdom is spiritual, the blessings must also be.

> If anyone objects and says that the prophet does not speak here allegorically, the answer is ready at hand, even this—that it is a manner of speaking everywhere found in Scripture, that a happy state is painted as it were before our eyes by setting before us the conveniences of the present life and earthly blessings: this may especially be observed in the prophets, for they accommodated [accommodabant] their style, as we have already stated, to the capacities of a rude and weak people.[38]

Why did God communicate in allegories? Partly to prevent the ungodly from understanding the message. "We know that God sometimes spoke enigmatically [aenigmatice] when unwilling to be understood by the impious and disbelieving."[39] But more importantly, the enigmatic nature of the allegory was intended to induce the people of Old Testament times to listen more carefully to the prophet's message. When the prophets used ordinary language, the people often ignored their message.[40] "If the prophet had spoken simply and in his accustomed language, they would not have been so attentive."[41] God's use of allegories is a gracious condescension to the ignorance of his people. The prophets "borrow their similitudes [similitudines] from an earthly kingdom, because our ignorance would make it almost impossible for us to comprehend, in any other way, the unspeakable treasure of blessings."[42] "Whenever the prophets speak of Christ's kingdom, they set before us an earthly form, because spiritual truth, without any figure [figura], could not have been sufficiently understood by a rude people in their childhood."[43] The prophets "accommodated [accommodabant] their style to the capacities of a rude and weak people."[44] When God offers us the conveniences of earthly life "it is not because he wishes that our attention should be confined to our present happiness, which alone hypocrites value, and which entirely occupies their minds, but in order that, by contemplation of it, we may rise to the heavenly life, and that, by tasting so much goodness, he may prepare us for the enjoyment of eternal happiness."[45]

> Christ's kingdom and his dignity cannot be perceived by carnal eyes, nor even comprehended by the human intellect. . . . Our minds cannot naturally comprehend these things. No wonder, then, if mortals judge

erroneously of Christ's kingdom, and are blind in the midst of light. Still there is no defect in the prophet's expressions, for they depict for us the visible image of Christ's kingdom, and accommodate [*accommodant*] themselves to our dullness. They enable us to perceive the analogy between things earthly and visible, and that spiritual blessedness which Christ has afforded to us, and which we now possess through hope in him.[46]

Calvin indicates that the difference between his approach and that of the allegorists is one of degree—he is moderate; they are excessive. In his commentary on Isaiah 55:13 ("Instead of the thorn shall come up the cypress; instead of the brier shall come up the myrtle; and it shall be to the LORD for a memorial, for an everlasting sign which shall not be cut off"), he distinguishes his spiritual exegesis from the allegorical approach, which he opposes. The passage is rightly interpreted as a promise of the spiritual kingdom of Christ. "When they say that these things relate to the kingdom of Christ and on that account ought to be understood spiritually [*spiritualiter*], I agree with them." But when the allegorists begin to draw meanings out of each of the particulars of the text, they have gone too far. "In expositions of that kind ingenuity is carried to excess."[47]

Calvin's principle for determining which Old Testament passages are allegories is this: if there has been no historical fulfillment of the promise, one should look for a fulfillment that is not literal. Since New Testament reality was often presented in an earthly, shadowy form in the Old Testament, it is reasonable to look for a spiritual interpretation of prophecies that were not literally fulfilled. Calvin's approach does not reflect a lack of concern for historical exegesis. On the contrary, it could be argued that his view is necessitated by that concern—specifically, by his failure to find an earthly historical fulfillment of Old Testament promises.

TYPOLOGY

Calvin's reservations about allegorical interpretation do not carry over to typological interpretation. In an exposition of Isaiah 33:17, where he argues that Hezekiah was a type of Christ, he expresses concern that someone might confuse his approach with allegorization. "Let no man imagine that I am here pursuing allegories, to which I am averse." Hezekiah, he believes, functioned as a type to lead the Jewish people to a knowledge of Christ. But this does not allow the interpreter to simply leap over Hezekiah to get to Christ.[48] In his explanation of the Old Testament sacrificial system, Calvin again distinguishes his typology from allegory. Typological interpretation of Old Testament cultic practices acknowledges that something more than purely historical interpretation is called for, yet differs from allegorical interpretation in not seeking meanings in all of the details of the ceremonies.

> All the ancient figures were sure testimonies of God's grace and of eternal salvation, and thus Christ was represented in them, since all the promises are in Him. . . . Yet it by no means follows from hence that there were mysteries hidden in all their details, since some, with mistaken acuteness, pass over no point, however trifling, without an allegorical exposition.[49]

Throughout the history of the church even opponents of allegorical interpretation have often found typology to be useful.[50] It has been adopted as a tool of twentieth-century biblical theology, and has thus escaped some of the criticism leveled at allegorical interpretation. It is considered by some to be acceptable because it is grounded in the historical meaning of the text.[51] Eichrodt argues that typology may have a legitimate role in modern exegesis.[52] Lampe agrees that legitimate histori-cal typology is useful in understanding scripture because, while not denying the role of historical exegesis, it provides a way of emphasizing the unity of scripture.

> If we admit the unity of Scripture in the sense that it is the literature of people whose thought was controlled by a single series of images, and that it is a body of writings whose explicit or implicit theme is the people and the Covenant, and if, further, we hold that Christ is the unifying centre-point of Biblical history, deliberately fulfilling the various images presented by that literature and bringing together different threads within it to form a consistent pattern, then we have no objection to a typology which seeks to discover and make explicit the real correspon-dences in historical events which have been brought about by the recurring rhythm of the divine activity.[53]

Frei agrees that the unity of scripture is the underlying presupposition of typological interpretation. Typology is actually literal interpretation "at the level of the whole biblical story," and thus may be regarded as "a natural extension of literal interpretation."[54]

That Calvin made extensive use of typological interpretation has been noted by many scholars. One writer states that without typology "Calvin would not be Calvin."[55] He has been faulted for having a "weakness for typology."[56] It has been charged that he "is often in danger of letting in allegory by the back-door of typology,"[57] and that he avoids allegory only by "falling into typology."[58] It should not be surprising that one who stresses the unity of scripture as strongly Calvin does would use typology extensively.

Typology for Calvin is true prophecy, albeit shadowy and somewhat obscure.[59] God chose to accommodate his revelation to the weakness and ignorance of his people in Old Testament times by presenting spiritual truth under earthly symbols. The symbols did not set forth the full truth, but directed the people toward the truth. The symbols varied, but in almost every instance they were intended as pictures of the redeemer who was to come.[60] Calvin believes an understanding of the symbolic nature of persons and institutions is absolutely indispensable if one is to profit fully from the study of the Old Testament.[61]

In conformity with much of the Christian exegetical tradition, Calvin views the ceremonial laws of the Old Testament as shadows of the coming Messiah. "The whole cultus of the law, taken literally and not as shadows and figures [*umbras et figuras*] corresponding to the truth, will be utterly ridiculous."[62] He finds typological significance in almost every ceremony. He learns from the New Testament that the Sabbath was typical. "We learn especially from Paul that the Sabbath day was enjoined in order that the people might look to Christ; for well known is the passage in Colossians 2:16 where he says that the Sabbath as well as other rites were shadows [*umbras*] of Christ to come, and that he was the substance of them."[63] Similarly, the passover is to be understood as a type of Christ:

> It is not to be wondered, therefore, that God should now require the Passover to be one year old, and without blemish, that the Israelites might know that in order to propitiate God, a more excellent price was required than could be discovered in the whole human race; and since such excellency could much less exist in a beast, the celestial perfection and purity of Christ was shown forth by this visible perfection of the lamb, or kid. It was with reference to this also that they were commanded to keep it up separate from the rest of the flock, from the tenth until the fourteenth day of the month. As to God's will, that the side-posts and lintel should be sprinkled with blood, by this sign He plainly taught them, that the sacrifice would profit none but those who were stained and marked with Christ's blood; for this sprinkling was equivalent to their bearing each one the mark of His blood upon their forehead.[64]

He adds of the paschal lamb that "there is no doubt that by this visible symbol, he raised up their minds to that true and heavenly exemplar, whom it would be absurd and profane to separate from the ceremonies of the law."[65]

The mediatorial function of the Levitical priesthood appears to Calvin to be an obvious picture of the priestly role of Jesus Christ. "It is unquestionable that the Levitical priests were the representatives of Christ, since, with respect to their office, they were even better than the very angels; which would be by no means reasonable, unless they had been the image [*imago*] of Him, who is Himself the head of the angels."[66] He finds a foreshadowing of the work of Jesus Christ in the detailed description of the Levitical garments.

This robe was above the oblong coat between that and the ephod, and from its lower edge hung the bells and pomegranates alternately. Although there was no smell in the pomegranates, yet the figure [*figura*] suggested this to the eyes, as if God required in that garment a sweet smell as well as a sound; and surely we who stink through the foulness of our sins are only a sweet smell unto God as being covered with the garment of Christ. But God would have the bells give a sound, because the garment of Christ does not procure favor for us except by the sound of the Gospel, which diffuses the sweet savor of the Head among all the members.

Calvin acknowledges that he has crossed the line in this interpretation from typology into allegory, so he hastens to insist that there is nothing speculative about his reasoning. "In this allegory there is nothing too subtle or far-fetched [*In hac allegoria nihil est nimis argutum, vel procul quaesitum*], for the similitude of the smell and the sound naturally leads us to the honoring of grace and to the preaching of the gospel."[67]

Although Calvin does in the case of the Levitical vestments elaborate on the particulars, as a general rule he suggests that one not seek a deeper meaning for every detail of the ceremonial law.

Nothing is better than to contain ourselves within the limits of edification, and it would be puerile to make a collection of the *minutiae* wherewith some philosophize, since it was by no means the intention of God to include mysteries in every hook and loop; and even although no part were without a mystical meaning, which no one in his senses will admit, it is better to confess our ignorance than to indulge ourselves in frivolous conjectures. Of this sobriety, too, the author of the Epistle to the Hebrews is a fit master for us, who, although he professedly shows the analogy between the shadows of the Law and the truth manifested in Christ, yet only sparingly touches upon some main points, and by this moderation restrains us from too curious disquisitions and deep speculations.[68]

As the Levitical priesthood typifies Christ as priest, so David and his descendants typify him in his kingly role. Calvin makes both points in his commentary on Jeremiah 33:17.

Now we know that in David was promised a spiritual kingdom, for what was David but a type of Christ [*Christi typus*]? As God then gave in David a living image of his only-begotten Son, we ought ever to pass from the temporal kingdom to the eternal, from the visible to the spiritual, from the earthly to the celestial. The same ought to be said of the priesthood; for no mortal can reconcile God to men, and make an atonement for sins; and further, the blood of bulls and goats could not pacify the wrath of God, nor incense, nor the sprinkling of water, nor any of the things which belonged to the ceremonial laws; they could not give the hope of salvation, so as to quiet trembling consciences. It then follows that the priesthood was shadowy [*umbratile*], and that the Levites represented Christ until he came.[69]

Not only David but also his royal successors typically represented Christ. Hezekiah was a type of Christ "as David and the rest of his successors also were."[70] And it was not just the pious kings of Old Testament times who served as types. All the posterity of David (and even his predecessor, Saul) represented Christ (*Christi imaginem*). In his exposition of Lamentations 4:20 Calvin explains, "Zedekiah is here rightly called the Christ of Jehovah, by which term Scripture designates all kings, and even Saul; and though his kingdom was temporary, and soon decayed, yet he is called 'the Anointed of Jehovah.' "[71] Joseph was a type of Christ.[72] Aaron was a type of Christ; the supreme power of Christ was represented in him.[73] Samson, who was set apart from his mother's womb and separated from the rest of the people by his Nazirite vow, was a type of Christ.[74] Joshua, the high priest, was a type of Christ, together with his successors.[75] Zerubbabel was a type of Christ, as one who was despised by the world, yet esteemed by God.[76] Even Cyrus was a type of Christ. In him things were foreshadowed that were ultimately fulfilled in the reign of Christ.[77]

In Jesus Christ the priestly and kingly are roles combined. The cult and government were given to ancient Israel by God so that they might not be ignorant of the basis of their salvation.

All our salvation depends upon these two points; first, that Christ has been given to us to be our priest, and, secondly, that he has been established king to govern us. This God showed to his ancient people under figures [*sub figuris*]. The sanctuary erected on mount Zion was intended to keep their faith fixed upon the spiritual priesthood of Christ; and in like manner, by the kingdom of David, there was presented to their view an image [*imago*] of the kingdom of Christ.[78]

Calvin recognizes that he is walking a very narrow path in his use of typology. He cannot follow the Jewish approach, which denies that the ceremonies and events of the Old Testament find their ultimate fulfillment in Jesus Christ. Nor can he follow Christian exegetes who disregard the significance of Old Testament history in their eagerness to find Christ in every passage. Jewish exegetes are guilty of maliciously misconstruing the words of the Bible in order to obscure the references to Jesus Christ in the Old Testament. Christians, unfortunately, give the Jews reason to object when they sophistically apply to Christ things that do not directly refer to him.[79]

In order to stifle any Jewish protest against his typological interpretations, Calvin attempts to substantiate the validity of his approach.[80] He depends on two basic arguments: first, the New Testament writers treat

Old Testament texts as prophecies that are fulfilled in Jesus Christ; second, the language does not suit the reign of David or any other Old Testament figure, yet it perfectly suits the reign of Christ.[81] These two arguments are his standard defense of typology throughout his Old Testament commentaries.

Calvin's primary argument is his appeal to the use of the Old Testament by Jesus[82] and the New Testament writers (most often the apostle Paul[83] and the writer of Hebrews),[84] yet he insists that he is able to make the case on Old Testament evidence alone. Arguments from the Old Testament itself are strong enough, he believes, to refute even those who reject the authority of the apostles. However, he doesn't think it is very productive to limit one's arguments to the Old Testament. He has little hope of convincing a skeptical Jew, but he does believe that his reasoning may strengthen the faith of the Christian who is perplexed by Jewish arguments. He suggests that when the language of the Old Testament writer does not seem appropriate for the Old Testament setting, it is normally a clue that the writer is presenting a type. The language of joyful submission to the king in Psalm 47 ("Clap your hands, all ye peoples; shout unto God with the voice of triumph") fits neither David nor Solomon. "Many nations were tributary to David, and to his son Solomon, but while they were so, they ceased not, at the same time, to murmur, and bore impatiently the yoke which was imposed upon them."[85] Isaiah 16:5 ("Then a throne will be established in steadfast love and on it will sit in faithfulness in the tent of David one who judges and seeks justice and is swift to do righteousness") was taken by the Jews as a prophecy of restoration under Hezekiah, but "the Psalmist is clearly speaking of a more important restoration of the Church than that which occurred in Hezekiah's reign."[86] In his exposition of Isaiah 33:6, Calvin writes that the kingdom of Hezekiah was "but a slender straw of the kingdom of Christ."[87] "In Christ alone is found the stability of that frail kingdom."[88]

Apart from the question of the size and strength of the kingdom, there are other descriptions that make little sense if applied to an Old Testament person or office but seem to fit Christ perfectly. The description of the Levitical priesthood as even better than angels certainly must be viewed typologically.[89] The qualities attributed to David in Jeremiah 33:17 could not fit any earthly king or priest: one who can reconcile God to men; one who can make atonement for sins; one who can quiet troubled consciences by giving them the hope of salvation.[90]

Finally, some Old Testament practices are simply absurd unless they are conceived as types—the Old Testament sacrificial system, for instance. In his exposition of Exodus 12:21, Calvin asks "what could be more childish than to offer the blood of an animal as a protection against the hand of God, or to seek from thence a ground of safety?"[91] In the same commentary he writes, "Surely if Christ be put out of sight, all the sacrifices that may be offered differ in no respect from mere profane butchery."[92] Only a typological fulfillment could explain why God says in Psalm 40:6 that sacrifices are of no value. Apart from leading people higher to the knowledge of the spiritual fulfillment in Christ, they were of no use.[93]

Although Calvin rarely appeals to the immediate literary context to justify his typological interpretations, he does do so on at least one occasion. Psalm 45 cannot refer primarily to Solomon because the context will not allow it. "As the Jews and other ungodly men refuse to submit cordially to the force of truth, it is important to show briefly from the context itself [*ex contextu*], the principal reasons from which it appears that some of the things here spoken are not applicable fully and perfectly to Solomon."[94]

Most of Calvin's arguments justifying typological exegesis are intended to support the faith of Christians in the face of Jewish objections to a christological reading of the Old Testament. But many Christians have no difficulty accepting the reality of Old Testament prophecies of Christ. More often their problem is that they see little else. He sometimes has to justify a typological interpretation to those who want to interpret a text as an explicit prophecy of Christ with no contextual referent. He is embarrassed by his fellow Christians' views concerning the referent of Psalm 72.

> Those who would interpret it simply as a prophecy of the kingdom of Christ, seem to put a construction upon the words which does violence to them; and then we must always beware of giving the Jews occasion of making an outcry, as if it were our purpose, sophistically, to apply to Christ those things which do not directly refer to him. . . . What is here spoken of everlasting dominion cannot be limited to one man, or to a few, nor even to twenty ages; but there is pointed out the succession which had its end and complete accomplishment in Christ.[95]

In his interpretation of Isaiah 61:1 ("The Spirit of the LORD God is upon me, because the LORD has anointed me to bring good tidings to the afflicted; he has sent me to bind up the brokenhearted, to proclaim liberty to the captives, and the opening of the prison to those who are bound") he again displays his sensitivity to criticism by the Jews.

> As Christ explains this passage with reference to himself (Luke 4:18), so commentators limit it to him without hesitation, and lay down this principle, that Christ is introduced as speaking, as if the whole passage related to him alone. The Jews laugh at this, as an ill-advised application to Christ of that which is equally applicable to other prophets.[96]

He counsels his fellow Christians that prophecy need not deny a historical referent in Old Testament times.[97] That is just the point with typology. It has an Old Testament referent, yet its perfect fulfillment comes later in the person of Christ. This approach allows Calvin to guard the unity of scripture without requiring him to discard historical exegesis.[98]

Calvin justifies his typological approach against both Jewish and Christian misinterpretations. The Jewish approach robs Jesus Christ of his honor; the Christian approach robs the Old Testament of significance for its original audience. A mediating position is necessary. His interpretations of Psalm 2, Psalm 22, Psalm 89, and Psalm 110 provide excellent examples of his method of exegetical reasoning as he tries to avoid the pitfalls often encountered by Jewish and Christian interpreters.

Calvin sees David in Psalm 2 boasting that his kingdom, though assailed by powerful enemies, will reach to the ends of the earth and last forever. All this he insists "is typical and contains a prophecy concerning the future kingdom of Christ [*Caeterum hic typus vaticinium continet de futuro Christi regno*]."

> As David's temporal kingdom was a kind of earnest to God's ancient people of the eternal kingdom, which at length was truly established in the person of Christ, those things which David declares concerning himself are not violently or even allegorically [*violenter vel allegorice*] applied to Christ but were truly predicted concerning him. If we attentively consider the nature of the kingdom, we will perceive that it would be absurd to overlook the end or scope [*fine vel scopo*], and to rest in the mere shadow [*umbra*].[99]

Calvin's proof of the correctness of a typological interpretation of the psalm begins with an appeal to the New Testament. "That the kingdom of Christ is here described by the spirit of prophecy is sufficiently attested to us by the apostles, who seeing the ungodly conspiring against Christ, arm themselves in prayer with this doctrine."

Calvin believes that the New Testament writer's use of Psalm 2 is an adequate demonstration that the psalm should be understood typologically. But apart from this explicit citation, it is still possible to prove that the psalm refers to Christ. "To place our faith beyond the reach of all cavils, it is plainly made manifest from all the prophets that those things which David testified concerning his own kingdom are properly applicable to Christ."[100] The language of verse 6 ("I have anointed my king upon my holy hill of Zion") has reference to David, yet more appropriately to Christ.

> Although David in these words had a regard to the promise of God, and recalled the attention of himself and others to it, yet, at the same time, he meant to signify that his own reign is holy and inseparably connected with the temple of God. But this applies more appropriately to the kingdom of Christ, which we know to be both spiritual and joined to the priesthood.[101]

Verse 7 ("I will tell of the decree of the LORD: He said to me, 'You are my son, today I have begotten you' ") again fits Christ much better than David. David "protests that he did not come to the throne without a sure and clear proof of his calling. . . . But this was more truly fulfilled in Christ, and doubtless, David, under the influence of the spirit of prophecy, had special reference to him." David "could with some propriety be called the son of God on account of his royal dignity."

> But here God, by the singularly high title with which he honours David, exalts him not only above all mortal men, but even above the angels. . . . David, individually considered, was inferior to the angels, but in so far as he represented the person of Christ, he is with good reason preferred far above them. By the Son of God in this place we are therefore not to understand one son among many, but his only begotten Son.[102]

The language of verse 8 ("Ask of me, and I will give thee the heathen for thine inheritance, and the uttermost parts of the earth for thy possession") cannot possibly be understood as fulfilled in the person of David. He had many great victories and conquered other nations, yet David's empire was not large compared with other monarchies. "Unless, therefore, we suppose this prophecy concerning the vast extent of the kingdom to have been uttered in vain and falsely, we must apply it to Christ, who alone has subdued the whole world to himself, and embraced all lands and nations under his dominion."[103] The language of verse 9 ("Thou shalt break them with a rod of iron, and dash them in pieces like a potter's vessel") also demands fulfillment in someone other than David. While it is true that David vanquished many enemies through military force, yet "the prediction is more fully verified in Christ, who, neither by sword nor spear, but by the breath of his mouth, smites the ungodly even to their utter destruction."[104]

For Calvin, Psalm 22 was unquestionably a prophecy of Christ.[105] The psalm opens with the words "My God! my God! why have you forsaken me?"—words which, according to Matthew 27:46, were uttered by the Savior while he was suffering on the cross. Calvin complains that older interpreters in their overenthusiasm for showing how the psalm teaches about Christ, could not even wait until they got beyond the psalm's heading before flying off into allegorical excesses. "They thought that Christ would not be sufficiently dignified and honored unless, putting a mystical or allegorical sense upon the word 'hind,' they viewed it as pointing out the various things which are included in a sacrifice." Calvin finds nothing solid (*nihil solidi*) in these subtleties. He opts for a more simple (*simplicius*) and genuine (*genuinum*) interpretation. The word *hind*, he suggests, is the beginning of some common psalm, and has no relation whatever to the subject matter.[106]

According to Calvin, David in Psalm 22 "sets before us, in his own person, a type of Christ." David understood "by the Spirit of Prophecy" that the things of which he wrote were true of the humiliation of Christ that took place prior to his exaltation.[107] Calvin insists he can prove that in this psalm "under the type [typo] of David, Christ has been shadowed forth [adumbratum]."[108] He explains that he is not trying to convince the Jews that David is a type of Christ. (They are too obstinate and opinionated to be reasonable.) He does, however, hope to demonstrate the truth of his interpretation to Christians who are in danger of being confused by the Jewish exegesis of the psalm. He is especially concerned with the Jewish charge that Christians have deliberately overthrown the literal sense of the psalm in their translation of verse 16 ("they have pierced"). He argues that if one accepts the Jewish reading of the text, the passage will be wrapped in obscurity.[109] He challenges the motives of the Jews, who he believes are guilty of tampering with the Old Testament text in order to rid it of whatever evidence there is that Christ is the redeemer. He is aware that, even if he wins the textual argument, he must still answer the Jewish argument that since David was never nailed to the cross, the language cannot refer to crucifixion. The answer to this is easy; the language must be metaphorical. David in the psalm declared "that he was not less afflicted by his enemies than the man who is suspended on a cross, having his hands and feet pierced through with nails."[110] Metaphorical language is also used in verse 17 ("They parted my garments among themselves, and cast lots for my cloak"). "It is as if he had said that all his goods have become a prey to his enemies, even as conquerors are accustomed to plunder the vanquished." In Matthew 8:16–17, the evangelist uses this verse of the psalm without the figure in reference to Christ—a perfectly legitimate practice if David is regarded as a type. "The heavenly Father intended that in the person of his Son those things should be visibly accomplished which were shadowed [adumbrata] forth in David."[111] If any question should remain about the propriety of viewing David as a type of Christ, all doubt is removed by verse 27 ("All the ends of the earth shall remember"). This language could never be applied to David's reign. First, David's kingdom was great, but not so great that it reached to the ends of the earth. Second, the nations David subdued were not converted to the true worship of God. The type reached fulfillment in Christ. With amazing speed his reign was extended to the Gentiles throughout the world. They were truly converted to his rule.

Calvin adopts the same line of argument in defending his typological interpretation of Psalm 89:26 ("He shall cry to me, Thou art my Father"). The language of the psalm best fits Christ—in fact, it can fit no one else. The psalmist presents God speaking of the king. This has to be a reference to Christ, because it was the privilege of "only one king in this world to be called the Son of God." If the description can fit anyone other than Christ, then the writer of Hebrews is reasoning inconclusively—even absurdly—when he uses this text to prove that Christ is superior to the angels. Calvin observes that in verse 27 David is given a dignity above men and angels when he is called the firstborn and one who is elevated above all the kings of the earth. Anticipating an objection to this comparison, he reasons: "If he is considered in himself, he cannot justly be elevated to the same rank with them, but with the highest propriety he may, in so far as for a time he represented the person of Christ."[112] The next two verses of the psalm picture David's descendants sitting upon the throne forever, a final proof that "this prophecy cannot have its full accomplishment in any till we come to Christ, in whom alone, in the strict and proper sense, this everlasting duration is to be found."[113] For Calvin a typological interpretation of this psalm is no uncertain matter. It is unquestionably correct for the same two reasons he highlights in his exposition of Psalm 22: first, the New Testament writer supports it; second, the language fits no one else.

> To limit what is here said to the ancient people of Israel is an exposition not only absurd, but altogether impious. In the first place, I take it as a settled point, which we have already had occasion often to consider, that this kingdom was erected to be a shadow [*umbratile*] in which God might represent the Mediator to his Church: and this can be proved, not only from the testimony of Christ and the apostles, but it may also be clearly and indubitably deduced from the thing considered in itself. If we set Christ aside, where will we find that everlasting duration of the royal throne of which mention is here made? . . . The obvious conclusion then is that perpetuity, as applied to this kingdom, can be verified in Christ alone.[114]

Calvin admits that the New Testament plays a major role in guiding him to a typological interpretation of this psalm. He does not concede, however, that he has no other reasons. Apart from the testimony of the writer of Hebrews, it is obvious that a typological interpretation is the only one that can do justice to the language of the text. Throughout the psalm he uses his normal justifications, especially arguing from context.[115] He apparently sees no tension between his typological approach and his usual method of determining the intention of the human writer through an understanding of language and a careful consideration of context.

Calvin launches his most sustained defense of typological interpretation in his exposition of Psalm 110.

> Having the testimony of Christ that this psalm was penned in reference to himself, we need not apply to any other quarter for the corroboration of this statement; and, even supposing we neither had his authority, nor the testimony of the apostle, the psalm itself would admit of no other

interpretation; for although we should have a dispute with the Jews, the most obstinate people in the world, about the right application of it, we are able, by solid arguments [*firmis rationibus*], to compel them to admit that the truths here stated relate neither to David nor to any other person than the Mediator alone.

Here again are Calvin's two recurring arguments for typological interpretation: the New Testament relates the psalm to Christ, and the language fits no one but Christ. Since Christ himself tells us the psalmist refers to him, no further substantiation should be required. Even the Jews, who refuse to accept the testimony of Christ or his apostles, have to admit that this can only be fulfilled in the mediator. "It cannot be asserted of him [David], or of any of his successors, that he should be a king whose dominion should be widely extended, and who, at the same time, was a priest, not according to the law, but according to the order of Melchizedek, and that for ever."[116] Though David did bring a few of the neighboring nations into subjection, "his kingdom, when contrasted with other monarchies, was always confined within narrow limits."[117] The problem of the priestly office fitting anyone in Old Testament times is twofold. First, another priestly office could not be established without depriving the Levites of their place of honor. Second, the longevity of the priesthood described here could not fit any one man—except Jesus Christ.[118]

It is thus clear from Calvin's defense of typology in his commentary on Psalms 2, 22, 89, and 110 that he believes typological interpretation as he practices it rests on a solid defensible base. He argues that the Jews are able to cite no adequate referent for the texts in Old Testament times, and thus a christological interpretation is necessary. Against fellow Christian exegetes he argues that one cannot tear a text out of its historical context in order to apply it to Christ.

PROPHECY

Jewish and Christian writers agreed that the Old Testament contained numerous explicit promises, predictions, or prophecies. Among these were assurances of deliverance from hardship and the restoration of God's blessing. Jewish exegetes believed these to be fulfilled either in some event before the Christian era (e.g., deliverance from the Babylonian captivity) or in the messiah for whom they were still waiting. In no case could the predictions be correctly related to Jesus Christ. Christians reasoned differently. Since Jesus Christ is the Messiah, promises of future deliverance may be taken as clear, direct prophecies of his life and work.

The dominant approach to interpreting Old Testament prophecy in the early church disregarded the setting in which the prophet lived and the circumstances in which he made his predictions. According to Greer:

> The exegesis by means of fulfillment of prophecy . . . tends so to see all events in terms of their fulfillment, that the events themselves become unimportant and meaningless. Prophecy then becomes not a speaking to the contemporary scene, but purely prediction of events to come in the distant future.[119]

Things had changed little by the Middle Ages. Preus indicates that a characteristic of much medieval Old Testament exegesis was that "the interpreter does not place himself with the Old Testament writer in time."[120] Calvin was uncomfortable with traditional Christian exegesis of Old Testament promises because he believed interpreters were wrong to ignore the historical circumstances in which the promises were originally given.

He finds something of value in both Jewish and Christian approaches. In his commentary on Isaiah 59:19 ("So they shall fear the name of the LORD from the west, and his glory from the rising of the sun; for he will come like a rushing stream which the wind of the LORD drives") he notes that the Jews refer the prophecy "exclusively to the deliverance from Babylon while the Christians refer it to Christ alone." His solution is to embrace elements of both views. "I join with both, so as to include the whole period after the return of the people along with that which followed down to the coming of Christ."[121] In his commentary on Isaiah 43:19 he argues that Christian commentators are undoubtedly mistaken in "referring absolutely to the coming of Christ." Jewish interpretations are no more correct in limiting the fulfillment to the return from the Babylonian captivity. "As I have frequently remarked, we ought here to include the whole period which followed the redemption from Babylon, down to the coming of Christ."[122]

It is the exclusivity of the positions that Calvin rejects. He opposes the "either/or" mentality that characterizes Jewish and Christian approaches to Old Testament promises. His approach recognizes the significance of the historical fulfillment in Old Testament times (return from Babylon) without divorcing it from the complete fulfillment that only comes in Christ.[123]

His comments on Isaiah 52:10 ("The LORD has bared his holy arm before the eyes of all the nations; and all the ends of the earth shall see the salvation of our God") show the middle way he found between Jewish and Christian views:

> This prophecy is maliciously restricted by the Jews to the deliverance from Babylon, and is improperly restricted by Christians to the spiritual

redemption which we obtain through Christ; for we must begin with the deliverance which was wrought under Cyrus (2 Chronicles 36:22, 23), and bring it down to our own time. Thus the Lord began to display his power among the Medes and Persians, but afterwards he made it visible to all the nations.[124]

Calvin finds the "either/or" approach of both Jewish and Christian interpreters to be defective in the interpretation of Joel 3:1–2 ("In those days and in that time, when I shall bring again the captivity of Judah and Jerusalem, I will also gather all nations").

This time the Jews limit to their return: they therefore think that when liberty to return was granted them by Cyrus and Darius, what the prophet declared here was fulfilled. Christian doctors apply this prediction to the coming of Christ, but both interpret the words of the prophet otherwise than the circumstances of the passage [circumstantia loci] require. The prophet, no doubt, speaks here of the deliverance we have just noticed, and at the same time includes the kingdom of Christ, and this, as we have seen in other parts, is very commonly done. While then the prophets testify that God would be the redeemer of his people, and promise deliverance from Babylonian exile, they lead the faithful, as it were, by a continuous train or course, to the kingdom of Christ. For what else was the Jewish restoration, but a prelude of that true and real redemption, afterwards effected by Christ? The prophet then does not speak only of the coming of Christ, or of the return of the Jews, but includes the whole of redemption, which was only begun when the Lord restored his people from the Babylonian exile; it will then go on from the first coming of Christ to the last day.[125]

Calvin also offers an "extended" interpretation in his comments on Jeremiah 32:37 ("Behold, I will gather them from all the countries to which I drove them in my anger and my wrath and in great indignation; I will bring them back to this place, and I will make them dwell in safety").

Whenever the prophets prophesied of the return of the people, they extended [extendunt] what they taught to the whole kingdom of Christ. For liberation from exile was no more than the beginning of God's favor: God began the work of true and real redemption when he restored his people to their own country, but he gave them but a slight taste of his mercy. This prophecy, then, with those which are like it, ought to be extended [extendi] to the kingdom of Christ."[126]

Another text misinterpreted by Jews and Christians alike was Jeremiah 32:41, in which God promised to "plant" his people in the land. Calvin sees a problem with the Christian approach in its failure to recognize a historical fulfillment in Old Testament times. The Jews, however, correctly saw the earthly fulfillment, but failed to see anything else. "The Jews, who reject

Christ, stop in that earthly deliverance." Calvin prefers an extended fulfillment that begins with the return of the people from exile and continues through the time of Christ. The prophets "set Christ also in the middle, that the faithful might know that the return was but a slight taste of the full grace, which was to be expected from Christ alone; for it was then, indeed, that God really planted his people." The fulfillment of this prophecy must be found in God's redemption of his people in Christ. Noting that Psalm 80 used similar language to describe the conquest of the land under Joshua, Calvin reasons that God initially planted his people in the land under Joshua's leadership. "God had brought his vine out of Egypt and planted it in the promised inheritance." But this was not the true planting, because the people did not put down firm roots. Jeremiah 32 promises something new and unusual—a perpetual planting that was based upon a covenant relationship. The planting after the exile was only a first step in the fulfillment of the promise. The complete fulfillment comes in Christ. The prophecy must be extended beyond what Jews and Christians traditionally say. "The Church was fixed in Judea until the coming of Christ, who brought in the real accomplishment of this plantation."[127]

Calvin believes that the fulfillment of Old Testament promises relating to the establishment of the kingdom sometimes extends as far as the final advent of Christ. Concerning Isaiah 26:19 ("The dead shall live, their bodies shall rise. O dwellers in the dust, awake and sing for joy! For thy dew is a dew of light, and on the land of the shades thou wilt let it fall") he writes: "Isaiah includes the whole reign of Christ; for, although we begin to receive the fruit of this consolation when we are admitted into the Church, yet we shall not enjoy it fully until that last day of the resurrection is come, when all things shall be most completely restored."[128] Concerning the promise of the restoration of God's people in Isaiah 60 he explains:

> The Prophet does not speak of a few years or a short period, but embraces the whole course of redemption, from the end of the captivity to the preaching of the gospel, and finally down to the end of the reign of Christ. . . . We know that this prediction was never accomplished in that external restoration of the people, or during the commencement of it, and even that the temple which was afterwards erected was far inferior to the former. It follows, therefore, that the Prophet, to whom a full redemption was exhibited in spirit, not only relates what shall happen immediately after the return of the people, but discourses concerning the excellence of the spiritual temple; that is, of the Church of Christ. We must, therefore, come down in uninterrupted succession to Christ, if we wish to understand this prophecy.[129]

In his commentary on Isaiah 66:10ff. ("Rejoice with Jerusalem, and be glad for her, all you who love her; . . . I will extend prosperity to her like a river, and the wealth of the nations like an overflowing stream") he explains his principle for treating prophecies of restoration: "We ought to abide by the general rule, of which we have often spoken already, namely, that those promises must be extended [*extendendas esse*] from the return of the people down to the reign of Christ, and to the full perfection of that reign."[130] He understands Ezekiel 17:22 ("I myself will take a sprig from the lofty top of the cedar, and will set it out; I will break off from the topmost of its young twigs a tender one, and I myself will plant it upon a high and lofty mountain") to be a prophecy of the reign of Christ. He explains: "When, therefore, the reign of Christ is treated, we must date its commencement from the period of the building of the temple after the people's return from their seventy years' captivity: and then we shall take its boundary, not at the Ascension of Christ, not yet in the first or second centuries, but through the whole progress of his kingdom, until he shall appear at the last day."[131] In his comments on Zephaniah 3:16–17 ("On that day it shall be said to Jerusalem: 'Do not fear, O Zion; let not your hands grow weak. The LORD, your God, is in your midst, a warrior who gives victory; he will rejoice over you with gladness, he will renew you in his love; he will exult over you with loud singing' ") he writes: "We must ever bear in mind what I have already stated—that it is not one year, or a few years, which are intended, when the prophets speak of future redemption; for the time which is now mentioned began when the people were restored from the Babylonian captivity, and continues its course to the final advent of Christ."[132]

Calvin's clearest explanation of why God might have his prophets speak in such a manner is found in his commentary on Isaiah 54:1 ("Sing, O barren one, who did not bear; break forth into singing and cry aloud, you who have not been in travail! For the children of the desolate one will be more than the children of her that is married, says the LORD"). Some Christian interpreters, he notes, believe the passage speaks of the church. Such interpreters are mistaken and "only succeed in increasing the obstinacy of the Jews, who perceive that the Prophet's meaning is twisted." In articulating his own position Calvin explains that the Old Testament period was the youth of the church and the period since Christ's advent is the adulthood. Only when this analogy is recognized is it possible to fully understand the prophets.

> This prophecy began to be fulfilled under Cyrus, who gave the people liberty to return, and afterwards extended to Christ in whom it has its full accomplishment. The church therefore conceived, when the people returned to their native country; for the body of the people was gathered together from which Christ should proceed, in order that the pure worship of God and true religion might again be revived. Hitherto, indeed, this fertility was not visible, for the conception was concealed, as

it were, in the mother's womb, and no outward appearance of it could be seen; but afterwards the people were increased, and after the birth the church grew from infancy to manhood, till the gospel was preached. This was the actual youth of the church; and next follows the age of manhood, down to Christ's last coming, when all things shall be fully accomplished.

All these things must be taken together if we wish to learn the prophet's genuine meaning [*genuinum prophetae sensum*].[133]

Calvin believes his views can be justified against the traditional interpretations of Jews and Christians. The rationale he offers for rejecting traditional Christian exegesis is grounded in his historical sensitivity. He rejects Christian interpretations that ignore the historical meaning of the text. In his commentary on Jeremiah 32:41 ("I will plant them in this land in faithfulness") he explains that prophecies belong first to the time in which they were given. "When Christians explain this passage and the like, they leave out the liberation of the people from Babylonian exile, as though these prophecies did not belong at all to that time; in this they are mistaken."[134] In his interpretation of Jeremiah 50:5 ("They shall ask the way to Zion, with faces turned toward it, saying, 'Come, let us join ourselves to the LORD in an everlasting covenant which will never be forgotten' ") Calvin does not follow Christian exegetes because the words need to be taken literally—"that God would never forget his covenant, so as to retain the Jews in the possession of the land." He contrasts his own view with the "allegorical" view, which does not allow for any fulfillment in Old Testament times. Yet he insists that the language must also be understood spiritually. The Jews had never received the favor of God to the degree described in this passage. Whenever the prophets spoke of the return of the people they referred not just to the return from Babylon; they also spoke of "the chief deliverance." While it is true that the passage does indicate that God will favor the Jews by putting them back in their land, "this would have been a very small thing had not Christ come to bring real happiness."[135] The fact that the Jews were suffering in the land suggests that the promise was not fulfilled then, yet their return to the land should be understood as the beginning of the fulfillment.

Calvin finds Christian interpreters of Micah 4 ("Arise and thresh, O daughter of Zion, for I will make your horn iron and your hoofs bronze; you shall beat in pieces many peoples, and shall devote their gain to the LORD, their wealth to the Lord of the whole earth") to be guilty of engaging in unnecessary allegorization—they again fail to see that the fulfillment of prophecies of the kingdom of Christ begins with the return of the Jews from foreign exile.[136] In his comments on Micah 7 ("The nations shall see and be ashamed of all their might; they shall lay their hands on their mouths; their ears shall be deaf; they shall lick the dust like a serpent, like the crawling things of the earth; they shall come trembling out of their strongholds, they shall turn in dread to the LORD our God, and they shall fear because of thee") he allows an interpretation that sees fulfillment taking place in the preaching of the gospel, but cautions that "deliverance must always be made to begin with the ancient people. For if anyone would have this to be understood exclusively of Christ, such a strained and remote exposition [*tam coacta et remota expositio*] would not be suitable."[137] Calvin rejects "exclusively" christological interpretations because they fail to grasp the historical meaning of the Old Testament text. The Old Testament must be interpreted historically because the prophets had their eyes on the Jews of that day so that they might give them hope in their difficult circumstances. The texts must be understood as partly fulfilled in Old Testament times when God freed the Jews from the domination of foreign despots, giving them a foretaste of the blessing that was to come in Jesus Christ.[138]

Calvin sharply rebukes some Christian interpreters in his interpretation of Jeremiah 31 ("Thus says the LORD of hosts, the God of Israel: 'Once more they shall use these words in the land of Judah and in its cities, when I restore their fortunes: 'The LORD bless you, O habitation of righteousness, O holy hill!' And Judah and all its cities shall dwell there together, and the farmers and those who wander with their flocks"). These interpreters fly into allegories without understanding what the prophecies would have meant to the people to whom they were originally delivered:

> Now, were anyone to ask, when was this fulfilled? We must bear in mind what has been said elsewhere—that the prophets, when speaking of the restoration of the Church, included the whole kingdom of Christ from the beginning to the end. And in this our divines go astray, so that by confining these promises to some particular time, they are compelled to fly to allegories, and thus they twist [*torquere*] and even pervert all the prophecies. But the prophets, as it has been said, include the whole progress of Christ's kingdom when they speak of the future redemption of the people. The people began to do well when they returned to their own country, but soon after distresses came as Daniel had predicted. It was, therefore, necessary for them to look for the coming of Christ. We now taste of these benefits of God as long as we are in the world. We hence see that these prophecies are not accomplished in one day, or in one year, no, not even in one age, but ought to be understood as referring to the beginning and the end of Christ's kingdom.[139]

Usually Calvin's defense of his exegesis of prophecy is aimed at refuting Jewish interpretations. In his commentary on Jeremiah 49:2 ("Therefore, behold, the days are coming, says the LORD, when I will cause the battle cry to be heard against Rabbah of the Ammonites; it shall become a desolate mound, and its villages shall be burned with fire; then

Israel shall dispossess those who dispossessed him, says the LORD") he justifies his "both/and" approach by arguing that the language of the prophecy cannot conceivably be regarded as having been fulfilled under the Old Testament kings.

> It may be asked, when was this prophecy fulfilled? God, indeed, under David, gave some indication of their future subjection, but Israel never possessed that land. Indeed, from that time Ammon had not been brought low until after the overthrow of Israel. It then follows that what Jeremiah predicted here was not fully accomplished except under the kingdom of Christ. David humbled that nation because he had received a great indignity from the king of Ammon, and he took also Rabbah, as it is evident from sacred history. He was yet satisfied with making the people tributary. From that time they not only shook off the yoke, but exercised authority within the borders of Israel; and that the Israelites had recovered what they had lost, we nowhere read. Then Israel began to possess power over the Ammonites when the kingdom of Christ was established; by which all heathen nations were not only brought into subjection and under the yoke, but all unworthy of mercy were also reduced to nothing.[140]

Concerning verse 6 of the same chapter ("But afterward I will restore the fortunes of the Ammonites, says the LORD") Calvin argues that the prophecy must refer to Christ because the calling of the Gentiles did not occur until Christ came.[141]

In his interpretation of Isaiah 60:21 ("Your people shall all be righteous; they shall possess the land forever") he again argues against the Jews that the language of the text was not fulfilled in Old Testament times—at least not perfectly. A later fulfillment is demanded. "This was not in every respect fulfilled in the Jews, but a beginning was made in them, when they were restored to their native country, that, by their agency, the possession of the whole earth might afterwards be given to them, that is, to the children of God."[142] Calvin finds the Jewish interpretation of Jeremiah 50:5 ("They shall ask the way to Zion, with faces turned toward it, saying, 'Come, let us join ourselves to the LORD in an everlasting covenant which will never be forgotten'") to be inadequate because "this would have been a very small thing, had not Christ come forth, in whom is found the real perpetuity of the covenant, because God's covenant cannot be separated from a state of happiness; for blessed are the people, as the Psalmist says, to whom God shows himself to be their God." Since the Jews were miserable rather than happy, it is evident that the fulfillment was not conspicuously present. "We must therefore come necessarily to Christ."[143]

So it is clear that in his treatment of allegory, typology, and prophecy in the Old Testament, Calvin adopts a moderate position in which he believes he has avoided the temptations that too often befell Jewish and Christian exegesis. He has not uprooted the Old Testament from its historical soil nor has he been content to look at the roots once the full flowering has taken place in Jesus Christ. He uses the New Testament interpretation of the Old to establish the meaning of the Old Testament text. Yet even if he could not find confirmation in the New Testament, he believes he can demonstrate through clear philological and historical reasoning that his interpretation is correct—and even necessary.

NOTES

1. Origen, *On First Principles*, trans. G. W. Butterworth (Gloucester, Mass.: Peter Smith, 1973), IV.2, 280.

2. Theodore of Mopsuestia, "Commentary on Galatians 4:22–31," in *Biblical Interpretation in the Early Church*, trans. and ed. Karlfried Froehlich, Sources of Early Christian Thought (Philadelphia: Fortress Press, 1984), 96. Frances Young has argued that a key to understanding the differences between Antiochene and Alexandrian exegesis is the training in rhetoric received by the Antiochenes ("The Rhetorical Schools and Their Influence on Patristic Exegesis," in *The Making of Orthodoxy*, ed. Rowan Williams [Cambridge: Cambridge University Press, 1989], 196).

3. Comm. Dan. 10:6 (C.O. 41.199).

4. Rowan A. Greer, *Theodore of Mopsuestia: Exegete and Theologian* (London: Faith Press, 1961), 94–95. Christian use of allegorical interpretation has in the past sometimes been viewed as finding its intellectual roots in Philo of Alexandria and later Clement and Origen, but in fact, it was already in use in the interpretation of pagan literature. Discussions of the early history of allegorical interpretation may be found in R. M. Grant, *The Letter and the Spirit* (London: SPCK, 1957); R.P.C. Hanson, *Allegory and Event: A Study of the Sources and Significance of Origen's Interpretation of Scripture* (Richmond: John Knox Press, 1959); M. J. Pépin, *Mythe et allégorie: Les origines grecques et les contestations judéo-chrétiennes*, rev. ed. (Paris, 1976).

5. Walther Eichrodt, "Is Typological Exegesis an Appropriate Method?" in *Essays in Old Testament Hermeneutics*, ed. Claus Westermann (Richmond: John Knox Press, 1963), 227. Barr has challenged the use of history as a criterion to make a clear and absolute distinction between typology and allegory: "The idea that allegory is definitely and ineluctably antihistorical does not seem to me to be true. It depends on the choice of examples." See James Barr, *Old and New in Interpretation: A Study of the Two Testaments* (London: SCM Press, 1982), 104, 105. Paul K. Jewett has also questioned the sharp distinction often drawn between allegory and typology ("Concerning the Allegorical Interpretation of Scripture," *Westminster Theological Journal* 17 [1954–55]: 1–20).

6. Torjesen effectively demonstrates that the allegorical approach of Origen was deeply rooted in his practical piety, and thus cannot be rejected on the basis that it is primarily a speculative exercise. Karen Jo Torjesen, "Hermeneutical Procedure and Theological Structure in Origen's Exegesis" (Ph.D. diss., Clare-

mont School of Theology, 1982); see also her essay " 'Body,' 'Soul,' and 'Spirit' in Origen's Theory of Exegesis," *Anglican Theological Review* 67 (January 1985): 17–31; Allan E. Johnson, "The Methods and Presuppositions of Patristic Exegesis in the Formation of Christian Personality," *Dialog* 16 (1977): 186–90.

7. Comm. Lev. 1:1 (C.O. 24.506).

8. Comm. Gen. 21:12 (C.O. 23.302).

9. Comm. 2 Cor. 3:6 (C.O. 49.40–41).

10. Comm. Gen. 2:8 (C.O. 23.37).

11. Comm. Gal. 4:22 (C.O. 50.236).

12. Comm. Gen. 1:6 (C.O. 23.18); 3:1 (C.O. 23.54); 3:14 (C.O. 23.68); 3:23 (C.O. 23.80); 49:1 (C.O. 23.590); 49:11 (C.O. 23.603); Comm. Ex. 17:10 (C.O. 24.180); 20:24 (C.O. 24.397); 31:18 (C.O. 25.80); Comm. Lev. 3:16 (C.O. 24.514); 11:9 (C.O. 24.349); Comm. Num. 17:8 (C.O. 25.231); Comm. Ps. 12:8 (C.O. 31.131); 22:1 (C.O. 31.219); 27:10 (C.O. 31.277); 36:6 (C.O. 31.362); 38:8 (C.O. 31.389–90); 74:11 (C.O. 31.696); 132:6 (C.O. 32.344); Comm. Isa. 13:12 (C.O. 36.264); 29:18 (C.O. 36.498); 42:16 (C.O. 37.70); 55:13 (C.O. 37.292–93); 66:20 (C.O. 37.452); Comm. Jer. 16:16 (C.O. 38.251); Comm. Ezek. 5:9–10 (C.O. 40.126); Comm. Hos. 1:8–9 (C.O. 42.215); 3:2–5 (C.O. 42.259); 4:12 (C.O. 42.282); Comm. Joel 3:7 (C.O. 42.588); Comm. Zech. 9:16 (C.O. 44.283); 10:2 (C.O. 44.287); 14:4 (C.O. 44.365); Comm. Mal. 2:12 (C.O. 44.449).

13. Comm. Gen. 6:14 (C.O. 23.123). What Calvin calls allegorical interpretation may be better categorized as typology.

14. Comm. Gen. 15:4 (C.O. 23.210).

15. Comm. Dan. 7:9 (C.O. 41.121).

16. Comm. Deut. 12:4 (C.O. 24.391).

17. Comm. Dan. 8:24–25 (C.O. 41.121).

18. Comm. Ex. 3:4 (C.O. 24.37).

19. Comm. Ezek. 16:10–13 (C.O. 40.343).

20. Comm. Hab. 3:10 (C.O. 43.577–78). He notes that the context is against the allegorical interpretation. Elsewhere he notes that allegorists seek to find meaning in small units and fail to interpret them in light of the larger context. They attempt to give "an ingenious exposition of every clause." Comm. Isa. 5:2 (C.O. 36.104). Barr argues that "de-contextualization" is one of the defining characteristics of the allegorical approach of the early church. "Ancient and mediaeval allegory is, in very large measure, de-contextualizing, and in two ways: firstly, in that it works from very small pieces of the text (as when each of Jacob's wives has an allegorical sense, but there isn't an allegorical sense for the passage as a whole) and interprets them in ways that are irreconcilable with the context within the books; secondly, that it uproots them from the culture in which they have meaning." Such an approach, he argues, has no validity. "All valid understanding of a passage as having allegorical features must depend on contextual considerations within the linguistic semantics, the literary context, the cultural background and the historical setting." James Barr, "The Literal, the Allegorical, and Modern Biblical Scholarship," *Journal for the Study of the Old Testament* 44 (1989): 14.

21. Comm. Zech. 6:1–3 (C.O. 44.202). Parker appears to be correct in observing that Calvin's "attacks on 'allegory' are directed against an over-elaborated use of allegory in its general sense of extended metaphor as well as against an allegorical interpretation imposed arbitrarily on a passage." T.H.L. Parker, *Calvin's Old Testament Commentaries* (Edinburgh: T. & T. Clark, 1986), 70.

22. Comm. Gal. 4:22 (C.O. 50.236).

23. Ibid.

24. See discussion in Alexandre Ganoczy and Stefan Scheld, *Die Hermeneutik Calvins: Geistesgeschichtliche Voraussetzungen und Grundzüge*, Veröffentlichungen des Instituts für Europäische Geschichte Mainz, Abteilung für Abendländische Religionsgeschichte, no. 114 (Wiesbaden: Franz Steiner Verlag, 1983), 157–59.

25. Comm. Ps. 19:4 (C.O. 31.198).

26. Comm. Rom. 10:18 (C.O. 48.207).

27. Comm. Ps. 104:4 (C.O. 32.86).

28. Comm. Jer. 31:15, 16 (C.O. 38.665).

29. Comm. Dan. 4:10–16 (C.O. 40.657). For Calvin's recognition of allegory as extended metaphor in the Old Testament, see also Comm. Isa. 9:15 (C.O. 36.204); 16:8 (C.O. 36.308); 22:22 (C.O. 36.382); 27:1 (C.O. 36.448); 44:27 (C.O. 37.125); 65:25 (C.O. 37.434); Comm. Ezek. 17:4 (C.O. 40.404); Comm. Dan. 7:7 (C.O. 41.47); Comm. Hos. 4:13–14 (C.O. 42.286).

30. Comm. Isa. 30:25 (C.O. 36.525).

31. Comm. Jer. 31:38–40 (C.O. 38.704).

32. Comm. Amos 9:15 (C.O. 43.176).

33. Comm. Zech. 14:8 (C.O. 44.375).

34. Comm. Joel 2:30–31 (C.O. 42.571).

35. Comm. Isa. 11:4 (C.O. 36.240).

36. Comm. Isa. 11:6 (C.O. 36.242).

37. Comm. Isa. 11:8 (C.O. 36.243).

38. Comm. Amos 9:15 (C.O. 43.176).

39. Comm. Ezek. 17:1–2 (C.O. 40.403).

40. Comm. Ezek. 17:11–16 (C.O. 40.408).

41. Comm. Ezek. 17:1–2 (C.O. 40.403).

42. Comm. Isa. 32:19 (C.O. 36.554).

43. Comm. Jer. 33:15 (C.O. 39.67).

44. Comm. Amos 9:15 (C.O. 43.176).

45. Comm. Isa. 1:19 (C.O. 36.47–48).

46. Comm. Dan. 7:27 (C.O. 41.82).

47. Comm. Isa. 55:13 (C.O. 37.292).

48. Comm. Isa. 33:17 (C.O. 36.572).

49. Comm. Ex. 20:8. See also Comm. Jer. 11:19 (C.O. 38.124).

50. Richard M. Davidson provides a concise, well documented survey of the history of typological interpretation in *Typology in Scripture: A Study of Hermeneutical ΤΥΠΟΣ Structures*, Andrews University Seminary Doctoral Dissertation Series, no. 2 (Berrien Springs, Mich.: Andrews University Press, 1981), 15–45. For the use of typology in the early church, see Jean Daniélou, *From Shadows to Reality: Studies in the Biblical Typology of the Fathers*, trans. Wulstan Hibberd (Westminster, Md.: Newman Press, 1960).

51. Francis Foulkes, *The Acts of God: A Study of the Basis of Typology in the Old Testament*, Tyndale Old Testament Lecture for 1955 (London: Tyndale Press, n.d.), 35–40.

52. Eichrodt, "Is Typological Exegesis an Appropriate Method?" 245.

53. G.W.H. Lampe, "The Reasonableness of Typology," in *Essays on Typology*, ed. G.W.H. Lampe and K. J. Woollcombe (Naperville, Ill.: Alec R. Allenson, 1957), 29.

54. Hans Frei, *The Eclipse of Biblical Narrative: A Study of Eighteenth and*

Nineteenth Century Hermeneutics (New Haven, Conn.: Yale University Press, 1974), 2.

55. Thomas M. Davis, "The Traditions of Puritan Typology," in *Typology and Early American Literature*, ed. Sacvan Berkovich (Amherst, Mass.: University of Massachusetts Press, 1972), 38.

56. Jackson Forstman, *Word and Spirit: Calvin's Doctrine of Biblical Authority* (Stanford, Calif.: Stanford University Press, 1962), 106.

57. Kemper Fullerton, *Prophecy and Authority: A Study in the History of the Doctrine and Interpretation of Scripture* (New York: Macmillan, 1919), 135.

58. Basil Hall, "Biblical Scholarship: Editions and Commentaries," in *The Cambridge History of the Bible*, vol. 3: *The West from the Reformation to the Present Day*, ed. S. L. Greenslade (Cambridge: Cambridge University Press, 1963), 88. Hall defends Calvin against this charge, arguing that his use of typology was sparing compared to that of others in his day—including Hunnius.

59. Davidson cautions that contemporary biblical typology should not be confused with the typology of earlier generations. While typological exegesis has experienced a revival in the Biblical Theology movement in the twentieth century, the modern understanding, which "describes typology in terms of historical *correspondences* retrospectively recognized within the consistent redemptive activity of God," is actually different than the typological interpretation of earlier writers, which "views typology in terms of divinely preordained and predictive *prefigurations.*" According to the older view, "God not only acts consistently but also has ordained and superintended specific persons/events/institutions to mutely predict the coming of Christ." The typical element is "already to be found within the context of the historical root event." According to the contemporary view, persons/events/institutions are only seen to be typical "in retrospect after the appearance of the antitype." Davidson, *Typology in Scripture*, 94–97. Calvin, not surprisingly, held the view of typology as predictive prophecy. In his exposition of Psalm 2 he insists that David prophesied concerning Christ—he knew his kingdom was merely a shadow of the future kingdom. If we carefully consider the nature of the kingdom we will see that it would be absurd to overlook the end and rest on the shadow only. Comm. Ps. 2: 1–3 (C.O. 31.42–43). See also Comm. Ps. 21:3 (C.O. 31.213); 22:1 (C.O. 31.219); 84:9 (C.O. 31.783); 89:18 (C.O. 31.817).

60. This view of the predictive nature of Old Testament ceremonies was opposed by Michael Servetus. See Jerome Friedman, "Servetus and the Psalms: The Exegesis of Heresy," in *Histoire de l'exégèse au XVIe siècle*, ed. Olivier Fatio and Pierre Fraenkel, Etudes de Philologie et d'Histoire, no. 34 (Geneva: Librairie Droz, 1978), 170.

61. Comm. Ps. 18:50 (C.O. 31.194).

62. *Inst.* II.vii.1 (O.S. 3.326–27).

63. Comm. Jer. 17:22 (C.O. 38.287).

64. Comm. Ex. 12:5 (C.O. 24.288).

65. Comm. Ex. 12:21 (C.O. 24.136).

66. Comm. Ex. 28:1ff. (C.O. 24.426).

67. Comm. Ex. 28:31 (C.O. 24.431–32).

68. Comm. Ex. 26:1 (C.O. 24.415).

69. Comm. Jer. 33:17 (C.O. 38.70).

70. Comm. Isa. 16:5 (C.O. 36.304).

71. Comm. Lam. 4:20 (C.O. 39.624).

72. Comm. Gen. 37:2 (C.O. 23.482). Calvin believes that careful attention to the context will prove his typological approach to be correct.

73. Comm. Num. 3:5 (C.O. 24.444).

74. Comm. Num. 6:2 (C.O. 24.304).

75. Comm. Zech. 3:6–7 (C.O. 44.174).

76. Comm. Hag. 2:20–23 (C.O. 44.122).

77. Comm. Isa. 60:10 (C.O. 37.361).

78. Comm. Ps. 122:4 (C.O. 32.305).

79. Comm. Ps. 72, pref. (C.O. 31.664).

80. Russell argues that a great deal of subjectivity is present in Calvin's approach to the Psalms. In his defense of typological exegesis Calvin succumbs to one of the chief pitfalls of typological exegesis: the temptation to account for discrepancies in description of type and antitype through the necessity of maintaining the difference between promise and fulfillment. This forces him to defend his typological exegesis through two contrary arguments: (a) the similarity of language and function between two realities shows they are related; (b) dissimilarity in language and function between two realities shows that one is superior in comparison to the other. S. H. Russell, "Calvin and the Messianic Interpretation of the Psalms," *Scottish Journal of Theology* 21 (1968): 42–43.

81. Bucer seems to have relied on the same arguments. See R. Gerald Hobbs, "How Firm a Foundation: Martin Bucer's Historical Exegesis of the Psalms," *Church History* 53 (December 1984): 489.

82. Comm. Ps. 110:1 (C.O. 32.160).

83. Comm. Ex. 20:8 (C.O. 24.577); Comm. Ps. 68:19 (C.O. 31.628); Comm. Jer. 17:22 (C.O. 38.287).

84. Comm. Ex. 20:8 (C.O. 24.577); 26:1 (C.O. 24.415).

85. Comm. Ps. 47:1 (C.O. 31.466).

86. Comm. Isa. 16:5 (C.O. 36.304).

87. Comm. Isa. 33:6 (C.O. 37.563).

88. Comm. Isa. 33:17 (C.O. 37.572).

89. Comm. Ex. 28:1–43 (C.O. 24.426).

90. Comm. Jer. 33:17, 18 (C.O. 38.70).

91. Comm. Ex. 12:21 (C.O. 24.136).

92. Comm. Ex. 29:38–46 (C.O. 24.489).

93. Comm. Ps. 40:7 (C.O. 31.410–11).

94. Comm. Ps. 45:1 (C.O. 31.449).

95. Comm. Ps. 72:1 (C.O. 31.664).

96. Comm. Isa. 61:1 (C.O. 37.371).

97. Comm. Ps. 109:6 (C.O. 32.148); Comm. Isa. 50:4 (C.O. 37.218).

98. Frei argues that "the reason for Calvin's confidence in the harmony of grammatical and pervasive Christological interpretation is his unquestioned assumption of a natural coherence between literal and figural reading, and the need of each for supplementation by the other." Calvin's "application of figural interpretation never lost its connection with literal reading of individual texts." Frei, *Eclipse of Biblical Narrative*, 27–31.

99. Comm. Ps. 2, pref. (C.O. 31.41).

100. Comm. Ps. 2:1–3 (C.O. 31.43).

101. Comm. Ps. 2:6 (C.O. 31.45).

102. Comm. Ps. 2:7 (C.O. 31.46). Ps. 2:7 had been used as a proof of the eternal

generation of the Son since the time of Origen. Calvin rejects this interpretation, arguing that Paul, "a more faithful and a better qualified interpreter of this prophecy," in Acts 13:33 relates this text to the time of the manifestation of the glory of Christ to men. In adopting this view Calvin maintains that these words have reference to David as well. Here Calvin uses the New Testament writer as an authoritative interpreter of the Old Testament, not against Jews, but against other Christian interpreters.

103. Comm. Ps. 2:8 (C.O. 31.47).

104. Comm. Ps. 2:9 (C.O. 31.48).

105. The typology of David and Christ is examined by Gilbert Vincent in "Calvin, commentateur du Psaume XXII," *Bulletin du Centre Protestant d'Etudes et de Documentation* 293 (July-August 1984): 32–52.

106. Comm. Ps. 22, pref. (C.O. 31.219).

107. Ibid.

108. Comm. Ps. 22:22 (C.O. 31.231).

109. See the discussion of what Calvin believes is a textual problem of this text, in "Criticism of Jewish Exegesis" in chapter 4.

110. Comm. Ps. 22:22 (C.O. 31.231).

111. Comm. Ps. 22:17 (C.O. 31.229).

112. Comm. Ps. 89:27–28 (C.O. 31.820–21).

113. Comm. Ps. 89:29–30 (C.O. 31.821).

114. Comm. Ps. 89:31 (C.O. 31.822).

115. Comm. Ps. 89, pref. (C.O. 31.811); 89:6 (C.O. 31.814); 89:7 (C.O. 31.814).

116. Comm. Ps. 110, pref. (C.O. 32.159–60).

117. Comm. Ps. 110:2 (C.O. 32.162).

118. Comm. Ps. 110, pref. (C.O. 32.159).

119. Rowan A. Greer, *Theodore of Mopsuestia: Exegete and Theologian* (London: Faith Press, 1961), 95.

120. James Samuel Preus, *From Shadow to Promise: Old Testament Interpretation from Augustine to the Young Luther* (Cambridge, Mass.: Belknap Press, 1969), 164.

121. Comm. Isa. 59:19 (C.O. 37.350).

122. Comm. Isa. 43: 19 (C.O. 37.94).

123. Calvin finds an extended fulfillment including an incomplete historical fulfillment near the time of the prophet and a later complete fulfillment in Jesus Christ in the following texts: Comm. Ex. 23:31 (C.O. 24.254–55); Comm. Num. 24:20 (C.O. 25.294); 61:6 (C.O. 31.583); 72:8 (C.O. 31.668); 102:22 (C.O. 32.71); Comm. Isa. 9:6 (C.O. 36.195); 11:13–14 (C.O. 36.248); 14:1 (C.O. 36.273); 14:25 (C.O. 36.288); 40:1 (C.O. 37.4); 41:19 (C.O. 37.48); 43:8 (C.O. 37.85–86); 46:1 (C.O. 37.153); 49:9–12 (C.O. 37.201–3); 49:19 (C.O. 37.207); 58:12 (C.O. 37.333); 60:10 (C.O. 37.361); 60:17 (C.O. 37.366); 60:21 (C.O. 37.368); 61:9 (C.O. 37.379); 62:11 (C.O. 37.390); 66:10 (C.O. 37.445); Comm. Jer. 3:17–18 (C.O. 37.566); 50:20 (C.O. 39.413); 50:39 (C.O. 39.429); Comm. Dan. 7:27 (C.O. 41.82–83); Comm. Micah 5:5 (C.O. 43.373); 7:12 (C.O. 43.421); Comm. Zeph. 3:10 (C.O. 44.62); 3:16–17 (C.O. 44.73); Comm. Zech. 3:10 (C.O. 44.180); 10:4 (C.O. 44.290–91); 14:13 (C.O. 44.380).

124. Comm. Isa. 52:10 (C.O. 37.249–50).

125. Comm. Joel 3:1–3 (C.O. 42.581).

126. Comm. Jer. 32:36, 37 (C.O. 39.37).

127. Comm. Jer. 32:41 (C.O. 39.45–46).

128. Comm. Isa. 26:19 (C.O. 36.442).

129. Comm. Isa. 60:15, 17 (C.O. 37.365).
130. Comm. Isa. 66:10 (C.O. 37.445).
131. Comm. Ezek. 17:22 (C.O. 40.417).
132. Comm. Zeph. 3:16–17 (C.O. 44.73).
133. Comm. Isa. 54:2 (C.O. 37.270).
134. Comm. Jer. 32:41 (C.O. 39.45–46).
135. Comm. Jer. 50:5 (C.O. 39.397).
136. Comm. Micah 4:11–13 (C.O. 43.362).
137. Comm. Micah 7:16–17 (C.O. 43.426).
138. Comm. Isa. 35:1 (C.O. 36.590).
139. Comm. Jer. 31:24 (C.O. 38.682).
140. Comm. Jer. 49:2 (C.O. 39.349).
141. Comm. Jer. 49:6 (C.O. 39.352).
142. Comm. Isa. 60:21 (C.O. 37.369).
143. Comm. Jer. 50:5 (C.O. 39.397). Calvin indicates in the following commentaries that the language of the prophets was not fulfilled in Old Testament times: Comm. Ps. 68:31 (C.O. 31.635); Comm. Isa. 11:11 (C.O. 36.246); 61:9 (C.O. 37.379); Comm. Jer. 32:36–37 (C.O. 39.36–37); 49:2–6 (C.O. 39.348–52); 50:3–5 (C.O. 39.392–97); Comm. Hos. 3:2–5 (C.O. 42.263); Comm. Amos 9:11 (C.O. 43.171); Comm. Obad. 19–20 (C.O. 43.198–200); Comm. Micah 5:9 (C.O. 43.398).

6

CONCLUSION

From the perspective of late-twentieth-century efforts toward Jewish-Christian dialogue Calvin could hardly be considered a friend of the Jewish people—much less a Judaizer. While his criticisms of Jews are perhaps not as harsh as Luther's diatribes, they are still quite severe. However, in the view of one of his sixteenth-century contemporaries, Aegidius Hunnius, Calvin made too many concessions to the Jews in his interpretation of scripture. He adopted interpretations of the Old Testament that did not offer the strongest direct support for Christian doctrines; he criticized Christian exegetes for twisting the meaning of the Old Testament away from its natural sense; he offered positive evaluations of Jewish exegesis; he admited that Jewish criticism of Christian interpretations was often valid. His approach thus appeared to be too much like that of the Jews.

Calvin's Jewish contemporaries, however, would have viewed the matter quite differently. To them his exegesis would have been virtually indistinguishable from that of other Christians. After all, he accused Jewish interpreters of blindness because they failed to find Jesus Christ in the Old Testament; he argued that the Old Testament contained direct prophecies that were fulfilled only in Jesus Christ; he argued that the priestly and kingly offices and the entire Old Testament cult existed to proclaim Christ. What could be more traditionally Christian than these views?

Battles has suggested that Calvin's attempt to find a middle way between opposing extremes is a prominent feature of the structure of his theology.[1] This study would support the thesis that Battles's observation may be extended from Calvin's theology (as expressed in his *Institutes*) to his exegesis (as expressed in his Old Testament commentaries), where the structural principle of the adoption of a middle way between what he regards as unacceptable extremes is still present.

Calvin unquestionably would have placed himself on the Christian end of any Jewish–Christian exegetical continuum. He was, however, troubled by the readiness of many of his fellow Christians to disregard literary and historical context in reading Christian teaching too directly into many Old Testament passages. In his method of exegetical reasoning, his desire to harmonize Old and New Testaments and his insistence on interpreting the biblical text in its most natural way contextually do not always coexist comfortably—but they do always coexist.

Scholars have long noted the tension in Calvin's approach to biblical interpretation between a traditional Christian approach that emphasizes the divine side of scripture and its unity and a more modern, critical approach that recognizes the human element and diversity to be found in scripture. Several of the writers I surveyed in chapter one of this study were particularly concerned with this tension. Kraeling and Forstman each concluded that Calvin's exegesis was governed by his theological commitment to the inspiration and unity of scripture. Thus his exegesis is viewed as more traditional than modern. Kraeling is too one-sided in his insistence that Calvin "Christianized the Old Testament."[2] Forstman is not as one-sided, yet his view too has problems. First, if, as he argues, the "natural meaning" that Calvin seeks is simply the one that upholds the unity of scripture, why did Calvin frequently label Christian interpretations that seem to be doing just that as "unnatural" or "violent"? Second, if the goal of his exegesis was simply to determine the meaning that does justice to the unity of scripture, why was his exegesis not appreciated by Hunnius, who desperately wanted to uphold the same?[3] Fullerton insists Calvin is much more modern than either Kraeling or Forstman believes. But he leans too far in the other direction in his insistence that for Calvin "the exegetical interest is convincingly demonstrated to be superior to the dogmatic."[4] Dowey seems to offer a more balanced perspective in suggesting that the tension in Calvin's approach is best left unresolved by scholars since Calvin left it unresolved. He finds in Calvin "an incomplete assimilation of a traditional doctrine with the new manner of approaching the text."[5]

The tension that all of these scholars have recognized in Calvin's exegesis may in part result from an untidiness in his exegetical presuppositions. Scripture has a divine side; it also has a human side. The Holy Spirit is the author of scripture; the human writer is also its author. The Holy Spirit chooses the words of scripture; the style of scripture is the style of the human writer. The interpreter must understand the Holy Spirit's intention; he must understand the human author's intention. Calvin affirms all of these propositions. He does not defend them. He does not explain how all of them can be true. He does not try to reconcile them. He holds them in tension. He is unwilling to be pulled too far in either direction. The divine side of scripture is a matter of faith—scripture is the Word of God. The human side is a matter of evidence—human hands have left their marks on scripture. Calvin's recognition of such tensions could hardly have failed to influence his exegesis.

Less tension is present in Calvin's view of the relation of Old and New Testaments—but it is present. The Old and New Testaments are one in substance; they proclaim the same message. Against the Jews (and to a lesser extent the Anabaptists) he insists that Christ is the true substance of the Old Testament. He does not, however, deny that Old and New Testament economies have their differences. While there is certainly nothing contradictory in Calvin's twin affirmations of the unity and diversity of scripture, the exegetical implications are potentially quite large. If his emphasis on biblical unity dominates his exegesis, we might expect to find him affirming traditional christological interpretations of the Old Testament. Calvin does concede that christological interpretations are useful and spiritually edifying, yet he sometimes rejects them when he believes that in arriving at them Christian exegetes have been guilty of ignoring the historical meaning.

Corresponding to Calvin's appreciation of the human side of scripture and the differences between the Old and New Testament economies is his insistence on historical exegesis. Corresponding to his recognition of the divine side of scripture and the unity of scripture is his insistence that the New Testament is a reliable guide to the interpretation of the Old Testament. Who better to interpret scripture than the one who authored scripture? Calvin believes that the Old Testament must be interpreted historically, yet he argues that Old Testament interpretation must be informed by the New Testament. He believes Christians may and should use the work of Jewish exegetes, yet argues that Christians must beware of malicious twisting of scripture by the Jews. The New Testament writers, he insists, were reliable interpreters of the Old Testament; yet he is compelled to admit that they sometimes appear to twist the Old Testament away from its historical meaning. In such cases, he may argue either that the New Testament writer's apparently strained interpretation is actually the true meaning of the Old Testament text or he may argue that it was not the purpose of the New Testament writer to explain the meaning of the Old Testament text. Calvin believes the New Testament, properly understood, is not—and cannot be—at odds with the true meaning of the Old Testament.

The tension present in Calvin's method is evident in his view of allegorical interpretation. He rejects Origen's speculative allegorical method because it has no solid basis. However, there really is allegory in the Old Testament. Calvin insists that his own limited use of allegorical interpretation is justifiable through philological and historical reasoning and is verified by the New Testament. His treatment of typology reflects the same tension. He justifies his typological exegesis by appealing to the use of the Old Testament by the New Testament writers, yet he believes it important to point out that he can prove the validity—even the necessity—of his interpretations apart from such confirmation. His arguments for the "extended" fulfillment of Old Testament prophecies provide some of the clearest examples of his attempt to interpret the Old Testament in a way that harmonizes his belief in the unity of scripture with his commitment to contextual interpretation. Against Jewish interpreters he argues that much of the language used by the Old Testament writers cannot possibly be understood as having been fulfilled in Old Testament times. Therefore, it must be fulfilled in Jesus Christ. Against Christian exegetes he believes he must insist on at least a partial fulfillment in Old Testament times. The text must have meaning for the people to whom it was originally delivered.

Calvin certainly feels the tug of the New Testament and of traditional Christian interpretation in his Old Testament exegesis, yet he is unwilling to follow the lead of earlier Christian exegetes in allowing a wedge to be driven between interpretations that are pious and edifying and those that are arrived at through sound reasoning. His arguments for his exegetical decisions suggest that he believes it is possible to interpret the Old Testament in a Christian way without leaving the sphere of objectively verifiable exegesis. Even in those cases where he recognizes that he embraces a spiritual interpretation rather than a literal one, he believes he can prove to any fair-minded reader that his interpretation is justifiable on historical grounds.

Thus far in this study I have dealt with the rational side of Calvin's exegesis. But the question may be asked, What role, if any, does the Holy Spirit play in Calvin's method of exegetical reasoning? One of his statements in his letter to Sadoleto seems to argue for the Spirit's involvement in biblical interpretation. "The Spirit goes before the Church, to enlighten her in understanding the Word, while the Word itself is like a Lydian stone, by which she tests all doctrines."[6]

The question of the Holy Spirit's role in the exegetical process may be expressed pointedly: "Is illumination by the Holy Spirit a necessary precondition for the proper understanding the Old Testament?" To this question Calvin's answer would seem to be "yes." He accuses the Jews of blindness, deceptiveness, obstinacy, and malice in their efforts to twist scripture away from its true christological meaning. While he finds much to approve in Jewish exegesis of the Old Testament, his approval is almost always restricted to lexical and grammatical matters. When the rabbis venture into other areas, he finds little reason to trust them. In short, the Jews do not understand scripture because they do not know Christ, who is the substance of scripture. The problems of Jewish exegesis that he highlights are rooted in their spiritual blindness. If, as Calvin teaches elsewhere,[7] the remedy for such blindness is the illuminating work of the Holy Spirit, then such illumination might be understood as a precondition of proper exegesis. If the Jews possessed the Spirit, they would understand that Christ is the substance of the Old Testament. If they possessed the Spirit, they would accept the authority of New Testament interpretations of the Old Testament. While Calvin believes he can justify his interpretations against the Jews on firm historical grounds, he also believes that the spiritual blindness of the Jews (and the related problem of spiritual rebellion) prevents them from weighing the exegetical evidence properly.[8]

Another question may now be asked: If absence of illumination by the Holy Spirit means one cannot truly understand the biblical text (as it does in the case of the Jews), does the presence of such illumination guarantee the correct understanding of the Old Testament? It would seem that if the message of the Old Testament is, as Calvin indicates, to set forth Christ, then the illumination by the Holy Spirit that all believers possess should guarantee the correct interpretation of the Old Testament as a whole. The evidence presented in this study does nothing to bring such an understanding into question. If the question is posed differently—Does the illumination of the Holy Spirit guarantee the correct understanding of specific texts?—the evidence is clear. Calvin is very critical of Christian exegetes, even Augustine and Luther, for adopting erroneous interpretations. He never argues that the Holy Spirit is directing his exegesis and not theirs. Instead he offers what he believes are firm, objective reasons for rejecting their interpretations. If Calvin believes that the Holy Spirit's illumination accounts for the correct interpretation of specific texts, then his frequent criticism of the views of fellow Christian interpreters is puzzling. After all, these interpreters presumably were led by the same Holy Spirit.

It thus seems that for Calvin illumination by the Holy Spirit and philological expertise are both needed by the biblical exegete. But they are not necessary in the same way. The exegete needs illumination in order to understand the meaning of the Old Testament as a whole—that is, as a witness to Jesus Christ. Apart from such illumination, any other understanding of the Old Testament is empty and useless. However, while this illumination guarantees that the interpreter will understand the message of the Old Testament as a whole, it in no way guarantees that he will understand the meaning of any specific text. Augustine and Luther certainly understood the Old Testament's witness to Jesus Christ, yet they often twisted the meaning of individual texts. The best exegesis of the Old Testament, in Calvin's view, combines piety and philological scholarship, but the relative charity of his comments about Christian exegesis as opposed to Jewish exegesis suggests that if one of these had to go, it would probably have to be scholarship.

Bouwsma, in his provocative study of Calvin, sees two Calvins living in tension. There was Calvin the philosopher, rationalist, and schoolman, who "tended toward static orthodoxy," was "singularly intolerant of what we now call 'cognitive dissonance,' " and "craved desperately for intelligibility, order and certainty." Then there was Calvin "the rhetorician and humanist, a skeptical fideist." This Calvin was "flexible to the point of opportunism, and a revolutionary in spite of himself." Calvin the rhetorician "asserted the primacy of experience over theory, and he had a considerable tolerance for individual freedom." Bouwsma argues that, in the struggle of the two Calvins, rhetoric triumphed over philosophy. "While philosophy has traditionally excluded rhetoric, rhetoric, intrinsically as impure as life itself, has generally been willing to appropriate, for the sake of utility, bits and pieces of philosophy."[9]

This study of Calvin's method of exegetical reasoning may be viewed as lending some support to Bouwsma's thesis—yet without the clear victory that Bouwsma sees of rhetoric over philosophy. On the one hand, Calvin does insist that Old Testament exegesis must do justice to the particulars of the text in their historical context—Christian exegetes often failed at this point. On the other hand, he consistently maintains an interest in preserving the uniformity of the message of scripture as a witness to Jesus Christ, displaying a marked intolerance for any exegesis that does not finally relate the message of the text to Christ—Jewish exegetes failed here.

One of Calvin's twentieth-century disciples describes a similar, yet modern, tension—the tension between critical biblical scholarship and the traditional Christian view of biblical inspiration:

> The historical-critical method of Biblical investigation has its rightful place. . . . But were I driven to choose between it and the venerable doctrine of Inspiration, I should without hesitation adopt the latter. . . . Fortunately, I am not compelled to choose between the two.[10]

It is clear that Calvin experienced similar tension in the sixteenth century—and adopted a similar approach. The tension present in his views on the authorship and unity of scripture are never transcended, and as a result, he adopts a "middle way" of exegesis that has both a "Jewish" and a "Christian" appearance. Were he driven to choose between a method that recognizes only the human side of scripture and its diversity or one that recognizes only the divine side of scripture and its unity, he would without hesitation adopt the latter. But he would not accept these as his options. He would probably want to say with Barth, "Fortunately, I am not compelled to choose between the two."

NOTES

1. Ford Lewis Battles, *Calculus Fidei: Some Ruminations on the Structure of the Theology of John Calvin* (Grand Rapids: Calvin Theological Seminary, 1978).

2. Emil K. Kraeling, *The Old Testament since the Reformation* (London: Lutterworth Press, 1955), 32.

3. H. Jackson Forstman, *Word and Spirit: Calvin's Doctrine of Biblical Authority* (Stanford, Calif.: Stanford University Press, 1962), 123.

4. Kemper Fullerton, *Prophecy and Authority: A Study in the History of the Doctrine and Interpretation of Scripture* (New York: Macmillan, 1919), 161.

5. Edward A. Dowey, Jr., *The Knowledge of God in Calvin's Theology*, 2d ed. (New York: Columbia University Press, 1965), 104.

6. *John Calvin and Jacopo Sadoleto: A Reformation Debate*, ed. John C. Olin (New York: Harper & Row, 1966), 61.

7. *Inst.* II.ii.19 (O.S. 3.261).

8. This may be analogous to Calvin's view of natural revelation. The evidence of God's existence and character is there for all to see. Only their blindness and rebellion keep people from receiving the revelation. *Inst.* I.iv (O.S. 3.40–44).

9. William J. Bouwsma, *John Calvin: A Sixteenth Century Portrait* (New York: Oxford University Press, 1988), 230–33.

10. Karl Barth, *The Epistle to the Romans*, trans. Edwyn C. Hoskyns, from the 6th ed. (London: Oxford University Press, 1933), 1.

APPENDIX

THE PREPARATION AND
PUBLICATION OF CALVIN'S
OLD TESTAMENT COMMENTARIES

Calvin preached, lectured, or wrote on almost every book in the Protestant Bible. His New Testament commentaries are preserved for every book except 2 and 3 John and Revelation.[1] In the Old Testament we are not so fortunate. Missing are expositions of Proverbs, Ecclesiastes, Song of Songs, Judges, and 1 Kings.[2] The extant expositions are preserved in the form of sermons, lectures to students in the Genevan academy, and commentaries proper.

Although Calvin preached on most of the Old Testament, many of his sermons were lost in the early nineteenth century.[3] Lost were the sermons on Judges, 1 Kings, much of Lamentations, almost all of the minor prophets, and substantial portions of the Psalms, Isaiah, Jeremiah, Ezekiel, and Daniel.[4] Fortunately, in the case of Calvin's lectures at the academy, no such disaster occurred. All of his known lectures on the Old Testament are extant.

Beginning in the late 1540s, Calvin began lecturing on the Old Testament.[5] Though the lectures were not initially intended for publication, in 1551 he allowed the first of these lectures to be published as his commentary on Isaiah.[6] In a letter dedicating the collection to Edward VI of England, he indicates that the recording was done by someone other than himself, but insists that the work was done in a "faithful and skillful" manner.[7] The work was revised eight years later and dedicated to Edward's sister Elizabeth I. Calvin's lectures on Genesis were published in 1554, four years after he had begun to teach the book. Initially, he intended to compose a commentary proper rather than simply publishing his lectures. The task, however, was too much for him to complete because of his many commitments, so the commentary was based upon his

147

lectures at the academy. He made his first venture into expounding the minor prophets in the mid-1550s. In 1557 his lectures on Hosea were first published. They were so well received that Calvin agreed to allow them to be reissued along with his lectures on the other minor prophets in 1559. He then began to lecture on the remaining prophets. In 1559 and 1560 he lectured on Daniel; from 1560 to 1563 on Jeremiah and Lamentations; and from 1563 until he was consigned to his deathbed in 1564 on the first twenty chapters of Ezekiel. Each lecture series was published within a year or two of its conclusion.

Calvin lectured extemporaneously and therefore was unable to provide any notes to serve as the basis for a written exposition. His secretary, Nicholas des Gallars, discovered a fairly efficient method for preserving his lectures on Isaiah. He took notes as Calvin lectured, later read to Calvin what he had written, and made whatever additions or deletions were requested.[8] In a letter to Dryander, who was anxiously awaiting publication of the lectures, Calvin describes the process. "They were written by des Gallars, because I have little time for writing. He takes down what I dictate to him and later arranges it at home. Then I read it over again and if anywhere he has not followed my meaning I restore the sense."[9]

Several years later an improved system was implemented. Three young colleagues took down what Calvin said (as well as they could), compared notes, and wrote a single version. The printer Jean Crispin gives a detailed account of the procedure.

> Each had his paper ready in the most convenient form, and each took down as quickly as possible what was said. If any word escaped one of them (which sometimes happened, especially on controversial matters and places expounded more vehemently) it was caught by another; and when this happened the author easily replaced it. For immediately after the lecture, Joinvillier took the papers of the other two, placed them before him, consulted his own, put them all together more accurately, and dictated to someone else what he had copied from their hasty writings. At the end he reread it, so that he might repeat it the next day to M. Calvin at home. When sometimes any little word was wanting, this was supplied, or if anything did not seem explained sufficiently, it was easily made clearer.[10]

Calvin assures his readers that his secretaries exercised great care in recording his words. "They did not permit themselves to replace one single word by a better." He expresses amazement at the reliability of the procedure: "I would not have believed, unless I had seen it with my own eyes, how, when they read it back to me the next day, their transcriptions did not differ from my spoken words. They recorded so faithfully what they heard me say that I can see no alteration." He even suggests that they may have recorded his words too perfectly. "It might perhaps have been better if they had used greater liberty and deleted superfluities, arranged other things into a better order, and made yet others more distinct or more stylish."[11]

Calvin was evidently pleased with the substance of his lectures, but he expressed reservations about publishing them in the lecture format. The annotations, which "were bearable as lectures but not worthy, as I thought, to be read, would never have been published on my initiative." He was glad to escape the chore of writing but not fully satisfied with the literary virtues of the product. Since it was only a transcript of his extemporaneous exposition of the text, it was much less polished than he desired for a written work bearing his name.

> I chose to allow this volume, as it is, taken from my lips, to go forth to the public, rather than by prohibition, to impose upon myself the necessity of writing; which I was forced to do as to the Psalms, before I found out, by that long and difficult work how unequal I am to so much writing. . . . I am one who is not easily pleased with works I finish with more labor and care. Had it been in my power, I should have rather tried to prevent the wider circulation of that extemporaneous kind of teaching, intended for the particular benefit of my hearers, and with which benefit I was abundantly satisfied.[12]

Calvin produced only three expositions of Old Testament books that were intended from the first for the written medium. In 1557 he published his commentary on the Psalms; in 1563, his *Harmony of the Last Four Books of Moses*. In 1565 his commentary on Joshua was published posthumously.

It was only at the persistent solicitation of others that he agreed to compose the Psalms commentary. At first, he planned to do nothing more than teach the Psalms in the academy; then he was encouraged to put something into writing. He had promised to write something in French for his countrymen but decided first to compose an exposition of one psalm in Latin. It received such a favorable reception that he extended it to other psalms. Finally, with some reluctance, he agreed to write a commentary on the entire book. He was compelled to produce the work more from apprehension that someone might publish the work behind his back than from any desire to do so.[13] We have no direct evidence from which to determine if the publication of his *Harmony of the Last Four Books of Moses* or the *Commentary on Joshua* was motivated by similar considerations.[14]

From the facts concerning the preparation of the commentaries on the Old Testament it is possible to conclude that even those commentaries which were simply transcriptions of his academy lectures are faithful representations of his thoughts, and even his very words. It is also true that, since the commentaries are mostly the product of the last decade of his life, they reflect his method after it has fully developed, and they reflect his mature thoughts on the subjects he addresses. Thus, the Old Testament commentaries provide an especially good source for the study of Calvin's method of exegetical reasoning.

NOTES

1. T.H.L. Parker in *Calvin's New Testament Commentaries* (Grand Rapids: Wm. B. Eerdmans Publishing Co., 1971), 75ff., argues convincingly that Calvin did not write on these books.

2. According to Parker, Calvin preached on Judges and 1 and 2 Samuel from February 1561 to February 1563 and 1 Kings from February 1563 to February 1564. T.H.L. Parker, *Calvin's Old Testament Commentaries* (Edinburgh: T. & T. Clark, 1986), 13. Parker's book contains a very thorough history of the composition of the Old Testament commentaries.

3. Ibid., 12. They were sold by weight, apparently because they were so difficult to read.

4. Ibid., 13.

5. These lectures are preserved in the form in which they were delivered. Parker argues that they were delivered to schoolboys, students thirteen to fifteen years old who had an elementary knowledge of the biblical languages and perhaps an intermediate knowledge of Latin, the language of the lecture. Ibid., 15–16. See also David C. Steinmetz, "John Calvin on Isaiah 6: A Problem in the History of Exegesis," *Interpretation* 36 (April 1982): 160.

6. All of Calvin's Old Testament commentaries were published after 1551: Isaiah (1551); Genesis (1554); Psalms (1557); Hosea (1557); Isaiah revision (1559); minor prophets (1559); Daniel (1561); Jeremiah and Lamentations (1563); Harmony of the Last Four Books of Moses (1563); Ezekiel (1565); Joshua (1565). Since all except for the first Isaiah commentary and the Genesis commentary date from the last six years of his life, we may be certain that they reflect his mature thought on the proper method of interpreting the Old Testament.

7. Letter of dedication to Edward VI (C.O. 14.30).

8. Des Gallars had the advantage of having taken down precise interpretations of key passages during Calvin's sermons on Isaiah several years earlier. Following the sermon, he returned to his house and gave as much time as he could to translating Calvin's interpretations from French to Latin. These notes, he relates, were of great assistance in the composition of the commentaries. Comm. Isa., Nicholas des Gallars's pref. (C.O. 36.11–14).

9. Calvin to Dryander (C.O. 13.536). Parker argues that the Genesis commentary was also put into written form by des Gallars (*Old Testament Commentaries*, 26).

10. Comm. minor prophets, Jean Crispen's pref. (C.O. 42.189–90).

11. Comm. minor prophets, pref. (C.O. 42.183–84).

12. Ibid.

13. Comm. Pss., pref. (C.O. 31.15). Such a concern was probably justifiable. Melanchthon had apparently experienced such a problem. See Robert Stupperich,

ed., *Melanchthons Werke* (Gütersloh: Gerd Mohn, 1965), vol. 5: *Römerbrief-Kommentar 1532*, ed. Rolf Schäfer, 26.

14. According to Parker, the three commentaries cover the same books as were discussed in the *Congrégations* (weekly meetings of ministers and other interested persons) after 1549, suggesting either that the *Congrégations* served as the basis of the commentaries or vice versa. Parker believes the *Congrégations* were organized to fit with whatever commentary was in progress (*Old Testament Commentaries*, 15).

SELECT BIBLIOGRAPHY

WORKS BY JOHN CALVIN

Texts

Ioannis Calvini opera quae supersunt omnia. (C.O.) Edited by W. Baum, E. Cunitz, and E. Reuss. 59 vols. Braunschweig, 1863–1900.

Ioannis Calvini Opera Selecta. (O.S.) Edited by P. Barth and W. Niesel. 5 vols. Munich: Chr. Kaiser Verlag, 1926–62.

Des Scandales. Edited by Olivier Fatio. Textes Littéraires Français. Geneva: Librairie Droz, 1984.

Calvin's Commentary on Seneca's De Clementia. Translated and edited by Ford Lewis Battles and André Malan Hugo. Renaissance Text Series. Leiden: E. J. Brill, 1969.

Translations

The Commentaries of John Calvin. 46 vols. Edinburgh: Calvin Translation Society, 1843–55. Reprint, 22 vols., Grand Rapids: Baker Book House, 1979.

Calvin's New Testament Commentaries. Edited by David W. Torrance and Thomas F. Torrance. 12 vols. Grand Rapids: Wm. B. Eerdmans Publishing Co., 1959–72.

Calvin: Commentaries. Translated and edited by Joseph Haroutunian. Library of Christian Classics, vol. 23. Philadelphia: Westminster Press, 1958.

Calvin: Institutes of the Christian Religion. (*Inst.*) Edited by John T. McNeill. Translated by Ford Lewis Battles. Library of Christian Classics, vols. 21–22. Philadelphia: Westminster Press, 1960.

On Scandals. Translated by John W. Fraser. Grand Rapids: Wm. B. Eerdmans Publishing Co., 1978.

John Calvin and Jacopo Sadoleto: A Reformation Debate. Edited by John C. Olin. New York: Harper & Row, 1966.

Treatises against the Anabaptists and Libertines. Translated and edited by Benjamin Wirt Farley. Grand Rapids: Baker Book House, 1982.

STUDIES ON CALVIN

Ashley, Clinton Matthew. "John Calvin's Utilization of the Principle of Accommodation and Its Continuing Significance for an Understanding of Biblical Language." Th.D. diss., Southwestern Baptist Theological Seminary, 1972.

Augsburger, Daniel. "Calvin et le second commandement." In *Histoire de l'exégèse au XVIe siècle*. Edited by Olivier Fatio and Pierre Fraenkel. Etudes de Philologie et d'Histoire, no. 34. Geneva: Librairie Droz, 1978.

Avis, P.D.L. "Moses and the Magistrate: A Study in the Rise of Protestant Legalism." *Journal of Ecclesiastical History* 26 (1975): 149–72.

Balke, Willem. "Calvijn over de geschapen werkelijkheid in zijn Psalmencommentaar." In *Wegen en gestalten in het gereformeerd protestantisme*. Edited by Willem Balke, C. Graafland, and H. Harkema. Amsterdam: Ton Bolland, 1976.

———. *Calvin and the Anabaptist Radicals*. Translated by William J. Heynen. Grand Rapids: Wm. B. Eerdmans Publishing Co., 1981.

———. "The Word of God and Experientia according to Calvin." In *Calvinus Ecclesiae Doctor*, edited by Wilhelm H. Neuser. Kampen: J. H. Kok, 1980.

Bandstra, Andrew John. "Law and Gospel in Calvin and in Paul." In *Exploring the Heritage of John Calvin*. Edited by David E. Holwerda. Grand Rapids: Baker Book House, 1976.

Baron, Salo. "John Calvin and the Jews." In *Ancient and Medieval Jewish History*, edited by Leon A. Feldman. New Brunswick, N.J.: Rutgers University Press, 1972.

Baroni, V. "Calvin à Oltramare: Deux commentaires genevois sur l'épitre aux Ephesiens." *Revue de Théologie et de Philosophie* 20 (1932): 191–210.

Bates, Gordon. "The Typology of Adam and Christ in John Calvin." *Hartford Quarterly* 5 (1965): 42–57.

Battles, Ford Lewis. *Calculus Fidei: Some Ruminations on the Structure of the Theology of John Calvin*. Grand Rapids: Calvin Theological Seminary, 1978.

———. "The Future of Calviniana." In *Renaissance, Reformation, Resurgence*, edited by Peter De Klerk. Grand Rapids: Calvin Theological Seminary, 1976.

———. "God Was Accommodating Himself to Human Capacity." *Interpretation* 31 (January 1977): 19–38.

Baumgartner, Ant. J. *Calvin Hébraïsant et interprète de l'Ancien Testament*. Paris: Librairie Fischbacher, 1889.

Baxter, Anthony G. "John Calvin's Use and Hermeneutics of the Old Testament." Ph.D. diss., University of Sheffield, 1987.

Benoît, Jean-Daniel. "Petit traité de l'amour du prochain d'après les sermons de Calvin sur Michée." *Le Christianisme au Vingtième Siècle* 94 (1965): 225–27.

Besse, Georges. "Saint Augustin dans les oeuvres exégétiques de Jean Calvin: Recherches sur l'autorité reconnue à saint Augustin par Calvin en matière d'exégèse." *Revue des Etudes Augustiniennes* 6 (1960): 161–72.

Bohatec, Josef. *Budé und Calvin*. Studien zur Gedankenwelt des französischen Frühhumanismus. Graz, 1950.

Bouwsma, William J. *Calvinism as Theologia Rhetorica*. Center for Hermeneutical Studies in Hellenistic and Modern Culture, Colloquy 54. Berkeley, Calif.: Center for Hermeneutical Studies, 1987.

———. *John Calvin: A Sixteenth Century Portrait*. New York: Oxford University Press, 1988.

Breen, Quirinus. *John Calvin: A Study in French Humanism*. 1931. Reprint, Hamden, Conn.: Archon Books, 1968.

————. "John Calvin and the Rhetorical Tradition." In *Christianity and Humanism: Studies in the History of Ideas*, edited by Nelson Peter Ross. Grand Rapids: Wm. B. Eerdmans Publishing Co., 1968.

Buehrer, Richard Lyle. "John Calvin's Humanistic Approach to Church History." Ph.D. diss., University of Washington, 1974.

Clavier, Henri. "Calvin commentateur biblique." In *Etudes sur le Calvinisme*. Paris: Librairie Fischbacher, 1936.

Coetzee, C. F. "Calvyn en die skopus van die skrif." Parts 1, 2. *Woord en Daad* 15 (February and March 1974): 16–17, 8–9.

Courvoisier, Jaques. "Calvin et les Juifs." *Judaica* 2 (1946): 203–8.

De Koster, Lester Ronald. "Living Themes in the Thought of John Calvin." Ph.D. diss., University of Michigan, 1964.

De Long, Irwin Hoch. "Calvin as an Interpreter of the Bible." *Reformed Church Review*, fourth series, 13 (1909): 165–82.

Doumergue, Emile. *Jean Calvin: Les hommes et les choses de son temps*. Vol. 4: *La pensée religieuse de Calvin*. Lausanne: G. Bridel, 1899–1927. Reprint, Geneva: Slatkine, 1969.

Dowey, Edward A., Jr. *The Knowledge of God in Calvin's Theology*. Revised ed. New York: Columbia University Press, 1965.

————. "The Structure of Calvin's Thought as Influenced by the Two-fold Knowledge of God." In *Calvinus Ecclesiae Genevensis Custos*, edited by Wilhelm H. Neuser. Frankfurt: Peter Lang, 1984.

Dubois, Claude-Gilbert. "Jean Calvin, commentaires sur le premier livre de Moyse." In *La conception de l'histoire en France au XVIe siècle (1560–1610)*. Paris: A. G. Nizet, 1977.

————. "Les leçons de Jean Calvin sur le livre des prophéties de Daniel." In *La conception de l'histoire en France au XVIe siècle (1560–1610)*. Paris: A. G. Nizet, 1977.

Duffield, Gervase E., ed. *John Calvin: A Collection of Essays*. Courtenay Studies in Reformation Theology, no. 1. Grand Rapids: Wm. B. Eerdmans Publishing Co., 1966.

Edwards, Felicity. "The Relation between Biblical Hermeneutics and the Formulation of Dogmatic Theology: An Investigation in the Methodology of John Calvin." Ph.D. diss., Oxford University, 1968.

Engelbrecht, B. "Is Christ the Scopus of Scripture?" In *Calvinus Reformator: His Contribution to Theology, Church, and Society*, edited by Wilhelm H. Neuser. Institute for Reformation Studies, series F, no. 17. Potchefstroom, South Africa: Potchefstroom University for Christian Higher Education, 1982.

Farrar, Frederic W. "Calvin as an Expositor." *The Expositor*, second series, 7 (1884): 426–44.

Floor, Lambertus. "Calvyn se hermeneutiek in sy betekenis vir ons tyd." *In die Skriflig* 4 (1970): 3–20.

————. "Calvyn se hermeneutiek in vergelyking met Ebeling en Fuchs." In *Aspekte van die Nuwe-Testamentiese hermeneutiek*. Pretoria: Universiteit van Pretoria, 1970.

————. "The Hermeneutics of Calvin." In *Calvinus Reformator: His Contribution to Theology, Church, and Society*, edited by Wilhelm H. Neuser. Institute for

Reformation Studies, series F, no. 17. Potchefstroom, South Africa: Potchefstroom University for Christian Higher Education, 1982.

Forstman, H. Jackson. *Word and Spirit: Calvin's Doctrine of Biblical Authority*. Stanford, Calif.: Stanford University Press, 1962.

Fuhrmann, Paul Traugott. "Calvin, the Expositor of Scripture." *Interpretation* 6 (1952): 188–209.

Gamble, Richard C. "Brevitas et Facilitas: Toward an Understanding of Calvin's Hermeneutic." *Westminster Theological Journal* 47 (1985): 1–17.

———. "Calvin as Theologian and Exegete—Is There Anything New?" *Calvin Theological Journal* 23 (1988): 178–94.

———. "Calvin's Theological Method: Word and Spirit, A Case Study." In *Calviniana: Ideas and Influence of Jean Calvin*, edited by Robert V. Schnucker. Sixteenth Century Essays and Studies, no. 10. Kirksville, Mo.: Sixteenth Century Journal Publishers, 1988.

———. "Exposition and Method in Calvin." *Westminster Theological Journal* 49 (1987): 153–65.

Ganoczy, Alexandre. "Calvin als paulinischer Theologe: Ein Forschungsansatz zur Hermeneutik Calvins." In *Calvinus Theologus*, edited by Wilhelm H. Neuser. Neukirchen: Neukirchener Verlag, 1976.

———. "Hermeneutische Korrelationen bei Calvin." In *Reformatio ecclesiae: Beiträge zu kirchlichen Reformbemühungen von der Alten Kirche bis zur Neuzeit*, edited by Remigius Bäumer. Paderborn, Germany: Ferdinand Schöningh, 1980.

———. *The Young Calvin*. Translated by David Foxgrover and Wade Provo. Philadelphia: Westminster Press, 1987.

Ganoczy, Alexandre, and Klaus Müller. *Calvins handscriftliche Annotationen zu Chrysostomus. Ein Beitrag zur Hermeneutik Calvins*. Veröffentlichungen des Instituts für Europäische Geschichte Mainz, Abteilung für Abendländische Religionsgeschichte, no. 102. Wiesbaden: Franz Steiner Verlag, 1981.

Ganoczy, Alexandre, and Stefan Scheld. *Die Hermeneutik Calvins: Geistesgeschichtliche Voraussetzungen und Grundzüge*. Veröffentlichungen des Instituts für Europäische Geschichte Mainz, Abteilung für Abendländische Religionsgeschichte, no. 114. Wiesbaden: Franz Steiner Verlag, 1983.

———. *Herrschaft Tugend-Vorsehung: Hermeneutische Deutung und Veröffentlichung handschriftlicher annotationen Calvins zu sieben Senecatragödien und der pharsalia Lucans*. Veröffentlichungen des Instituts für Europäische Geschichte Mainz, Abteilung für Abendländische Religionsgeschichte, no. 105. Wiesbaden: Franz Steiner Verlag, 1982.

Gerrish, B. A. "The Word of God and the Words of Scripture: Luther and Calvin on Biblical Authority." In idem, *The Old Protestantism and the New: Essays on the Reformation Heritage*. Chicago: University of Chicago Press, 1982.

Giradin, Benoît. *Rhétorique et théologique: Calvin, le commentaire de l'Epîtyr aux Romains*. Théologie Historique, no. 54. Paris: Editions Beauchesne, 1979.

Goetz, Ronald. "Joshua, Calvin, and Genocide." *Theology Today* 2 (1975/76): 263–74.

Gore, R. J., Jr. "Calvin's Doctrine of Inspiration." *Reformation Review* 27 (1982): 100–114.

Gotch, F. W. "Calvin as a Commentator." *Journal of Sacred Literature* 3 (1849): 222–36.

Graafland, Cornelis. *Het vaste verbond: Israel en het Oude Testament bij Calvijn en het gereformeerd protestantisme*. Amsterdam: Ton Bolland, 1978.

Grin, Edmond. "L'unité des deux Testaments selon Calvin." *Theologische Zeitschrift* 17 (1961): 175–86.

Groenewald, Evert Philippus. "Calvyn en die Heilige Skrif." *Nederduitse Gereformeerde Teologiese Tydskrif* 5 (1964): 131–41.

Hagen, Kenneth. "John Calvin (1509–64)." In *Hebrews Commenting from Erasmus to Bèze, 1516–1598.* Beiträge zur Geschichte der biblischen Exegese, no. 23. Tübingen: J.C.B. Mohr (Paul Siebeck), 1981.

Hall, Basil. "Calvin and Biblical Humanism." *Huguenot Society of London Proceedings* 20 (1959–64): 195–209.

Harbison, Elmore Harris. "Calvin's Sense of History." In *Christianity and History.* Princeton, N.J.: Princeton University Press, 1964.

Hartvelt, Gerrit Pieter. "Calvijn: Exegese tussen oud en nieuw." In *Omgaan met het verleden: Tussen ja-zeggers en nee-zeggers.* Kampen: J. H. Kok, 1981.

Hasler, R. A. "The Influence of David and the Psalms upon John Calvin's Life and Thought." *Hartford Quarterly* 5 (1965): 7–18.

Helm, Paul. "Calvin and the Covenant: Unity and Continuity." *Evangelical Quarterly* 55 (1983): 65–81.

Hesselink, I. John. "Calvin and Heilsgeschichte." In *Oikonomia: Heilsgeschichte als Thema der Theologie,* edited by Felix Christ. Hamburg-Bergstedt: Reich, 1967.

Howorth, H. H. "The Origin and Authority of the Biblical Canon according to the Continental Reformers." Parts 1, 2. *Journal of Theological Studies* (1908, 1909): 188–230, 183–232.

Jellema, Dirk William. "God's 'Baby-Talk': Calvin and the 'Errors' in the Bible." *Reformed Journal* 30 (April 1980): 25–27.

Jülicher, A. "Calvin als Schriftausleger." *Die Christliche Welt* 23 (1909): 655–57.

Karlberg, Mark W. "Reformed Interpretation of the Mosaic Covenant." *Westminster Theological Journal* 43 (fall 1980): 1–57.

Kraus, Hans-Joachim. "Calvin's Exegetical Principles." *Interpretation* 31 (1977): 8–18.

———. "Vom Leben und Tod in den Psalmen: Eine Studie zu Calvins Psalmen-Kommentar." In *Biblisch-theologische Aufsätze.* Neukirchen-Vluyn: Neukirchener Verlag, 1972.

Kreck, Walter. "Wort und Geist bei Calvin." In *Festschrift für Günther Dehn,* edited by Wilhelm Schneemelcher. Neukirchen: Verlag des Buchhandlung des Erziehungsvereins, 1957.

Krusche, Werner. *Das Wirken des Heiligen Geistes nach Calvin.* Göttingen: Vandenhoeck & Ruprecht, 1957.

Leith, John H. "John Calvin—Theologian of the Bible." *Interpretation* 25 (1971): 329–44.

Lobstein, P. "Les commentaires de Calvin." *Revue de Théologie et de Philosophie* 8 (1920): 84–90.

Locher, Gottfried W. "Calvin spricht zu den Juden." *Theologische Zeitschrift* 23 (1967): 180–96.

———. *Testimonium internum: Calvins Lehre vom Heiligen Geist und das hermeneutische Problem.* Theologische Studien, no. 81. Zurich: EVZ-Verlag, 1964.

Long, J. H. "Calvin as an Interpreter of the Bible." *Reformed Church Review* 13 (1909): 165–82.

McKane, William. "Calvin as an Old Testament commentator." *Nederduitse Gereformeerde Teologiese Tydskrif* 25 (1984): 250–59.

McKee, Elsie Anne. "Exegesis, Theology, and Development in Calvin's *Institutio*." In *Probing the Reformed Tradition: Historical Studies in Honor of Edward A. Dowey, Jr.*, edited by Elsie Anne McKee and Brian G. Armstrong. Louisville, Ky.: Westminster/John Knox Press, 1989.

McNeill, John T. "The Significance of the Word of God for Calvin." *Church History* 28 (June 1959): 131–46.

Marichal, Walter W. "J. Calvin et l'écriture sainte." *Les Cahiers Calvinistes* 22 (December 1964): 1–6.

Martin, Alain-Georges. "Comment Calvin lisait le récit de la Tour de Babel." *La Revue Réformée* 33 (1982): 16–19.

Martin-Achard, R. "Calvin et les Psaumes." *Les Cahiers Protestants* 40 (1960): 102–12.

Mays, James Luther. "Calvin's Commentary on the Psalms: The Preface as Introduction." In *Calvin Studies IV*, edited by W. Stacy Johnson. Richmond: Union Theological Seminary in Virginia, 1988.

Mickelsen, John K. "The Relationship between the Commentaries of John Calvin and His *Institutes of the Christian Religion*, and the Bearing of that Relationship on the Study of Calvin's Doctrine of Scripture." *Gordon Review* 5 (1959): 155–68.

Müller, E. F. Karl. "Reformatorische, insbesondere reformierte Schriftauslegung, 3: Calvin." In *Für Christus und die Gemeinde*, edited by W. A. Lagenohl. Neukirchen: Erziehungsverein, 1928.

Muller, Richard A. "The Foundation of Calvin's Theology: Scripture as Revealing God's Word." *Duke Divinity School Review* 44 (winter 1979): 14–23.

———. "The Hermeneutic of Promise and Fulfillment in Calvin's Exegesis of the Old Testament." In *The Bible in the Sixteenth Century*, edited by David C. Steinmetz. Duke Monographs in Medieval and Renaissance Studies. Durham, N.C.: Duke University Press, 1990.

Murray, John. "Calvin as Theologian and Expositor." In *Collected Writings*, Vol. 1, *The Claims of Truth*. Edinburgh: Banner of Truth, 1976.

Neugebauer, Richard. "Exegetical Structure in the *Institutes of the Christian Religion* and the Biblical Commentaries of John Calvin: A Study of the *Commentary on the Four, Last Books of Moses arranged in the Form of a Harmony*." M.A. thesis, Columbia University, 1968.

Neuser, Wilhelm H. "Calvins Stellung zu den Apokryphen des Alten Testaments." In *Text-Wort-Glaube: Studien zur Überlieferung, Interpretation und Autorisierung biblischer Text*, edited by Kurt Aland and Martin Brecht. Arbeiten zur Kirchengeschichte, no. 50. Berlin: Walter de Gruyter, 1980.

Newport, J. P. "An Investigation of the Factors Influencing John Calvin's Use of the Linguistic and Historical Principles of Biblical Exegesis." Ph.D. diss., Edinburgh, 1953.

Nicole, P. D. "De l'exégese à l'homilétique: Evolution entre le commentaire de 1551, les sermons de 1559 sur le prophéte Esaïe." In *Calvinus Ecclesiae Genevensis Custos*, edited by Wilhelm H. Neuser. Frankfurt: Peter Lang, 1984.

Nicole, Roger. "John Calvin and Inerrancy." *Journal of the Evangelical Theological Society* 25 (December 1982): 425–44.

Niesel, Wilhelm. "Calvins Stellungnahme zu den Juden," *Reformierte Kirchenzeitung* 120 (1979): 181–83.

Paluku Rabinga, Nyanza N. "Calvin commentateur du prophète Isaïe: Le commentaire sur Isaïe, un traité de son herméneutique." Doctorat en Sciences Religieuses, Université des Sciences Humaines de Strasbourg, 1978.

Parker, T.H.L. "Calvin the Biblical Expositor." In *John Calvin: A Collection of Essays,* edited by Gervase E. Duffield. Grand Rapids: Wm. B. Eerdmans Publishing Co., 1966.

———. "Calvin the Exegete: Change and Development." In *Calvinus Ecclesiae Doctor,* edited by Wilhelm H. Neuser. Kampen: J. H. Kok, 1980.

———. *Calvin's Doctrine of the Knowledge of God.* Revised ed. Grand Rapids: Wm. B. Eerdmans Publishing Co., 1959.

———. *Calvin's New Testament Commentaries.* Grand Rapids: Wm. B. Eerdmans Publishing Co., 1971. (2d ed., Edinburgh: T. & T. Clark, 1993; Louisville, Ky.: Westminster John Knox Press, 1993.)

———. *Calvin's Old Testament Commentaries.* Edinburgh: T. & T. Clark, 1986; Louisville, Ky.: Westminster John Knox Press, 1993.

———. *John Calvin: A Biography.* Philadelphia: Westminster Press, 1975.

———. "The Shadow and the Sketch." In *Calvinus Reformator: His Contribution to Theology, Church, and Society,* edited by Wilhelm H. Neuser. Institute for Reformation Studies, series F, no. 17. Potchefstroom: Potchefstroom University for Christian Higher Education, 1982.

Partee, Charles. *Calvin and Classical Philosophy.* Studies in the History of Christian Thought, no. 14. Leiden: E. J. Brill, 1977.

Peter, Rodolphe. "Calvin and Louis Budé's Translation of the Psalms." In *John Calvin: A Collection of Essays,* edited by Gervase E. Duffield. Grand Rapids: Wm. B. Eerdmans Publishing Co., 1966.

Polman, Andries Derk Rietema. "Calvin on the Inspiration of Scripture." In *John Calvin Contemporary Prophet,* edited by Jacob T. Hoogstra. Grand Rapids: Baker Book House, 1959.

Potgieter, P. C. "Calvin as Scriptural Theologian." In *Calvinus Reformator: His Contribution to Theology, Church, and Society,* edited by Wilhelm H. Neuser. Institute for Reformation Studies, series F, no. 17. Potchefstroom, South Africa: Potchefstroom University for Christian Higher Education, 1982.

Prust, Richard C. "Was Calvin a Biblical Literalist?" *Scottish Journal of Theology* 20 (1967): 312–28.

Pury, R. de. "Pour marquer les distances: Simple note sur une exégèse de Calvin et de Luther." *Foi et Vie* 65 (1966): 42–45.

Quack, Jürgen. "Calvins Bibelvorreden (1535–1546)." In *Evangelische Bibelvorreden von der Reformation bis zur Aufklärung.* Quellen und Forschungen zur Reformationsgeschichte, no. 43. Gütersloh: Gerd Mohn, 1975.

Reuss, E. "Calvin considéré comme exégète." *Revue de Théologie* 6 (1853): 223–48.

Reynolds, Blair. "Calvin's Exegesis of Jeremiah and Micah: Use or Abuse of Scripture." *Proceedings* 11 (1991): 81–91.

Robert, Daniel. "Le rôle historique de Calvin." *La Revue Réformée* 15 (1964): 42–48.

Robertson, A. T. "Calvin as an Interpreter of Scripture." *Review and Expositor* 6 (1909): 577–78.

Robinson, William Childs. "The Theologian of the Reformation; John Calvin, Interpreter of God's Word." In *The Reformation: A Rediscovery of Grace.* Grand Rapids: Wm. B. Eerdmans Publishing Co., 1962.

Rossouw, Hendrik Willem. "Calvin's Hermeneutics of Holy Scripture." In *Cal-*

vinus Reformator: His Contribution to Theology, Church, and Society, edited by Wilhelm H. Neuser. Institute for Reformation Studies, series F, no. 17. Potchefstroom: Potchefstroom University for Christian Higher Education, 1982.

Röthlisberger, Hugo. "Calvin und der Dekalog." In *Kirche am Sinai: Die Zehn Gebote in der christlichen Unterweisung.* Studien zur Dogmengeschichte und systematischen Theologie, no. 19. Zurich and Stuttgart: Zwingli Verlag, 1965.

Runia, Klaus. "The Hermeneutics of the Reformers." *Calvin Theological Journal* 17 (fall 1984): 121–53.

Russell, S. H. "Calvin and the Messianic Interpretation of the Psalms." *Scottish Journal of Theology* 21 (1968): 37–47.

Scalise, Pamela. "The Reformers as Biblical Scholars." *Review and Expositor* 86 (1989): 23–28.

Schaff, P. "Calvin as a Commentator." *Presbyterian and Reformed Review* 3 (July 1892): 462–69.

Schellong, Dieter. *Calvins Auslegung der synoptischen Evangelien.* Forschungen zur Geschichte und Lehre des Protestantismus 10, no. 38. Munich: Chr. Kaiser Verlag, 1969.

———. *Das evangelische Gesetz in der Auslegung Calvins.* Theologische Existenz Heute, no. 152. Munich: Chr. Kaiser Verlag, 1968.

Schreiner, Susan E. "Exegesis and Double Justice in Calvin's Sermons on Job." *Church History* 58 (September 1989): 322–38.

———. " 'Through a Mirror Dimly': Calvin's Sermons on Job." *Calvin Theological Journal* 21 (November 1986): 175–193.

Simon, M. "Die Beziehung zwischen Altem und Neuem Testament in der Schriftauslegung Calvins." *Reformierte Kirchenzeitung* 82 (1932): 17–21, 25–28, 33–35.

Smid, T. D. "Enkele bibliografische opmerkingen betreffende Calvijn en zijn commentaar op Jeremia." *Gereformeerd theologisch tijdschrift* 61 (1961): 156–65.

Smits, Lucesius. *Saint Augustin dans l'oeuvre de Jean Calvin.* 2 vols. Assen, Netherlands: Van Gorcum, 1951–58.

Stauffer, Richard. *Dieu, la création et la providence dans la prédication de Calvin.* Basler und Berner Studien zur historischen und systematischen Theologie, no. 33. Bern: Peter Lang, 1978.

———. "Un texte de Calvin inconnu en français: Le Sermon sur le Psaume 46/1–6." *La Revue Réformée* 15 (1964): 1–15.

Steinmetz, David C. "Calvin and Abraham: The Interpretation of Romans 4 in the Sixteenth Century." *Church History* 57 (December 1988): 443–55.

———. "John Calvin on Isaiah 6: A Problem in the History of Exegesis." *Interpretation* 36 (April 1982): 156–70.

Stroup, George W. "Narrative in Calvin's Hermeneutic." In *Calvin Studies III*, edited by John H. Leith. Richmond: Union Theological Seminary in Virginia, 1986.

Tholuck, August. "Die Verdienste Calvins als Ausleger der heiligen Schrift." In *Vermischte Schriften größtentheils apologetischen Inhalts.* Hamburg: Friedrich Perthes, 1839.

Todd, William Newton. "The Function of the Patristic Writings in the Thought of John Calvin." Th.D. diss., Union Theological Seminary, 1964.

Torrance, Thomas F. *The Hermeneutics of John Calvin.* Edinburgh: Scottish Academic Press, 1988.

Van der Walt, Frans. "Calvyn oor die hermeneutiese reël ten opsigte van nuuskierigheid en spekulasie." *In die Skriflig* 6 (September 1972): 36–38.

van Rooy, H. F. "Calvin's Genesis Commentary—Which Bible Text Did He Use?" In *Our Reformational Tradition: A Rich Heritage and Lasting Vocation.* Institute for Reformation Studies, series F, no. 21. Potchefstroom, South Africa: Potchefstroom University for Christian Higher Education, 1984.

Verhoef, Pieter A. "Luther's and Calvin's Exegetical Library." *Calvin Theological Journal* 3 (April 1968): 5–20.

Vincent, Gilbert. "Calvin, commentateur du Psaume XXII." *Bulletin du Centre Protestant d'Etudes et de Documentation* 293 (July-August 1984): 32–52.

Vischer, Wilhelm. "Calvin, exégète de l'Ancien Testament." *Etudes Théologiques et Religieuses* 40 (1965): 213–31.

Visser, Anne Jippe. *Calvijn en de Joden.* The Hague: Boekencentrum, 1963.

Volz, H. "Beiträge zu Melanchthons und Calvins Auslegungen des Propheten Daniel." *Zeitschrift für Kirchengeschichte* 67 (1955–56): 93–118.

Vos, Clarence John. "Calvin's View of Man in the Light of Genesis 2,15 or Man: Earth's Servant or Lord." In *Calvinus Reformator: His Contribution to Theology, Church, and Society,* edited by Wilhelm H. Neuser. Institute for Reformation Studies, series F, no. 17. Potchefstroom, South Africa: Potchefstroom University for Christian Higher Education, 1982.

Walchenbach, John Robert. "The Influence of David and the Psalms on the Life and Thought of John Calvin." Th.M. thesis, Pittsburgh Theological Seminary, 1969.

————. "John Calvin as Biblical Commentator: An Investigation into Calvin's Use of John Chrysostom as an Exegetical Tutor." Ph.D. diss., University of Pittsburgh, 1974.

Wallace, Ronald S. *Calvin's Doctrine of the Word and Sacrament.* Grand Rapids: Wm. B. Eerdmans Publishing Co., 1957.

Warfield, Benjamin Breckinridge. "Calvin's Doctrine of the Knowledge of God." *Princeton Theological Review* 7 (1909): 219–325.

Weber, Otto. "Die Einheit der Kirche bei Calvin." In *Die treue Gottes in der Geschichte der Kirche, in Gesammelte Aufsätze II.* Beiträge zur Geschichte und Lehre der reformierten Kirche, no. 29. Neukirchen-Vluyn: Neukirchener Verlag des Erziehungsvereins, 1968.

Wendel, François. *Calvin: Origins and Development of His Religious Thought.* Translated by Philip Mairet. New York: Harper & Row, 1963.

————. *Calvin et l'humanisme.* Cahiers de la Revue d'Histoire et de Philosophie Religieuses, no. 45. Paris: Presses Universitaires de France, 1976.

Willis-Watkins, David. "Calvin's Prophetic Reinterpretation of Kingship." In *Probing the Reformed Tradition: Historical Studies in Honor of Edward A. Dowey, Jr.,* edited by Elsie Anne McKee and Brian G. Armstrong. Louisville, Ky.: Westminster/John Knox Press, 1989.

Wolf, Hans Heinrich. *Die Einheit des Bundes: Das Verhältnis von Altem und Neuem Testament bei Calvin.* Beiträge zur Geschichte und Lehre der reformierten Kirche, no. 10. Neukirchen: Verlag der Buchhandlung des Erziehungsvereins, 1958.

Woudstra, Marten H. "Calvin Interprets What 'Moses Reports': Observations on Calvin's Commentary on Exodus 1–19." *Calvin Theological Journal* 21 (November 1986): 151–74.

————. *Calvin's Dying Bequest to the Church: A Critical Evaluation of the Commentary on Joshua.* Calvin Theological Seminary, monograph series, no. 1. Grand Rapids: Calvin Theological Seminary, 1960.

Wright, David F. "Calvin's Pentateuchal Criticism: Equity, Hardness of Heart, and Divine Accommodation in the Mosaic Harmony Commentary." *Calvin Theological Journal* 21 (April 1986): 33–50.

————. "Woman before and after the Fall: A Comparison of Luther's and Calvin's Interpretation of Genesis 1—3." *Churchman* 98 (1984): 126–35.

Youngblood, Ronald F. "From Tatian to Swanson, from Calvin to Bendavid: The Harmonization of Biblical History." *Journal of the Evangelical Theological Society* 25 (1982): 415–23.

GENERAL WORKS

Aldridge, John William. *The Hermeneutic of Erasmus.* Basel Studies of Theology, no. 2. Richmond: John Knox Press, 1966.

Augsburger, Daniel. "Calvin et le second commandement." In *Histoire de l'exégèse au XVIe siècle,* edited by Olivier Fatio and Pierre Fraenkel. Etudes de Philologie et d'Histoire, no. 34. Geneva: Librairie Droz, 1978.

————. "Pierre Viret on the Sabbath Commandment." *Andrews University Seminary Studies* 20 (1982): 91–101.

Augustine. *De doctrina Christiana.* In *Corpus Christianorum,* Series Latina, vol. 32. Turnhout, Belgium: Brepols, 1962.

Baker, D. L. *Two Testaments, One Bible: A Study of Some Modern Solutions to the Theological Problem of the Relationship between the Old and New Testaments.* Downers Grove, Ill.: InterVarsity, 1976.

Baker, Joshua, and Nicholson, Ernest W., ed. *The Commentary of Rabbi David Kimchi on Psalms CXX–CL.* Cambridge: Cambridge University Press, 1973.

Baron, Salo W. "Medieval Heritage and Modern Realities in Protestant-Jewish Relations." In *Ancient and Medieval Jewish History,* edited by Leon A. Feldman. New Brunswick, N.J.: Rutgers University Press, 1972.

————. *A Social and Religious History of the Jews.* 16 vols. New York: Columbia University Press, 1969.

Barr, James. "The Literal, the Allegorical, and Modern Biblical Scholarship." *Journal for the Study of the Old Testament* 44 (1989): 3–17.

————. "Literality." *Faith and Philosophy* 6 (October 1989): 412–28.

————. *Old and New in Interpretation: A Study of the Two Testaments.* London: SCM Press, 1982.

Bedoulle, Guy. *Lefèvre d'Etaples et l'intelligence des Ecritures.* Travaux d'Humanisme et Renaissance, no. 171. Geneva: Librairie Droz, 1979.

————. *Le quincuplex Psalterium de Lefèvre d'Etaples: Un guide de lecture.* Travaux d'Humanisme et Renaissance, no. 152. Geneva: Librairie Droz, 1976.

Bentley, Jerry H. *Humanists and Holy Writ: New Testament Scholarship in the Renaissance.* Princeton, N.J.: Princeton University Press, 1983.

Berger, David, trans. and ed. *The Jewish Christian Debate in the High Middle Ages: A Critical Edition of the Nizzahon Vetus.* Philadelphia: Jewish Publication Society of America, 1979.

Berger, Samuel. *La Bible au XVIe siècle.* Nancy, 1879.

Black, C. Clifton, II. "Unity and Diversity in Luther's Biblical Exegesis: Psalm 51 as a Test-Case." *Scottish Journal of Theology* 38 (1985): 325–45.

Blaising, Craig Alan. "Athanasius of Alexandria: Studies in the Theological Contents and Structure of the *Contra Arianos* with Special Reference to Method." Ph.D. diss., University of Aberdeen, 1987.

Blowers, Paul M. "Origen, the Rabbis, and the Bible: Toward a Picture of Judaism and Christianity in Third-Century Caesarea." In *Origen of Alexandria: His World and His Legacy*, edited by Charles Kannengiesser and William L. Peterson. Christianity and Judaism in Antiquity, no. 1. Notre Dame, Ind.: University of Notre Dame Press, 1988.

Bock, Darrell L. "Evangelicals and the Use of the Old Testament in the New." *Bibliotheca Sacra* 142 (1965): 209–23, 306–19.

Bohlmann, Ralph Arthur. *Principles of Biblical Interpretation in the Lutheran Confessions.* Revised ed. St. Louis: Concordia Publishing House, 1983.

Bornkamm, Heinrich. *Luther and the Old Testament.* Translated by Eric W. and Ruth C. Gritch. Philadelphia: Fortress Press, 1969.

Braverman, Jay. *Jerome's Commentary on Daniel: A Study of Comparative Jewish and Christian Interpretations of the Hebrew Bible.* The Catholic Biblical Quarterly Monograph Series, no. 7. Washington, D.C.: Catholic Biblical Association of America. 1978.

Bright, Pamela. *The Book of Rules of Tyconius: Its Purpose and Inner Logic.* Notre Dame, Ind.: University of Notre Dame Press, 1988.

Brooks, Roger. "Straw Dogs and Scholarly Ecumenism: The Appropriate Jewish Background for the Study of Origen." In *Origen of Alexandria: His World and His Legacy*, edited by Charles Kannengiesser and William L. Peterson. Christianity and Judaism in Antiquity, no. 1. Notre Dame, Ind.: University of Notre Dame Press, 1988.

Brown, Raymond E. "The History and Development of the Theory of a Sensus Plenior." *Catholic Biblical Quarterly* 15 (1953): 141–62.

———. "The Problems of the Sensus Plenior." In *Exégèse et théologie: Les Saintes Ecritures et leur interprétation théologique*, edited by G. Thils and R. E. Brown. Gembloux: J. Duculot, 1968.

———. "The Sensus Plenior in the Last Ten Years." *Catholic Biblical Quarterly* 25 (1963): 262–85.

———. *The Sensus Plenior of Sacred Scripture.* Baltimore: St. Mary's University, 1955.

Busser, Fritz. "Zwingli the Exegete: A Contribution to the 450th Anniversary of the Death of Erasmus." In *Probing the Reformed Tradition: Historical Studies in Honor of Edward A. Dowey, Jr.*, edited by Elsie Anne McKee and Brian G. Armstrong. Louisville, Ky.: Westminster/John Knox Press, 1989.

Carson, D. A., and H.G.M. Williamson. *It Is Written: Scripture Citing Scripture.* Cambridge: Cambridge University Press, 1988.

Cambridge History of the Bible. 3 vols. Cambridge: Cambridge University Press, 1963–70.

Chenu, M. D. *Nature, Man, and Society in the Twelfth Century: Essays on New Theological Perspectives in the Latin West.* Translated and edited by Jerome Taylor and Lester K. Little. Chicago: University of Chicago Press, 1968.

Childs, Brevard S. *Old Testament Books for Pastor and Teacher.* Philadelphia: Westminster Press, 1977.

————. "The Sensus Literalis of Scripture: An Ancient and Modern Problem." In *Beiträge zur alttestamentlichen Theologie*, edited by Herbert Donner, Robert Hanhart, and Rudolf Smend. Göttingen: Vandenhoeck & Ruprecht, 1977.

Cranfield, C.E.B. *A Critical and Exegetical Commentary on the Epistle to the Romans.* International Critical Commentary. Edinburgh: T. & T. Clark, 1975.

Daniélou, Jean. *From Shadows to Reality: Studies in the Biblical Typology of the Fathers.* Translated by Wulstan Hibberd. London: Burns & Oates, and Westminster, Md.: Newman Press, 1960.

Davidson, Richard M. *Typology in Scripture: A Study of Hermeneutical* ΤΥΠΟΣ *Structures.* Andrews University Seminary Doctoral Dissertation Series, no. 2. Berrien Springs, Mich.: Andrews University Press, 1981.

Davis, Thomas M. "The Traditions of Puritan Typology." In *Typology and Early American Literature*, edited by Sacvan Bercovitch. Amherst, Mass.: University of Massachusetts Press, 1972.

Deist, Ferdinand. *Mosaïek van Moses: Pentateug-navorsing sedert die reformasie.* Kaapstad, South Africa: Tafelberg-Uitgewers, 1976.

Demerson, G. "Un mythe des libertins spirituels: Le prophète Elie." In *Aspects du libertinisme au XVIe siècle.* Actes du Colloque International de Sommières. De Pétrarque à Descartes, no. 30. Paris: J. Vrin, 1974.

Diestel, Ludwig. *Geschichte des Alten Testaments in der christlichen Kirche.* Jena, 1869.

Encyclopedia Judaica. Jerusalem: Keter, 1971. S.v. "Abrabanel," by Avraham Grossmann.

Erasmus, Desiderius. *Christian Humanism and the Reformation: Selected Writings of Erasmus.* Edited by John C. Olin. New York: Fordham University Press, 1975.

Erdei, Klára A. "Méditations calvinistes sur les psaumes dans la littérature française du XVIe siècle." *Acta Litteraria Academiae Scientiarum Hungaricae* 24 (1982): 117–55.

Evans, G. R. *The Language and Logic of the Bible*, vol. 1: *The Earlier Middle Ages.* Cambridge: Cambridge University Press, 1984.

————. *The Language and Logic of the Bible*, vol. 2: *The Road to Reformation.* Cambridge: Cambridge University Press, 1985.

Farkasfalvy, Denis. "The Case for Spiritual Exegesis." *Communio* 10 (winter 1983): 332–50.

Farrar, Frederic W. *History of Interpretation.* E. P. Dutton, 1886. Reprint, Grand Rapids: Baker Book House, 1961.

Feinberg, John S., ed. *Continuity and Discontinuity: Perspectives on the Relationship between the Old and New Testaments.* Westchester, Ill.: Crossway Books, 1988.

Feld, Helmut. *Die Anfänge der modernen biblischen Hermeneutic in der spätmittelalterlichen Theologie.* Wiesbaden: Franz Steiner Verlag, 1977.

Fishbane, Michael. *Biblical Interpretation in Ancient Israel.* Oxford: Clarendon Press, 1985.

Florovsky, Georges. "The Fathers of the Church and the Old Testament." In *The Collected Works of Georges Florovsky.* Vol. 4: *Aspects of Church History.* Belmont, Mass.: Nordland, 1975.

Forde, Gerhard O. "Law and Gospel in Luther's Hermeneutic." *Interpretation* 37 (July 1983): 240–52.

Foulkes, Francis. *The Acts of God: A Study of the Basis of Typology in the Old Testament.* Tyndale Old Testament Lecture for 1955. London: Tyndale Press, n.d.

Frei, Hans W. *The Eclipse of Biblical Narrative: A Study of Eighteenth and Nineteenth Century Hermeneutics.* New Haven, Conn.: Yale University Press, 1974.

———. "The 'Literal Reading' of Biblical Narrative in the Christian Tradition: Does It Stretch or Will It Break?" In *The Bible and the Narrative Tradition,* edited by Frank McConnell. New York: Oxford University Press, 1986.

Friedman, Jerome. *Michael Servetus: A Case Study in Total Heresy.* Geneva: Librairie Droz, 1978.

———. "Michael Servetus: Exegete of Divine History." *Church History* 43 (December 1974): 460–69.

———. "Michael Servetus: The Case for a Jewish Christianity." *Sixteenth Century Journal* 4 (April 1973): 87–110.

———. *The Most Ancient Testimony: Sixteenth-Century Christian-Hebraica in the Age of Renaissance Nostalgia.* Athens, Ohio: Ohio University Press, 1983.

———. "The Reformation and Jewish Anti-Christian Polemics." *Bibliothèque d'Humanisme et Renaissance* 41 (1979): 85–97.

———. "Sebastian Münster, the Jewish Mission, and Protestant Antisemitism." *Archiv für Reformationsgeschichte* 70 (1979): 238–59.

———. "Servetus and the Psalms: The Exegesis of Heresy." In *Histoire de l'exégèse au XVIe siècle,* edited by Olivier Fatio and Pierre Fraenkel. Etudes de Philologie et d'Histoire, no. 34. Geneva: Librairie Droz, 1978.

———. "Sixteenth-Century Christian-Hebraica: Scripture and the Renaissance Myth of the Past." *Sixteenth Century Journal* 11 (1980): 67–85.

Froehlich, Karlfried. " 'Always to Keep the Literal Sense in Holy Scripture Means to Kill One's Soul': The State of Biblical Hermeneutics at the Beginning of the Fifteenth Century." In *Literary Uses of Typology from the Late Middle Ages to the Present,* edited by Earl Miner. Princeton, N.J.: Princeton University Press, 1977.

Froehlich, Karlfried, trans. and ed. *Biblical Interpretation in the Early Church.* Sources of Early Christian Thought. Philadelphia: Fortress Press, 1984.

Fullerton, Kemper. *Prophecy and Authority: A Study in the History of the Doctrine and Interpretation of Scripture.* New York: Macmillan, 1919.

Gesigora, Gerd. "Probleme humanistischer Psalmenexegese, dargestellt am Beispiel des Reformbischofs und Kardinals Jacopo Sadoleto." In *Der Kommentar in der Renaissance,* edited by August Buck and Otto Herding. Deutsche Forschungsgemeinschaft. Boppard am Rhein: Harald Boldt Verlag, 1975.

Goldingay, John. *Approaches to Old Testament Interpretation.* Issues in Contemporary Theology. Downers Grove, Ill.: InterVarsity, 1981.

———. "Luther and the Bible." *Scottish Journal of Theology* 35 (1982): 33–58.

Gosselin, Edward Alberic. "David and the Reformation." In *The King's Progress to Jerusalem: Some interpretations of David during the Reformation Period and Their Patristic and Medieval Background.* Humana Civilitas, no. 2. Malibu, Calif.: Undena Publications, 1976.

Grant, Robert M. *The Letter and the Spirit.* London: SPCK, 1957.

Grant, Robert M., and David Tracy. *A Short History of the Interpretation of the Bible.* 2d ed. Philadelphia: Fortress Press, 1984.

Greenspahn, Frederick E., ed. *Scripture in the Jewish and Christian Traditions: Authority, Interpretation, Relevance.* Nashville: Abingdon Press, 1982.

Greer, Rowan A. *Theodore of Mopsuestia: Exegete and Theologian.* London: Faith Press, 1961.

Gritch, Eric W. "The Cultural Context of Luther's Interpretation." *Interpretation* 37 (July 1983): 266–76.

Hailperin, Herman. "Intellectual Relations between Jews and Christians in Europe before 1500 A.D. Described Mainly according to the Evidences of Biblical Exegesis with Special Reference to Rashi (1040–1105) and Nicolas De Lyra (1270–1349)." *University of Pittsburgh Bulletin*, Nov. 15, 1933, 128–45.

———. *Rashi and the Christian Scholars.* Pittsburgh: University of Pittsburgh Press, 1963.

Halperin, David J. "Origen, Ezekiel's Merkabah, and the Ascension of Moses." *Church History* 50 (1981): 261–75.

Hanson, R.P.C. *Allegory and Event: A Study of the Sources and Significance of Origen's Interpretation of Scripture.* Richmond: John Knox Press, 1959.

Harbison, E. Harris. *The Christian Scholar in the Age of the Reformation.* New York: Charles Scribner's Sons, 1956.

Hayes, John H., and Frederick C. Prussner. *Old Testament Theology: Its History and Development.* Atlanta: John Knox Press, 1985.

Heine, Ronald E. "Gregory of Nyssa's Apology for Allegory." *Vigiliae Christianae* 38 (1984): 360–70.

Hendrix, Scott H. "Luther against the Background of the History of Biblical Interpretation." *Interpretation* 37 (July 1983): 229–39.

Herminjard, A. L., ed. *Correspondance des Réformateurs dans les pays de la langue française.* 7 vols. Geneva, Paris, 1866.

Hirschfield, H. *The Literary History of Hebrew Grammarians and Lexicographers.* London, 1926.

Hobbs, R. Gerald. "Martin Bucer on Psalm 22: A Study in the Application of Rabbinic Exegesis by a Christian Hebraist." In *Histoire de l'exégèse au XVI siècle,* edited by Olivier Fatio and Pierre Fraenkel. Etudes de Philologie et d'Histoire, no. 34. Geneva: Librairie Droz, 1978.

———. "How Firm a Foundation: Martin Bucer's Historical Exegesis of the Psalms." *Church History* 53 (December 1984): 477–91.

———. "Monitio amica: Pellican à Catiton sur le danger des lectures rabbiniques." In *Horizons Européens de la Réforme en Alsace,* edited by Marijn de Kroon and Marc Leinhard. Strasbourg: Librairie Istra, 1980.

Hunnius, Aegidius. *Calvinus Iudaizans, Hoc est: Iudaicae Glossae et Corruptilae, Quibus Iohannes Calvinus illustrissima Scripturae sacrae loca & Testimonia, de gloriosa Trinitate, Deitate Christi, & Spiritus sancti, eum primis autem vaticinia Prophetarum de Adventu Messiae, nativitate eius, passione, resurrectione, ascensione in coelos & sessione ad dextram Dei, detestandum in modum corrumpere non exhorruit. Addita est corruptelarum confutatio.* Wittenberg, 1595.

Jackson, B. Darrell. "The Theory of Signs in St. Augustine's De Doctrina Christiana." *Revue de Etudes Augustiniennes* 15 (1969): 9–49.

Jewett, Paul K. "Concerning the Allegorical Interpretation of Scripture." *Westminster Theological Journal* 17 (1954–55): 1–20.

Johnson, Allan E. "The Methods and Presuppositions of Patristic Exegesis in the Formation of Christian Personality." *Dialog* 16 (1977): 186–90.

Kannengiesser, Charles. *Holy Scripture and Hellenistic Hermeneutics in Alexandrian Christology: The Arian Crisis.* Center for Hermeneutical Studies in Hellenistic and Modern Culture, Colloquy 41. Berkeley, Calif.: Center for Hermeneutical Studies, 1982.

Kannengiesser, Charles, and William L. Petersen, eds. *Origen of Alexandria: His World and His Legacy.* Notre Dame, Ind.: University of Notre Dame Press, 1988.

Karlberg, Mark W. "Reformed Interpretation of the Mosaic Covenant." *Westminster Theological Journal* 43 (fall 1980): 1–57.

Kerrigan, Alexander. *St. Cyril of Alexandria: Interpreter of the Old Testament.* Analecta Biblica: Investigationes Scientificae in Res Biblicas, no. 2. Rome: Pontifico Instituto Biblico, 1952.

Kittelson, J. *Wolfgang Capito: From Humanist to Reformer.* Leiden: E. J. Brill, 1975.

Klassen, William. *Covenant and Community: The Life, Writings, and Hermeneutics of Pilgrim Marpeck.* Grand Rapids: Wm. B. Eerdmans Publishing Co., 1968.

Kraeling, Emil G. *The Old Testament since the Reformation.* London: Lutterworth Press, 1955.

Kraus, Hans-Joachim. *Geschichte der historisch-kritischen Erforschung des Alten Testaments.* Neukirchen-Vluyn: Neukirchener Verlag, 1969.

Kugel, James L. *The Idea of Biblical Poetry: Parallelism and Its History.* New Haven, Conn.: Yale University Press, 1981.

Kugel, James L., and Rowan A. Greer. *Early Biblical Interpretation.* Library of Early Christianity. Philadelphia: Westminster Press, 1986.

Kukenheim, Louis. *Contributions à l'histoire de la grammaire grecque, latine, et hébraïque à l'époque de la Renaissance.* Leiden: E. J. Brill, 1951.

Lampe, G.W.H. *A Patristic Greek Lexicon.* Oxford: Clarendon Press, 1961. S.v. σκοπός.

———. "The Reasonableness of Typology." In *Essays on Typology,* edited by G.W.H. Lampe and K. J. Woollcombe. Naperville, Ill.: Alec R. Allenson, 1957.

LeClercq, Jean. *The Love of Learning and the Desire for God: A Study of Monastic Culture.* Translated by Catharine Misrahi. New York: Fordham University Press, 1982.

Lehmann, Paul. "The Reformer's Use of the Bible." *Theology Today* 3 (October 1946): 328–44.

Longenecker, Richard. *Biblical Exegesis in the Apostolic Period.* Grand Rapids: Wm. B. Eerdmans Publishing Co., 1975.

Lubac, Henri de. *Exégèse médiévale: Les quatre sens de l'Ecriture.* 4 vols. Paris: Aubier, 1959–64.

———. *Histoire et esprit: L'intelligence de l'Ecriture d'après Origène.* Paris: Editions Montaigne, 1950.

Luther, Martin. *D. Martin Luthers Werke, Kritische Gesamtausgabe.* Weimar, 1883–.

McKane, William. *Selected Christian Hebraists.* Cambridge: Cambridge University Press, 1989.

McNally, Robert E. *The Bible in the Early Middle Ages.* Woodstock Papers, no. 4. Westminster, Md.: Newman Press, 1959.

McNeil, David O. *Guillaume Budé and Humanism in the Reign of Francis I.* Geneva: Librairie Droz, 1975.

Manning, Stephen. "Scriptural Exegesis and the Literary Critic." In *Typology and Early American Literature,* edited by Sacvan Bercovitch. Amherst, Mass.: University of Massachusetts Press, 1972.

Melanchthon, Philip. *Melancthons Werke.* Edited by Robert Stupperich. Gütersloh: Gerd Mohn, 1955–84.

Merrill, Eugene H. "Rashi, Nicholas de Lyra, and Christian Exegesis." *Westminster Theological Journal* 38 (1975): 66–79.

Moo, Douglas J. "The Problem of Sensus Plenior." In *Hermeneutics, Authority, and Canon*, edited by D. A. Carson and John Woodbridge. Grand Rapids: Zondervan Publishing House, 1986.

Mulder, Martin Jan, and Harry Sysling, eds. *Mikra: Text, Translation, Reading, and Interpretation of the Hebrew Bible in Ancient Judaism and Early Christianity*. Compendia Rerum Iudaicarum ad Novum Testamentum, vol. 1, section 2. Philadelphia: Fortress Press, 1988.

Müller, Johannes. *Martin Bucers Hermeneutik*. Quellen und Forschungen zur Reformationsgeschichte, no. 32. Gütersloh: Gerd Mohn, 1965.

Münster, Sebastian. *Mikdash YHWH: Hebraica Biblia*. Basel, 1546.

Newman, Louis Israel. *Jewish Influence on Christian Reform Movements*. Columbia University Oriental Studies, no. 23. New York: Columbia University Press, 1925.

Oberman, Heiko Augustinus. *Forerunners of the Reformation: The Shape of Late Medieval Thought Illustrated by Key Documents*. Philadelphia: Fortress Press, 1981.

Origen. *On First Principles*. Translated by G. W. Butterworth. Gloucester, Mass.: Peter Smith, 1973.

————. *Origen: Spirit and Fire, a Thematic Anthology of His Writings*. Edited by Hans Urs von Balthasar. Translated by Robert J. Daly. Washington, D.C.: Catholic University Press of America, 1984.

Osborn, Eric. "Philo and Clement." *Prudentia* 19 (May 1987): 35–49.

Pépin, M. J. *Mythe et allégorie: Les origines grecques et les contestations judéo-chrétiennes*. Revised ed. Paris, 1976.

Poythress, Vern Sheridan. "Divine Meaning of Scripture." *Westminster Theological Journal* 48 (1986): 241–79.

Preus, James Samuel. *From Shadow to Promise: Old Testament Interpretation from Augustine to the Young Luther*. Cambridge, Mass.: Belknap Press, 1969.

Pulvermacher, D. *Sebastian Münster als Grammatiker*. Berlin, 1892.

Rabil, Albert, Jr. *Erasmus and the New Testament: The Mind of a Christian Humanist*. San Antonio, Tex.: Trinity University Press, 1972.

Rad, Gerhard von. "Typological Interpretation of the Old Testament." Translated by John Bright. *Interpretation* 15 (1961): 174–92.

Rashkow, Ilona N. "Hebrew Bible Translation and the Fear of Judaization." *Sixteenth Century Journal* 21 (1990): 217–33.

Reid, J.K.S. *The Authority of Scripture: A Study of the Reformation and Post-Reformation Understanding of the Bible*. 1957. Reprint, Westport, Conn.: Greenwood Press, 1981.

Rendtorff, Rolf. "Towards a New Christian Reading of the Hebrew Bible." *Immanuel* 15 (winter 1982–83): 13–21.

Reuss, E. *Geschichte der Heiligen Schriften des Alten Testaments*. Braunschweig, 1890.

Reventlow, Henning Graf. *Problems of Biblical Theology in the Twentieth Century*. Translated by John Bowden. Philadelphia: Fortress Press, 1986.

Richardson, Alan, and John Bowden, eds. *The Westminster Dictionary of Christian Theology*. Philadelphia: Westminster Press, 1983. S.v. "Sensus Plenior," by G. R. Evans.

Ricoeur, Paul. "Preface to Bultmann." In *Essays on Biblical Interpretation*, edited by Lewis S. Mudge. Philadelphia: Fortress Press, 1980.

Rogers, Jack B., and Donald K. McKim. *The Authority and Interpretation of the Bible: An Historical Approach*. New York: Harper & Row, 1979.

Rogerson, John, Christopher Rowland, and Barnabas Lindars. *The Study and Use of the Bible*. History of Christian Theology, no. 2. Grand Rapids: Wm. B. Eerdmans Publishing Co., 1988.

Rosenthal, Erwin I. J. "Sebastian Muenster's Knowledge and Use of Jewish Exegesis." In *Essays in Honour of the Very Rev. Dr. J. H. Hertz*, edited by I. Epstein, E. Levine, and C. Roth. London: Edward Goldston, 1942.

Rosenthal, Frank. "Christian Hebraists of Latin Europe." Ph.D. diss., University of Pittsburgh, 1945.

————. "The Rise of Christian Hebraism in the Sixteenth Century." *Historia Judaica* 7 (April 1945): 167–91.

Roussel, B. "Histoire de l'église et histoire de l'exégèse au XVIe siècle." *Bibliothèque d'Humanisme et Renaissance* 37 (1975):181–92.

Sadoleto, Jacopo. *Jacobi Sadoleti: Cardinalis et Episcopi Carpentoractensis viri disertissimi, Opera quae extant omnia*. 4 vols. Verona, 1738.

————. *Jacobi Sadoleti S. R. E. Cardinalis Epistolae quotquot extant proprio nomine scriptae nunc primum duplo auctiores in lucem editae*. Edited by U. A. Costanz. 3 vols. Rome, 1760–64.

Scalise, Charles J. "Origen and the Sensus Literalis." In *Origen of Alexandria: His World and His Legacy*, edited by Charles Kannengiesser and William L. Peterson. Christianity and Judaism in Antiquity, no. 1. Notre Dame, Ind.: University of Notre Dame Press, 1988.

————. "The 'Sensus Literalis': A Hermeneutical Key to Biblical Exegesis." *Scottish Journal of Theology* 42 (1989): 45–65.

Scheper, George L. "Reformation Attitudes toward Allegory and the Song of Songs." *Publications of the Modern Language Association of America* 89 (1974): 551–62.

Schwarz, Werner. *Principles and Problems of Bible Translation: Some Reformation Controversies and Their Background*. Cambridge: Cambridge University Press, 1955.

Servetus, Michael. *The Two Treatises of Servetus on the Trinity*. Translated by Earl Morse Wilbur. Harvard Theological Studies, no. 24. Cambridge, Mass.: Harvard University Press, 1932.

Shotwell, Willis A. *The Biblical Exegesis of Justin Martyr*. London: SPCK, 1965.

Silva, Moisés. *Has the Church Misread the Bible? The History of Interpretation in the Light of Current Issues*. Foundations of Contemporary Interpretation, vol. 1. Grand Rapids: Zondervan Publishing House, 1987.

Simon, Richard. *Histoire critique du Vieux Testament*. Rotterdam, 1689.

Smalley, Beryl. *The Study of the Bible in the Middle Ages*. Notre Dame, Ind.: University of Notre Dame Press, 1964.

————. "William of Auvergne, John of la Rochelle, and St. Thomas Aquinas on the Old Law." In *Studies in Medieval Thought and Learning: From Abelard to Wyclif*. History Series, no. 6. London: Hambledon, 1981.

Smolinsky, H. "The Bible and Its Exegesis in the Controversies about Reform and Reformation." In *Creative Biblical Exegesis: Christian and Jewish Hermeneutics through the Centuries*, edited by Benjamin Uffenheimer and Henning Graf Reventlow. Journal for the Study of the Old Testament, Supplement Series 59. Sheffield: JSOT Press, 1988.

Stacey, David. *Interpreting the Bible*. New York: Hawthorn Books, 1977.

Stauffer, Richard. *Interprètes de la Bible: Etudes sur les Réformateurs du XVIe siècle*. Théologie Historique, no. 57. Paris: Editions Beauchesne, 1980.

Stead, G. C. "St. Athanasius on the Psalms." *Vigiliae Christianae* 39 (1985): 65–78.

Steinmetz, David C. "Hermeneutic and Old Testament Interpretation in Staupitz and the Young Martin Luther." *Archiv für Reformationsgeschichte* 70 (1979): 24–58.

―――. "Scripture and the Lord's Supper in Luther's Theology." *Interpretation* 37 (July 1983): 253–65.

―――. "The Superiority of Precritical Exegesis." *Theology Today* (1980): 27–38.

Stek, John Henry. "The Modern Problem of the Old Testament in the Light of Reformation Perspective." *Calvin Theological Journal* 2 (1967): 202–25.

Stuhlmacher, Peter. *Historical Criticism and Theological Interpretation of Scripture: Toward a Hermeneutics of Consent*. Philadelphia: Fortress Press, 1977.

Tavard, George H. *Holy Writ or Holy Church*. New York: Harper & Brothers, 1959.

Timmer, David E. "Biblical Exegesis and the Jewish-Christian Controversy in the Early Twelfth Century." *Church History* 58 (September 1989): 309–21.

Torjesen, Karen Jo. " 'Body,' 'Soul,' and 'Spirit' in Origen's Theory of Exegesis." *Anglican Theological Review* 67 (January 1985): 17–31.

―――. "Hermeneutical Procedure and Theological Structure in Origen's Exegesis." Ph.D. diss., Claremont School of Theology, 1982.

Torrance, Thomas F. "The Hermeneutics of Erasmus." In *Probing the Reformed Tradition: Historical Studies in Honor of Edward A. Dowey, Jr.*, edited by Elsie Anne McKee and Brian G. Armstrong. Louisville, Ky.: Westminster/John Knox Press, 1989.

Vander Goot, Henry. *Interpreting the Bible in Theology and the Church*. New York: Edwin Mellen, 1984.

―――. "*Tota scriptura*: The Old Testament in the Christian Faith and Tradition." In *Life is Religion*, edited by Henry Vander Goot. St. Catharines, Ontario: Paideia, 1981.

VanGemeren, Willem A. "Israel as the Hermeneutical Crux in the Interpretation of Prophecy." Parts I and II. *Westminster Theological Journal* 45, 46 (1983, 1984): 132–44, 254–97.

Wallace-Hadrill, D. S. *Christian Antioch: A Study of Early Christian Thought in the East*. Cambridge: Cambridge University Press, 1982.

Walzer, Michael. "Exodus 32 and the Theory of Holy War: The History of a Citation." *Harvard Theological Review* 61 (1968): 1–14.

Westermann, Claus, ed. *Essays in Old Testament Hermeneutics*. Translated by James Luther Mays. Richmond: John Knox Press, 1963.

Wilkin, Robert L. *Judaism and the Early Christian Mind: A Study of Cyril of Alexandria's Exegesis and Theology*. Yale Publications in Religion, no. 15. New Haven, Conn.: Yale University Press, 1971.

Wood, Arthur Skevington. *The Principles of Biblical Interpretation; as Enunciated by Irenaeus, Origen, Augustine, Luther, and Calvin*. Grand Rapids: Zondervan Publishing House, 1967.

Würthwein, Ernst. *The Text of the Old Testament*. Translated by Erroll F. Rhodes. Grand Rapids: Wm. B. Eerdmans Publishing Co., 1979.

Young, Frances. "The Rhetorical Schools and Their Influence on Patristic Exegesis." In *The Making of Orthodoxy*. Edited by Rowan Williams. Cambridge: Cambridge University Press, 1989.

INDEX OF SCRIPTURE REFERENCES

GENERAL INDEX

Aaron, 117
Abrabanel, Don Isaac, 84
Abraham, 39, 89
accommodation, 11, 40, 43, 51 n.110, 80
  n.106, 112–14
Advent
  first advent of Christ, 17, 126–27
  second advent of Christ, 16, 126–29
allegory/allegorical, 9, 54, 105–10, 112–
  14, 116, 120–21, 129–30, 132 n.5, 133
  nn.20, 21; 134 n.29, 141–42
  See also prophecy; typology
Ammon, 131
Amos, 47 n.22
Anabaptist interpretation, 16, 37, 49
  n.79, 141
anagogy, 69, 80–81 n.114, 109
analogy, 68, 80–81 n.114, 113, 116, 128
Antichrist, 69
Antiochus, 69–70
apostles, 27, 42
  apostolic interpretation, 27–28, 32,
  35, 38, 57, 86, 88–94, 97–99, 112,
  118
application, 66, 68–70, 96–98
Aristotle, 7, 83
Athanasius, 3
Augustine, 4, 15, 54–55, 66, 74 n.16, 107,
  143

authorship
  divine, 11, 25–31, 45, 46 n.5, 47 n.24,
  48 n.24, 91, 100, 140–41, 144
  human, 25, 27–29, 45, 48 n.24, 140–41,
  144

Babylon, 70, 72, 125–26, 128–29
Balke, Willem, 49 n.79
Baron, Salo, 78 n.64, 84
Barr, James, 132 n.5, 133 n.20
Battles, Ford Lewis, 51 n.110, 59, 73 n.4,
  139
Baumgartner, J., 75 n.27
Bomberg, Daniel, 78 n.64
Bornkamm, Heinrich, 55, 75 n.23
Bouwsma, William J., 16, 73 n.4, 144
Bucer, Martin, 22 n.65, 49–50 n.79, 58, 74
  n.12, 78 n.64

Cabala, 57
Canaan, 38
Capito, Wolfgang, 56, 58, 76 n.44
Chaldeans, 70
Childs, Brevard, 8
Christ
  as foundation of covenant of grace,
  44–45,
  as fulfillment, 42, 111, 114–15, 117,
  119–27, 129, 142

175